The Law Commission
(LAW COM No 273)

EVIDENCE OF BAD CHARACTER IN CRIMINAL PROCEEDINGS

Report on a reference under section 3(1)(e) of the Law Commissions Act 1965

Presented to the Parliament of the United Kingdom by the Lord High Chancellor by Command of Her Majesty
October 2001

LONDON: The Stationery Office
£20.60

Cm 5257

The Law Commission was set up by the Law Commissions Act 1965 for the purpose of promoting the reform of the law.

The Law Commissioners are:

> The Honourable Mr Justice Carnwath CVO, *Chairman*
> Professor Hugh Beale
> Mr Stuart Bridge
> Professor Martin Partington
> Judge Alan Wilkie QC

The Secretary of the Law Commission is Mr Michael Sayers and its offices are at Conquest House, 37-38 John Street, Theobalds Road, London WC1N 2BQ.

The terms of this report were agreed on 8 August 2001.

The text of this report is available on the Internet at:

> http://www.lawcom.gov.uk

© Crown Copyright 2001

The text in this document may be reproduced free of charge in any format or media without requiring specific permission. This is subject to the material not being used in a derogatory manner or in a misleading context. The source of the material must be acknowledged as Crown copyright and the title of the document must be included when being reproduced as part of another publication or service.

Any enquiries relating to the copyright in this document should be addressed to HMSO, The Copyright Unit, St. Clements House, 2–16 Colegate, Norwich NR3 1BQ. Fax: 01603-723000 or e-mail: copyright@hmso.gov.uk.

THE LAW COMMISSION

EVIDENCE OF BAD CHARACTER IN CRIMINAL PROCEEDINGS

CONTENTS

	Paragraph	Page
PART I: INTRODUCTION AND SUMMARY		1
The background to this report	1.1	1
The area of law covered in this report	1.3	1
Our approach	1.4	2
Our main recommendations	1.12	4
The structure of this report	1.24	6
PART II: THE PRESENT LAW		8
Exceptions to the rule of exclusion:		
(I): Adducing evidence of a defendant's bad character in chief	2.3	8
"Similar fact" evidence	2.4	8
Res gestae and background evidence	2.9	10
Can evidence of propensity be admitted as similar fact evidence?	2.10	10
How can similar fact evidence be used to rebut a defence?	2.13	11
Does the prosecution have to wait and see what defence is to be relied upon before adducing similar fact evidence?	2.16	12
Is there a special rule for sexual offences against persons of the same sex, or children?	2.18	13
Is there a discretion to exclude similar fact evidence?	2.19	13
Supervening discretions: section 78, and the common law	2.20	14
Identity cases		
Striking similarity	2.23	15
How the evidence is to be approached	2.24	15

	Paragraph	Page
Special cases where bad character evidence is admissible in chief		
Section 27(3) of the Theft Act 1968	2.27	16
The application of section 27(3)	2.29	17
Section 1(2) of the Official Secrets Act 1911	2.31	17
Special cases where bad character evidence is inadmissible in chief		
Spent convictions	2.33	18
(II): Evidence adduced by the defendant	2.39	20
Evidence adduced against a co-accused	2.40	20
Is there a discretion to exclude defence evidence?	2.41	20
(III): Adducing bad character evidence in cross-examination	2.43	21
The meaning of section 1(f)	2.45	22
The relationship between section 1(e) and section 1(f)	2.48	22
Section 1(f)(i)	2.50	23
The first limb of section 1(f)(ii): asserting good character	2.53	24
What is an assertion of good character?	2.55	24
Character is indivisible	2.59	25
The discretion to exclude	2.61	26
Common law rules	2.62	26
The second limb of section 1(f)(ii): casting imputations against prosecution witnesses	2.63	26
The pre-conditions	2.64	27
Sexual cases	2.68	28
The discretion to exclude	2.71	29
Similarity of offences	2.73	30
Where the convictions do not reveal dishonesty	2.74	30
Defence necessarily involving imputations	2.75	31
Section 1(f)(iii): attacking a co-defendant	2.77	32
"has given evidence"	2.78	32
"against any other person charged in the same proceedings"	2.80	33
When section 1(f)(iii) is invoked	2.85	34

	Paragraph	Page
Severance of defendants	2.88	35
Section 1(f)(iii) and separate trials	2.89	35
Severance of counts/informations	2.91	36

PART III: THE EUROPEAN CONVENTION ON HUMAN RIGHTS — 38

	Paragraph	Page
The structure of Article 6	3.2	38
Article 6 and rules of evidence	3.4	39
The fairness of the admission of previous convictions *per se*	3.7	40
Loss of shield by casting imputations	3.9	41
Victims of crime and the Convention	3.14	42
The effect of incorporation	3.21	44
The distinctive nature of Article 6	3.25	45
HRA, section 3	3.29	46
Reading down	3.32	47
Reading in	3.33	47
Conclusion	3.36	48

PART IV: DEFECTS OF THE PRESENT LAW — 49

	Paragraph	Page
The principal defects		49
The problems in detail (I): Evidence in chief		
Lack of clarity in the "similar fact evidence" rules	4.2	50
Evidence of propensity admitted as similar fact evidence	4.7	51
Background evidence	4.11	52
Section 27(3) of the Theft Act 1968		
The justification for section 27(3)	4.13	53
The defects of section 27(3)	4.17	54
The problems in detail (II): Cross-examination of the defendant	4.24	56
Section 1(f)(i)	4.25	56
The first limb of section 1(f)(ii): assertions of good character	4.26	57
(i) The doctrine that character is indivisible	4.27	57
(ii) The use that can be made of bad character evidence	4.28	57
(iii) It is unclear what kinds of assertions will trigger the loss of the shield	4.30	58

		Paragraph	Page
(iv)	Previous convictions of other possible culprits	4.32	58

The second limb of section 1(f)(ii): imputations against prosecution witnesses and deceased victims

		Paragraph	Page
Summary		4.33	59
(i)	No exception for necessary imputations	4.34	59
(ii)	Over-reliance on judicial discretion	4.44	63
(iii)	The foundations for the second limb of section 1(f)(ii) are unsound	4.47	63
	(a) Credibility	4.48	64
	(b) Fairness	4.51	65
	(c) Deterring attacks on prosecution witnesses	4.53	65
(iv)	Non-testifying defendants	4.60	67
(v)	A temptation to fabricate	4.66	68
(vi)	Inconsistent prosecution practice	4.67	68
(vii)	Lack of clarity	4.68	69
Section 1(f)(iii): cross-examination of a co-accused		4.70	70
(i)	Lack of judicial discretion	4.71	70
(ii)	Defendants may be inhibited in their defence or may be deterred from testifying	4.76	72
(iii)	The court may be misled	4.78	72
The hearsay exception for reputation		4.79	73
The need for change		4.80	73

PART V: GENERAL PRINCIPLES   75

PART VI: THE GENERAL APPROACH: THE OPTIONS   78

	Paragraph	Page
Option 1: adduce the defendant's criminal record at the start of every trial	6.3	78
Arguments in favour of option 1	6.4	78
Simplicity	6.5	79
Removal of injustices and anomalies in the current law	6.8	79
Avoiding the prejudicial effect of revealing the defendant's record in cross-examination	6.9	79

	Paragraph	Page
The relevance of the record	6.10	80
Relevance to the defendant's propensity to act in the manner alleged	6.11	80
Relevance to the defendant's propensity to lie	6.14	81
The fact-finders know anyway	6.18	82
Is this true?	6.20	83
Is option 1 the only solution?	6.23	84
Is option 1 the best solution?	6.27	85
Arguments against option 1	6.30	86
Irrelevance	6.31	86
The risk of prejudice	6.33	86
The research	6.37	88
Minimising the prejudicial effect of automatic disclosure	6.43	89
The perceived risk of prejudice	6.46	90
Longer trials	6.47	90
Distraction	6.49	90
The fairness of the criminal justice system	6.50	91
Conclusion	6.53	92
Option 1A: adduce the defendant's record of *similar* offences at the start of every trial	6.54	92
Option 2: adduce the defendant's record of sex offences in sex cases	6.57	93
Option 3: allow evidence of the defendant's previous misconduct to be adduced *only* where it is an ingredient of the offence charged	6.62	94
Option 4: a single inclusionary rule with an exception for evidence whose likely prejudicial effect outweighs its probative value	6.64	95
Option 5: an exclusionary rule with a single exception for evidence whose probative value outweighs its likely prejudicial effect	6.66	95
Conclusion: the general approach we recommend	6.67	96

PART VII: OVERVIEW OF OUR RECOMMENDATIONS   97

Inside or outside the central set of facts	7.4	97
"Substantial" probative value	7.8	98
Taking factors into account	7.18	102

	Paragraph	Page
The purpose of the evidence	7.20	102
Who is adducing the evidence?	7.21	102

PART VIII: BAD CHARACTER AND THE LEAVE REQUIREMENT — 104

	Paragraph	Page
Defining evidence of bad character		
The options considered in the consultation paper	8.4	105
Objections to our provisional proposal	8.9	106
Evidence of criminal offences	8.10	107
Evidence of bad character not amounting to an offence	8.12	107
Disposition	8.18	109
Our recommendation	8.19	109
Bad character evidence not subject to the exclusionary rule	8.20	110
The central set of facts	8.20	110
Evidence which all parties agree should be admitted	8.29	112
Evidence of a defendant's bad character, adduced by that defendant	8.30	112
Our recommendations	8.31	112

PART IX: EXCEPTIONS APPLICABLE TO NON-DEFENDANTS — 115

	Paragraph	Page
The current position	9.3	115
Judicial control	9.5	116
The option put forward in the consultation paper	9.8	116
The views of respondents	9.10	117
The dangers of bad character evidence		
Its irrelevance	9.14	119
Its prejudicial effect	9.16	120
The effect of a statutory test of enhanced relevance	9.24	123
Would a test of enhanced relevance prevent the defendant from having a fair trial?	9.28	123
Our conclusion	9.35	125
Formulating the test of enhanced relevance	9.36	126
The importance of the matter in issue	9.38	126

	Paragraph	Page
Ensuring a fair trial	9.40	127
Our recommendations		
Exceptions: non-defendants: substantial probative value	9.41	127
Exceptions: non-defendants: substantial explanatory value	9.42	127
The consequences for the defendant	9.44	128
The relationship with section 41 Youth Justice and Criminal Evidence Act 1999	9.45	128

PART X: THE EXPLANATORY EXCEPTION — 129

	Paragraph	Page
The defects of the current law		
Res gestae and background evidence	10.1	129
Our analysis	10.3	130
Evidence which is part of the narrative of the offence	10.4	130
Explanatory evidence	10.7	131

PART XI: THE INCRIMINATORY EXCEPTION — 134

	Paragraph	Page
Introduction	11.1	134
The options for reform and the response on consultation	11.3	134
Option 2: adducing bad character evidence to prove mens rea	11.4	134
Option 3: adducing bad character evidence to show disposition	11.8	135
Option 4: the Australian common law test, namely whether there is any reasonable explanation for the similar fact evidence other than that the defendant is guilty	11.11	136
Option 5: the scheme of the Australian Evidence Act 1995	11.14	137
Option 6	11.20	138
Our conclusions		
A test of enhanced relevance	11.22	138
The relationship between probative value and prejudicial effect	11.23	138
The importance of the matter in issue	11.31	140
The defendant's propensity to be untruthful	11.32	141
The credibility of a defence	11.34	141
The additional value of the evidence	11.38	142
Statutory guidance	11.40	143
Provisional proposals on statutory guidelines	11.41	143

	Paragraph	Page
The recommendation: evidence of substantial probative value	11.46	145
The Theft Act 1968, section 27(3)	11.48	145
The defects of the current law and the proposals in the consultation paper	11.49	145
The response on consultation	11.53	146
The Official Secrets Act 1911, section 1(2)	11.56	146
The effect of an earlier acquittal	11.62	148

PART XII: THE CREDIBILITY EXCEPTION — 149

	Paragraph	Page
Introduction	12.1	149
The recommendation		
The defendant will have obtained leave to attack the other's character	12.3	149
The comparison	12.7	150
The test of enhanced relevance	12.8	150
The interests of justice test	12.9	151
Attacks which do not relate to the person's propensity to tell the truth	12.22	153

PART XIII: THE CORRECTIVE EXCEPTION — 155

	Paragraph	Page
When a defendant is responsible for the misleading impression	13.3	156
The non-testifying defendant	13.9	157
Implied and non-verbal assertions	13.13	158
The corrective evidence must have substantial value		
Divisibility of character	13.22	159
The interests of justice test	13.29	162
Factors to take into account	13.30	162
Practice in the magistrates' courts	13.37	163
Use of the evidence	13.38	164
The recommendations	13.48	165
Where the defendant sets up a false or misleading comparison	13.51	166

Paragraph *Page*

PART XIV: THE CO-DEFENDANT EXCEPTION — 168

Introduction	14.1	168
Our provisional proposals	14.4	169
Bad character evidence adduced by a co-defendant	14.5	169
Cross-examination of a co-defendant	14.6	169
Attacks on a co-accused by a defendant who does not testify	14.12	170
The views of respondents		
A question of balance	14.13	170
Cross-examination of a co-defendant	14.17	171
Our proposal	14.22	172
Who should be able to apply?	14.26	173
Attacks on D2 by D1 where D1 does not testify	14.28	173
Relevance of bad character to guilt as well as credibility	14.31	174
Our recommendation	14.36	175
The operation of the exception	14.49	177
Severance	14.52	178

PART XV: THE QUALITY OF TENDERED EVIDENCE — 179

Introduction	15.1	179
What are contamination and collusion?	15.3	179
The quality of evidence and admissibility	15.8	180
The current law	15.9	181
The options in the consultation paper and the response on consultation	15.10	181
The policy considerations	15.15	182
What approach is a court to adopt to bad character evidence generally?	15.25	185
The recommendation	15.26	185
A duty to withdraw the case from the jury	15.27	186
Responses on consultation	15.32	186
The recommendation	15.37	188

Paragraph *Page*

PART XVI: SEVERANCE OF COUNTS OR INFORMATIONS 189

The response on consultation	16.3	189
Joinder and fairness	16.6	190
Option 1	16.9	191
Option 2	16.13	192
Option 3	16.16	194
The recommendation	16.21	195
Special rules for cases involving sexual offences?	16.24	195

PART XVII: PROCEDURAL AND ANCILLARY MATTERS 197

A notice requirement	17.1	197
Pre-trial rulings	17.6	198
A duty to give reasons		
The common law	17.8	199
The ECHR jurisprudence	17.12	201
Conclusion	17.14	201
Warnings to the jury		
A warning against speculation	17.17	202
A warning against placing too much weight on evidence of past misconduct	17.18	202
Service courts and professional tribunals	17.21	203

PART XVIII: THE COLLECTED RECOMMENDATIONS AND CONCLUSIONS 204

DRAFT BILL AND EXPLANATORY NOTES 209

APPENDIX A: RESEARCH: THE EFFECT ON MAGISTRATES OF KNOWING OF A DEFENDANT'S CRIMINAL RECORD 235

APPENDIX B: PERSONS AND ORGANISATIONS WHO COMMENTED ON THE CONSULTATION PAPER 244

ABBREVIATIONS

In this paper we use the following abbreviations:

the 1898 Act: the Criminal Evidence Act 1898

the ALRC: the Australian Law Reform Commission

Archbold: *Archbold Criminal Pleading, Evidence and Practice* (2001 ed, ed P J Richardson)

Blackstone: *Blackstone's Criminal Practice* (2001 ed, ed P Murphy)

the CLRC: the Criminal Law Revision Committee

the CLRC Evidence Report: CLRC, Eleventh Report: Evidence (General) (1972) Cmnd 4991

the consultation paper: Evidence in Criminal Proceedings: Previous Misconduct of a Defendant (1996) Law Commission Consultation Paper No 141

the Convention: the European Convention on Human Rights

Cross and Tapper: *Cross and Tapper on Evidence* (9th ed 1999, ed C Tapper)

the Evidence Act 1995 (Cth): the Australian Evidence Act 1995 of the Commonwealth

the HRA 1998: the Human Rights Act 1998

the JSB: the Judicial Studies Board

the Jury Study: the report of the mock jury research conducted by Dr S Lloyd-Bostock of the Centre for Socio-Legal Studies of the University of Oxford in 1995

the NZLC: the New Zealand Law Commission

PACE: the Police and Criminal Evidence Act 1984

the Royal Commission: the Royal Commission on Criminal Justice (Chairman: Viscount Runciman of Doxford CBE FBA)

the Report of the Royal Commission: (1993) Cm 2263

the Strasbourg Commission: the European Commission of Human Rights

the Strasbourg Court: the European Court of Human Rights

THE LAW COMMISSION

Report on a reference under section 3(1)(e) of the Law Commissions Act 1965

EVIDENCE OF BAD CHARACTER IN CRIMINAL PROCEEDINGS

To the Right Honourable the Lord Irvine of Lairg, Lord High Chancellor of Great Britain

PART I
INTRODUCTION AND SUMMARY

THE BACKGROUND TO THIS REPORT

1.1 On 28 April 1994, the Home Secretary made a reference to this Commission[1] in the following terms:

> to consider the law of England and Wales relating to hearsay evidence[2] and evidence of previous misconduct in criminal proceedings; and to make appropriate recommendations, including, if they appear to be necessary in consequence of changes proposed to the law of evidence, changes to the trial process.

1.2 We published our consultation paper on 10 July 1996 and we are grateful to all those who took the trouble to respond their views have been very valuable. We should also like to record our thanks to our consultant on this report, Professor Di Birch, of Nottingham University.

THE AREA OF LAW COVERED IN THIS REPORT

1.3 Presently, evidence of misconduct of the defendant on an occasion other than that leading to the charge may be introduced by the prosecution as evidence of "similar fact" or by the prosecution or the co-defendant in the limited circumstances provided for by statute, principally under section 1 of the Criminal Evidence Act 1898. Evidence of a person's bad character may, however, also be introduced by a defendant in respect of witnesses who are not co-defendants or in respect of people who are not witnesses. The only limitation to this freedom is the requirement that the evidence be "relevant". We consider each of these instances of the introduction of evidence of bad character.

---

[1] This reference was made pursuant to a recommendation made in the Report of the Royal Commission, ch 8 para 30, and Recommendation 191.

[2] A consultation paper was issued on this subject in 1995 and our report published in June 1997: Evidence in Criminal Proceedings: Hearsay and Related Topics (1997) Law Com No 245. The Government has accepted all the recommendations in that report, and implemented one.

OUR APPROACH

1.4 We are aware that some of those who are interested in this report may approach it by focusing on the question: "Will this report, if carried into effect, result in a significant increase in the number of occasions when fact-finders will be told about a defendant's previous convictions?" If we had taken the approach of recommending that previous convictions should, as a rule, be presented to the fact-finders however marginally relevant they might be and regardless of how prejudicial they might be, or conversely, of recommending that they should never be adduced save where it would be an affront to common sense to exclude them, then we might have been able to answer such a question with confidence.

1.5 In our view we would have been mistaken to have taken either of these approaches. Their apparently attractive simplicity ignores the complexity and variety of factual situations to which they would have to apply. Each of them would run the risk of endangering the vital interests of the individuals involved: whether defendant, complainant, witness, or investigator. The former would run the risk of wrongful convictions based on prejudice rather than evidence which would be liable to being overturned on appeal with consequential damage to the reputation of the criminal justice system.

1.6 In our judgment, the question: "Should the fact-finders hear or not hear about the previous convictions of a defendant or a witness?" is not, in practice, sensibly addressed as one of a priori principle. Questions of admissibility of bad character arise in criminal trials daily, case by case, affecting the vital interests of those involved. It is our view that those individuals deserve that these important questions be decided by the careful and consistent application to each case by the court of a structured process, which reflects the fact that often a person's misconduct will have significance for determining the matters in issue, but also recognises that fact-finders, whether lay or professional, are susceptible, however much they may try to avoid it, to having their good judgment either overborne or distorted by prejudice. Such a process requires that the court, performing the exercise of balancing countervailing considerations, should be given sufficient guidance to enable it to reach decisions which are consistent and, to an extent, predictable but which focus on the judgment of the individual decision-taker who is in the best position to make a sound judgment as to where the interests of justice lie.

1.7 The present law suffers from a number of defects which we identify in a later chapter of this report. In summary, however, they constitute a haphazard mixture of statute and common law rules which produce inconsistent and unpredictable results, in crucial respects distort the trial process, make tactical considerations paramount and inhibit the defence in presenting its true case to the fact-finders whilst often exposing witnesses to gratuitous and humiliating exposure of long forgotten misconduct.

1.8 In constructing a process which we believe meets the requirements we have set ourselves, we have placed a number of key principles at the centre of our scheme and we summarise them below:

(1) All parties to the trial should feel free to present their case on the central facts in issue free from the fear that this will automatically result in previous misconduct being exposed.

(2) Insofar as the context permits, defendants and non-defendants should be equally protected from having their previous misconduct revealed for no good reason.

(3) Evidence of a person's bad character extraneous to the central set of facts should only be presented to the fact-finders if the court gives permission; and if the evidence is within the central set of facts, the court's permission is not needed.

(4) In considering whether to give permission the court must be satisfied that a test has been met, having regard to identified factors.

(5) No such evidence may be adduced unless it is of substantial value for determination of the case (the enhanced relevance test).

(6) A person's character should not be regarded as indivisible. If certain parts of it are sufficiently relevant to be revealed to the fact-finders then so be it but no more should be revealed than is necessary for the interests of justice to be served.

(7) If it is to be revealed it will be for the fact-finders to make of it what they will, with appropriate guidance on the risks inherent in such evidence.

(8) If a defendant's character should be revealed to the fact-finders he or she should not be able to avoid it by taking tactical steps such as not giving evidence.

1.9 We intend that our recommendations will contribute to making the law fairer in a number of ways:

(1) All the rules will be in one statute and will therefore be accessible.

(2) They will give greater protection for non-defendants.

(3) They will result in the elimination of "tit-for-tat"[3] unfairness thereby giving greater protection for defendants.

(4) A co-defendant with a criminal record is less likely to suffer the admission of that record where it is not warranted.

(5) Judges will have to give and juries seek to comply with fewer nonsensical directions drawing bizarre and unreal distinctions between credibility and propensity.

(6) The establishment of consistent statutory tests coupled with guidance for courts when ruling on admissibility will result in greater consistency of decisions.

---

[3] A defendant's criminal record can be admitted on a "tit-for-tat" basis where the defendant has attacked the character of a prosecution witness.

1.10 We are unable to say whether, if our scheme were carried into effect, more or less bad character evidence would be presented to fact-finders. We can see aspects of the scheme which might lead to less call for such evidence to be admitted on a "tit-for-tat" basis because witnesses are given greater protection from gratuitous attack and, under our scheme, the whole of a defendant's bad character is not automatically admissible if the defence attack a witness's character. On the other hand, we can also see that making a final break from formulae such as those requiring that bad character evidence be "strikingly similar" may mean that more evidence of bad character would become potentially admissible, subject always to the court's judgment on the impact of its potentially prejudicial effect.

1.11 Our inability to make such a prediction does not trouble us because, as we have said, we have not started from a position that the admittance of more or less bad character evidence should be the outcome of our recommendations. We have sought, rather, to construct a consistent and balanced process under which the conflicting interests of the various parties may best be advanced and protected, and the fairness of criminal trials generally enhanced.

OUR MAIN RECOMMENDATIONS

1.12 Fundamental to the scheme we recommend is the idea that, in any given trial, there is a *central set of facts* about which any party should be free to adduce relevant evidence without constraint – even evidence of bad character. Evidence falls within this central set of facts if it has to do with the offence charged, or is of misconduct connected with the investigation or prosecution of that offence. We recommend that evidence of bad character which falls outside this category should only be admissible if the court gives leave for it to be adduced.[4]

1.13 An important feature of our scheme is that this basic rule applies equally whether the evidence is of the bad character of a defendant or of anyone else. Thus witnesses, no less than the defendant, will be protected against allegations of misconduct extraneous to the events the subject of the trial, which have only marginal relevance to the facts of the case. For the purpose of deciding whether the evidence has sufficient enhanced relevance so that leave might be granted, the same criteria will apply to defendants and non-defendants. Defendants will have additional protection from the prejudicial impact of such evidence to reflect the fact that it is their liability to criminal sanction which is at stake.

1.14 Under our scheme, leave may be given to adduce evidence of the bad character of a *non-defendant* if it has substantial explanatory value, or it has substantial probative value in relation to a matter in issue in the proceedings which is of substantial importance in the context of the case as a whole.

1.15 Leave may be given to adduce evidence of the bad character of a *defendant* in four situations, the first two of which correspond to those in which evidence of the bad character of a non-defendant may be admitted.

---

[4] Or all parties agree to its admission, or it is evidence of a *defendant's* bad character and it is that defendant who wishes to adduce it.

1.16 First, leave may be given to any party if the evidence has the same degree of explanatory value as would be required in the case of a non-defendant, but in addition it is only admissible if the interests of justice *require* it to be admissible, even taking account of its potentially prejudicial effect.

1.17 Secondly, leave may be given *to the prosecution* if

(1) the evidence has substantial probative value in relation to a matter in issue which is itself of substantial importance, and

(2) the interests of justice require it to be admissible, even taking account of its potentially prejudicial effect.

If it has probative value only in showing that the defendant has a propensity to be untruthful, leave may not be given unless, *in addition*,

(3) the defendant has suggested that another person has a propensity to be untruthful, and

(4) adduces evidence in support of that suggestion of that person's bad character which falls outside the central set of facts, and

(5) without the evidence of the defendant's bad character the fact-finders would get a misleading impression of the defendant's propensity to be untruthful in comparison with that of the other person.

1.18 Thirdly, leave may be given *to the prosecution* if

(1) the defendant is responsible for an assertion which creates a false or misleading impression about the defendant,

(2) the evidence has substantial probative value in correcting that impression, and

(3) the interests of justice require it to be admissible, even taking account of its potentially prejudicial effect.

1.19 Fourthly, leave may be given *to a co-defendant* (D2) to adduce evidence of the bad character of a defendant (D1) if the evidence has substantial probative value in relation to a matter in issue between D2 and D1 which is itself of substantial importance in the context of the case as a whole. If it has probative value only in showing that D1 has a propensity to be untruthful, leave may not be given unless, *in addition*, D1's case is such as to undermine that of D2.

1.20 Where the court is required, for the purpose of any of the above rules, to assess either the probative value of evidence of a person's bad character, or whether the interests of justice require the evidence to be admissible taking account of the risk of prejudice, it will be required to have regard to factors which are set out in the Bill.

1.21 In assessing the probative value of such evidence the court must assume its truth – *unless* it appears, on the basis of any material before the court, that no court or jury could reasonably find it to be true.

1.22 We recommend a number of procedural safeguards, designed to ensure a fair trial:

(1) Where a party is required to seek permission to adduce evidence of the defendant's bad character, rules of court may require notice to be given of their intention to do so but the court may have a discretion to dispense with that requirement.

(2) In a trial on indictment, where evidence of the defendant's bad character has been admitted with leave and the judge is satisfied that the evidence is contaminated such that, considering the importance of the evidence to the case against the defendant, a conviction would be unsafe, the judge would be required to discharge the jury or direct the jury to acquit.

(3) Where a court gives a ruling on the admissibility of bad character evidence, or on whether the case should be stopped under safeguard (2) above, it must give the reasons for the ruling in open court and those reasons must be recorded.

(4) Where a defendant is charged with more than one offence, and evidence of the defendant's bad character is admissible on one of the offences charged but not on another, the court should grant any defence application for severance of the charges unless satisfied that the defendant can receive a fair trial.

1.23 We also conclude that the jury may need to be given warnings by the judge in two situations: first, where no evidence has been adduced about the defendant's character and there is a danger of speculation about it, and second, where there is a danger that the jury will give undue weight to bad character evidence which is admitted.

THE STRUCTURE OF THIS REPORT

1.24 Parts II and III introduce the reader to the law in this area as it currently stands. We described the English law in some detail in the consultation paper, and do not go into the same degree of detail in the report. We trust that enough information is given for the reader to follow what effects our recommendations would have. The case for changing the law is argued in Part IV.

1.25 In Part V we set out the principles which have informed our criticisms of the law and our recommendations. In Part VI we consider the range of broad options on which we consulted and our views upon them following upon the consultation.

1.26 In the subsequent Parts, we describe our recommendations. Part VII provides an overview of the scheme of our recommendations. Part VIII describes one of the central elements of the scheme, namely our identification of "the central facts" as an envelope of inquiry within which evidence of bad character will be admissible without leave. Outside that envelope, evidence of bad character may only be introduced with leave. Part IX explains when leave may be given in respect of the evidence of bad character of *non*-defendants. Parts X, XI, XII, XIII and XIV respectively describe the different circumstances in which leave may be given in respect of the bad character of defendants, namely where the evidence:

is explanatory, is incriminatory, goes to credibility, or has corrective value, and where evidence may be adduced by a co-defendant.

1.27 Parts XV, XVI and XVII concern trial issues. Part XV addresses the quality of tendered evidence. The question of severance of counts on an indictment, or informations in a summary trial, is considered in Part XVI. Procedural requirements as to notice and the duty to give reasons are dealt with in Part XVII.

1.28 Part XVIII contains all our recommendations. The Bill to give effect to those recommendations follows (with explanatory notes). Appendix A gives a summary of recent important research. Appendix B lists all those who responded to our consultation paper.

PART II
THE PRESENT LAW

2.1 In this Part we seek to set out the main features of the legal landscape with enough detail to give the general reader an understanding of the relevant law. We have not sought to answer every question that might be asked, nor to give an account of how the law came to be what it is. The exceptions to the exclusionary rule fall into three categories: those which relate to evidence that may be adduced in chief against the defendant, those relating to evidence which a defendant may adduce, and those relating to evidence which may be adduced in cross-examination of a defendant. They are described at paragraphs 2.3 – 2.38, 2.39 – 2.42 and 2.43 – 2.86 respectively. We then set out the circumstances in which separate trials of co-defendants might have to be ordered at paragraphs 2.88 – 2.90. Finally, we explain the rules as to when counts on an indictment (or informations in the magistrates' court) may be severed at paragraphs 2.91 – 2.95.

2.2 The prosecution may not, in general, adduce evidence of the defendant's bad character (other than that relating to the offence charged) nor of the defendant's propensity to act in a particular way even if relevant. This is a derogation from the general rule that all relevant evidence is admissible, and has been described as "one of the most deeply rooted and jealously guarded principles of our criminal law".[1] There are two bases for this exclusion of evidence of bad character: it is often irrelevant in showing guilt; insofar as it *is* relevant, its prejudicial effect outweighs its probative value.

EXCEPTIONS TO THE RULE OF EXCLUSION

(I): Adducing evidence of a defendant's bad character in chief

2.3 Evidence which discloses previous misconduct which is an ingredient of the offence is not subject to an exclusionary rule (for example commission of an earlier driving offence for the charge of driving while disqualified, contrary to section 103(1)(b) of the Road Traffic Act 1988). There are also charges where an allegation of previous misconduct cannot be avoided (such as absconding on bail, contrary to section 6(1) of the Bail Act 1976).

"Similar fact" evidence

2.4 The main exception to the exclusionary rule is known (somewhat misleadingly) as "the similar fact rule". The term "similar fact" evidence[2] covers evidence of misconduct by the defendant, whether arising before or after the offence charged, which is said to be evidence of his or her propensity or disposition to misconduct himself or herself either in general or in specific ways. It extends to evidence of

---

[1] *Maxwell v DPP* [1935] AC 309, 317, *per* Viscount Sankey LC.

[2] This term is still causing confusion: in *Beedles* the defence submitted that the "similar fact evidence" should be excluded, partly because it did not disclose a similar incident: 31 July 1996, CA No 96/1855/W4, 8.

bad character or conduct which is not criminal.[3] For the history of the evolution of this rule, see paragraphs 2.14 – 2.34 of the consultation paper.

2.5 The leading authority is *DPP v P* in which Lord Mackay LC held,

> ... the essential feature of evidence which is to be admitted is that its probative force ... is sufficiently great to make it just to admit the evidence, notwithstanding that it is prejudicial to the accused in tending to show that he was guilty of another crime.[4]

2.6 Before *DPP v P* the leading authority was the decision of the House of Lords in *Boardman v DPP*.[5] In that case there was a shift in emphasis in the criterion for admitting similar fact evidence from the purpose of the evidence to the amount of relevance it bore to the matter in issue.[6] The notion that the similar fact evidence should have "striking similarity" to be admissible was developed in their Lordships' speeches in *Boardman v DPP*,[7] and it came to be understood that such evidence *must* have that quality to be admissible.

2.7 In *DPP v P*, the "striking similarity" test used in *Boardman* was stated to be only one of the ways in which the enhanced relevance required of similar fact evidence may be found. It was said that to regard "striking similarity" as an essential qualification for the admissibility of similar fact evidence is "to restrict the operation of the principle in a way which gives too much effect to a particular manner of stating it".[8] The circumstances in which there may be sufficient probative force are not restricted to cases involving "striking similarities" but can be derived from some other sources, such as a relationship in time or circumstance.[9] The most significant development of the case law since the consultation paper has been in relation to cases where identification is in issue, and the previous misconduct is being tendered to prove the identity of the perpetrator. That is set out in paragraphs 2.23 – 2.26 below.

---

[3] *Ball* [1911] AC 47.

[4] [1991] 2 AC 447, 460E–F. This authority is considered in detail at paragraphs 2.35 – 2.83 of the consultation paper.

[5] [1975] AC 421, 462, *per* Lord Salmon:
> It has never ... been doubted that if the crime charged is committed in a uniquely or strikingly similar manner to other crimes committed by the accused the manner in which the other crimes were committed may be evidence upon which a jury could reasonably conclude that the accused was guilty of the crime charged. The similarity would have to be so unique or striking that common sense makes it inexplicable on the basis of coincidence.

[6] See D W Elliott, "The Young Person's Guide to Similar Fact Evidence – I" [1983] Crim LR 284, 285.

[7] See [1975] AC 421, 462 *per* Lord Salmon (n 5 above), 441D *per* Lord Morris of Borth-y-Gest, 444D *per* Lord Wilberforce, 455D *per* Lord Hailsham and 460E *per* Lord Cross of Chelsea.

[8] *DPP v P* [1991] 2 AC 447, 460G, *per* Lord Mackay LC.

[9] *DPP v P* [1991] 2 AC 447, 460.

2.8 The following sections address some specific points of difficulty in the current law.

RES GESTAE AND BACKGROUND EVIDENCE

2.9 The similar fact rule does not apply to res gestae nor to evidence which forms part of the background to the offence charged. The parameters of these two categories are not clear. Background evidence is admitted because of the close connection between it and the facts in issue, but, as *Cross and Tapper* points out,[10] this approach is potentially dangerous because it can be used to smuggle in similar fact evidence which would otherwise be inadmissible. Evidence has been admitted without application of the rule in *DPP v P* where it was part of the res gestae, showed a pre-existing relationship between the victim and the accused, revealed a motive for the offence charged, or where, without that evidence, "the totality of ... the account would be incomplete or incomprehensible".[11]

CAN EVIDENCE OF PROPENSITY BE ADMITTED AS SIMILAR FACT EVIDENCE?

2.10 The traditional view is that evidence of mere propensity to commit crimes of a certain type is inadmissible.[12] Lord Hailsham, in *Boardman*,[13] spoke of "the forbidden chain of reasoning", which was any chain of reasoning leading directly from propensity to guilt.

2.11 This view has been criticised[14] on the grounds that evidence of disposition *may* occasionally have sufficient probative value to merit admission.[15] In the consultation paper[16] we provisionally concluded that the admissibility of bad character evidence in chief should depend upon the probative value of the evidence, and not on the purpose for which it is proposed to adduce it; and that the evidence should not, therefore, be inadmissible merely because it is relevant

---

[10] *Cross and Tapper*, p 343.

[11] *Per* Purchas LJ in the unreported case of *Pettman*, 2 May 1985, CA No 5048/C/82. See further paras 4.11 – 4.12 below.

[12] See, eg, *A-G of Hong Kong v Siu Yuk-Shing* [1989] 1 WLR 236, 239F, *per* Lord Griffiths; and Lord Herschell LC's dictum in *Makin* [1894] AC 57, 65: evidence should not be adduced which tends to show that the accused has committed other criminal acts, for the purpose of leading to the conclusion that the accused is likely from such conduct or character to have committed the offence for which he is being tried.

[13] *Boardman* [1975] AC 421, 453E–G.

[14] *Boardman* [1975] AC 421, 456–457, *per* Lord Cross of Chelsea.

[15] An example is *Straffen* [1952] 2 QB 911, where the charge was of murdering a young girl by strangling in unusual circumstances: no attempt had been made to assault her sexually or to conceal her body. The defendant came under immediate suspicion because he had previously strangled two other girls, with each murder having the same peculiar feature. He had also been in the neighbourhood at the time, having just escaped from Broadmoor, and he admitted having seen the murdered girl. In those circumstances, very little other evidence was required to convict him of the third murder. An attempt is currently being made to have this case referred to the Court of Appeal by the Criminal Cases Review Commission.

[16] At paras 2.54, 10.14 and Part XVI, provisional proposal 14.

only to propensity. Support for this view can be found in the dicta of Lord Mackay LC in *DPP v P*.[17]

2.12 It is by no means clear, however, that this view has been universally adopted by the courts. It seems that there remains a reluctance to accept the proposition that propensity reasoning is not *necessarily* "forbidden" in all cases. We discuss this issue when we consider the defects in the current law.[18]

HOW CAN SIMILAR FACT EVIDENCE BE USED TO REBUT A DEFENCE?

2.13 Where similar fact evidence is sought to be admitted to rebut a defence, its purpose is to put a different complexion on what occurred – perhaps by demonstrating a criminal purpose[19] or knowledge,[20] or by showing that a death is attributable not to natural causes but to the actions of the accused.[21] The evidence is admissible if it is clear that the link between the events cannot be put down to coincidence.

2.14 Similar fact evidence must be directed to an issue in the case.[22] Clear identification of the issue to which it is said to be relevant is important, because evidence may bear on one issue, but not on another. There are various cases in which it has been suggested that similar fact evidence would *necessarily* be *inadmissible* if the defence was a general denial of the prosecution's case. One such case is *Lewis*[23] where evidence of paedophile tendencies was held *admissible* in relation to counts where the defendant said that the touching was innocent or accidental, but *inadmissible* in relation to an incident which he denied had ever

---

[17] *DPP v P* [1991] 2 AC 447, 460.

[18] See paras 4.7 – 4.10 below.

[19] Eg, in *Bond* [1906] 2 KB 389 the prosecution case was that a doctor had operated upon a woman who was pregnant with his child, with intent to procure her miscarriage. To rebut the defence that he was carrying out a lawful medical examination of the woman, the prosecution was allowed to rely on the evidence of another woman who claimed that nine months previously the defendant had operated on her when she had become pregnant by him, with the intention of terminating her pregnancy, and that he had told her that he had "put dozens of girls right".

[20] Eg, in *Peters* [1995] 2 Cr App R 77 the defendant was charged with importing amphetamine sulphate. He denied any involvement with drugs and claimed that the drugs must have been concealed in his car without his knowledge. Evidence was admitted that small quantities of cannabis had been found at his address. The Court of Appeal held that the evidence was relevant and admissible because the jury were entitled to consider the coincidence that an accused who denied knowledge of the drugs in his car also had drugs at his home.

[21] Thus in *Smith* (1915) 11 Cr App R 229 the defendant, charged with the murder of his wife, claimed that she had drowned in the bath through natural causes. To rebut this defence, the prosecution was permitted to adduce evidence that two other women whom the defendant had induced to marry him had met with the same fate, and that, in each case, the defendant had insured the woman's life, with the result that he benefited from their deaths.

[22] Thus in *Lunt* (1987) 85 Cr App R 241, 245, it was said that in order to decide whether evidence is positively probative in relation to the crime charged, it is first necessary to identify the issue to which it relates. In our provisional proposal 16 we suggested that the specific fact in issue be identified when a court considered whether bad character evidence should be admissible.

[23] (1983) 76 Cr App R 33.

taken place.[24] More recently, a similar approach was taken in *Wright*.[25]

2.15 At one time it was thought that when Lord Herschell said that evidence may be sufficiently relevant to be admissible "if it bears upon the question whether the acts alleged to constitute the crime charged in the indictment were designed or accidental, or to rebut a defence which would otherwise be open to the accused",[26] he was proposing a closed list of defences in which it might be possible to adduce similar fact evidence in rebuttal.[27] The House of Lords has repeatedly made it clear that no such closed list exists.[28] We believe the law to be, consistent with the principle set out by Lord Mackay in *DPP v P*,[29] that although in cases where the defence is a general denial it may often be the case that the similar fact evidence will not be sufficiently probative to outweigh its prejudicial effect, there should be no absolute bar to its admission. It should be noted, however, that in *B(RA)*[30] – a decision post-dating *DPP v P* – *Lewis* and *Wright* were approved on this point. We discuss the difficulties of *B(RA)* in further detail below.[31]

DOES THE PROSECUTION HAVE TO WAIT AND SEE WHAT DEFENCE IS TO BE RELIED UPON BEFORE ADDUCING SIMILAR FACT EVIDENCE?

2.16 Similar fact evidence can be adduced only if it goes to one of the issues in the case, not if it merely goes to "strengthen the evidence of a fact ... which was not denied and, perhaps, could not be the subject of rational dispute".[32] In most cases where a defence statement is provided,[33] the defence disclosure will make the prosecution aware of the matters with which the defence intends to take issue. If the defence is not known, then the test for deciding whether the similar fact evidence is relevant to the prosecution's case is whether the defence in question "may fairly be said to be open to the accused on the facts as they appear from the

---

[24] See also *Flack* [1969] 1 WLR 937, 943B–C, *per* Salmon LJ, in which the defendant was charged with incest with three of his sisters. His defence was a blank denial. It was held that the evidence on each count was inadmissible to prove the other two since "No question of identity, intent, system, guilty knowledge, or of rebutting a defence of innocent association ever arose."

[25] (1990) 90 Cr App R 325.

[26] *Makin v A-G for New South Wales* [1894] AC 57, 65.

[27] See, eg, *Flack* [1969] 1 WLR 937 and *Chandor* [1959] 1 QB 545, where evidence was excluded on the basis that the defence did not fall within the specific list, due to a misunderstanding of the decision in *Makin*.

[28] See, eg, *Harris v DPP* [1952] AC 694, 705–706, *per* Lord Simon LC.

[29] See para 2.5 above.

[30] [1997] 2 Cr App R 88.

[31] See paras 4.8 – 4.9 below.

[32] *Noor Mohamed* [1949] AC 182, 191, *per* Lord Du Parcq.

[33] Defence statements are compulsory in Crown Court cases, but voluntary before summary trial: Criminal Procedure and Investigations Act 1996 ss 5, 7. A defence statement summarises the defendant's case including those matters within the prosecution case with which the defendant takes issue.

evidence available to the prosecution".[34] We believe this to be a fair principle because it is always open to the accused to say that a particular defence will *not* be taken, or that a particular fact is not in issue, thus obviating the need for similar fact evidence to be called.[35]

2.17 While the case law suggests that evidence in rebuttal of a defence fairly open to the accused should be given as part of the prosecution's case, the courts have also, exceptionally, permitted what has been called the "short-circuiting" of this process, allowing the prosecution to put questions in rebuttal of the accused's defence in cross-examination without having led the evidence as part of its own case.[36] This is a course which should be avoided wherever possible.[37] It is preferable that the similar fact evidence should be adduced in chief rather than in the course of cross-examination with all its attendant prejudice to the witness.[38] This can be achieved by permitting the prosecution to re-open its case.

IS THERE A SPECIAL RULE FOR SEXUAL OFFENCES AGAINST PERSONS OF THE SAME SEX, OR CHILDREN?

2.18 The present position is as stated by the Court of Appeal in *Clarke*:[39] there is no specific category of offences against children for the purpose of similar fact evidence, because to assert that such offences are so rare as to justify admissibility is to ignore the regrettable fact that they are not uncommon. The more recent case of *Musquera*[40] confirmed that where the only significant similarity between two groups of offences was that they were sexual in nature, this was not sufficient to allow the evidence of one group to be admitted in respect of the other group pursuant to the rule in *DPP v P*.[41] In *Musquera*, having refused severance, the judge should have directed the jury to treat the charges separately.

Is there a discretion to exclude similar fact evidence?

2.19 The courts have traditionally had a discretion to exclude similar fact evidence even if it passes the test of admissibility. This discretion "flows from the duty of the judge when trying a charge of crime to set the essentials of justice above the

---

[34] *Blackstone*, para F12.11. This is borne out by the comments of Lord Sumner in *Thompson* [1918] AC 221, 232, that "The prosecution cannot credit the accused with fancy defences in order to rebut them at the outset", subsequently explained by Lord Du Parcq in *Noor Mohamed* [1949] AC 182, 191–2.

[35] See, eg, *A-G of Hong Kong v Siu Yuk-Shing* [1989] 1 WLR 236, 240H, *per* Lord Griffiths: "The defence ... had the opportunity if they so desired to admit knowledge of the Triad significance of the articles. If the defence had made this admission knowledge would no longer have been in issue and no proper purpose would have been served by proof of the previous conviction."

[36] See *Anderson* (1988) 87 Cr App R 349, 358, *per* Lord Lane CJ.

[37] *Jones v DPP* [1962] AC 635, 685, *per* Lord Morris.

[38] Such as the ability to ask leading questions and the proof of previous inconsistent statements.

[39] (1978) 67 Cr App R 398.

[40] [1999] Crim LR 857.

[41] [1991] 2 AC 447.

technical rule if the strict application of the latter would operate unfairly against the accused".[42] In the consultation paper[43] we suggested that the principle stated by the House of Lords in *DPP v P*[44] has the character of a rule of law – at least in cases where the prosecution seeks to rely on the evidence as proof of the defendant's disposition, or where there is a risk that the jury will regard it as such – and we questioned the existence of a residual discretion. There is no room for any discretion which entails the weighing of probative value against prejudicial effect, because that is itself the test of admissibility.[45]

SUPERVENING DISCRETIONS: SECTION 78, AND THE COMMON LAW

2.20 Section 78(1) of PACE reads:

> In any proceedings the court may refuse to allow evidence on which the prosecution proposes to rely to be given if it appears to the court that, having regard to all the circumstances, including the circumstances in which the evidence was obtained, the admission of the evidence would have such an adverse effect on the fairness of the proceedings that the court ought not to admit it.

2.21 The scope of section 78 is not limited merely to the balance of relevance and prejudice. Extrinsic considerations of fairness come into play, such as the way in which the evidence was obtained. It is therefore possible that the defence would seek to exclude some item of bad character evidence on these grounds.[46]

2.22 Section 82(3) of the same Act preserves the common law discretion to exclude evidence, which is founded on the duty of the judge to ensure that every accused person has a fair trial.[47] As with section 78, this discretion is not limited to excluding evidence which is more prejudicial than probative, but extends to excluding evidence which might be unfair to the accused for some other reason.[48] However, in nearly all cases the role formerly played by the common law discretion has been subsumed within the new statutory regime.

---

[42] *Harris v DPP* [1952] AC 694, 707, *per* Viscount Simon.

[43] At para 2.41.

[44] *DPP v P* [1991] 2 AC 447.

[45] As Peter Mirfield has said: "The judge is likely to invite counsel to explain to him how evidence which, for the purposes of the similar fact rule, has more probative value than prejudicial effect, can possibly be more prejudicial than probative as a matter of discretion." Mirfield, "Proof and Prejudice in the House of Lords" (1996) 112 LQR 1, 7-8.

[46] In *H* [1995] 2 AC 596 both Lord Mackay LC at p 612H and Lord Nicholls at p 627E made the point that, even where evidence is admissible under the similar fact rules, the trial judge can always use the s 78 discretion to exclude the evidence where appropriate.

[47] See *Sang* [1980] AC 402, 452, *per* Lord Scarman; 447, *per* Lord Fraser; 445, *per* Lord Salmon.

[48] Such as confessions and other evidence obtained after the alleged commission of the offence by improper or unfair means.

IDENTITY CASES

Striking similarity

2.23 It was said in *DPP v P* that where the identity of the perpetrator was in issue, "something in the nature of what has been called ... 'a signature' or other special feature would be necessary".[49] This proposition has been further considered in the recent decision of *W*[50] where it was held that this dictum should be interpreted as applying only to cases "where the only evidence of any substance against a defendant on a count was 'a signature' or other very striking similarity."[51] Thus, in the majority of cases where identification is in issue, there is no longer any special rule.

How the evidence is to be approached

2.24 The traditional approach to identity cases can be called the "sequential approach": where crimes A and B are strikingly similar, such that they are likely to have been committed by the same person, and the prosecution can prove that D committed crime B, the prosecution can use this evidence to prove that D also committed crime A, as in *Straffen*.[52]

2.25 This type of reasoning is frequently employed where D has already been convicted in respect of crime B.[53] However, there is no reason why the same reasoning should not also be employed where D's guilt of crime B is also in issue in the proceedings. It seems to have been employed, for example, in *Ruiz*[54] where D was alleged to have followed the same *modus operandi* in respect of separate incidents concerning two victims, to each of whom a stupefying drug was administered to enable D to rob them. One victim died. The identity of the killer was in issue, and the purpose of adducing evidence of the robbery by D of the surviving victim was to suggest that a pattern could be deduced which showed that D was also the murderer.

2.26 A relatively recent line of cases has emerged which adopts a different approach to similar fact evidence where identification is in issue. It can be conveniently labelled the "cumulative approach".[55] Unlike the "sequential approach" there is

---

[49] [1991] 2 AC 447, 462, *per* Lord Mackay LC.

[50] *John W* [1998] 2 Cr App R 289.

[51] *Per* Hooper J, affirming the approach adopted in *Ruiz* [1995] Crim LR 151. The case of *Straffen* [1952] 2 QB 911 was cited as an example of such an approach. See n 15 above.

[52] [1952] 2 QB 911. See n 15 above.

[53] See, eg, *Black* [1995] Crim LR 640, where D's previous conviction in respect of the "Stow incident" in Scotland in 1990 was used to identify him as the perpetrator of three strikingly similar murders and a kidnapping in England.

[54] [1995] Crim LR 151.

[55] Following the wording in *John W* [1998] 2 Cr App R 289, reported as *Wharton* [1998] Crim LR 668. The validity of this type of reasoning was first acknowledged by the Court of Appeal in *Downey* [1995] 1 Cr App R 547. The phrase "pooling" approach is also used: see R Pattenden, "Similar Fact Evidence and Proof of Identity" (1996) 112 LQR 446.

no need to establish independently[56] that D was responsible for crime B in order for the evidence concerning that offence to be used to support the evidence relating to crime A. Rather, the two crimes are "welded together"[57] and *all the available evidence* is used cumulatively in order to establish the identity of the perpetrator. The legitimacy of this approach was confirmed in *Brown*[58] and in *W*,[59] but it was said in the latter case that where the *only* evidence on count A is the striking similarity with count B, it would be necessary to adopt the sequential approach.[60]

Special cases where bad character evidence is admissible in chief

SECTION 27(3) OF THE THEFT ACT 1968

2.27 Section 27(3) of the Theft Act 1968 provides:

> Where a person is being proceeded against for handling stolen goods (but not for any offence other than handling stolen goods), then at any stage of the proceedings, if evidence has been given of his handling or arranging to have in his possession the goods the subject of the charge, or of his undertaking or assisting in, or arranging to undertake to assist in, their retention, removal, disposal or realisation, the following evidence shall be admissible for the purpose of proving that he knew or believed the goods to be stolen goods:–
>
> (a) evidence that he has had in his possession, or has undertaken or assisted in the retention, removal, disposal or realisation of, stolen goods, from any theft taking place not earlier than twelve months before the offence charged; and
>
> (b) (provided seven days' notice in writing has been given to him of the intention to prove the conviction) evidence that he has within

---

[56] In other words, in isolation from the evidence pertaining to the other counts. Under the cumulative approach the evidence in relation to each count is, *ex hypothesi*, inconclusive to prove the identity of the perpetrator of that particular count – if it were otherwise the sequential approach would be employed.

[57] An expression first used by counsel for the Crown in *Downey* [1995] 1 Cr App R 547 and adopted by the Court of Appeal in the course of its judgment.

[58] [1997] Crim LR 502. This case concerned the identification of a gang of offenders. In his commentary to this case, Ormerod points out that the cumulative approach may be dangerous in group identification cases, since the personnel involved may alter between offences. He notes that the dangers are particularly acute where the similar fact evidence is not specific to the particular defendant, but to the group as a whole: [1997] Crim LR 502, 504.

[59] [1998] 2 Cr App R 289, reported as *Wharton* [1998] Crim LR 668.

[60] The Court of Appeal has warned that it is dangerous to elevate what is essentially a matter of relevance and common sense to a proposition of law; and that the process by which it is ascertained whether the defendant committed the offences may well contain aspects of both the cumulative and sequential approaches: *Gourde* 31 July 1997, CA 96/5746/X5, *per* Evans LJ. His Honour also said: "it would be wrong to lose sight of the reasons why similar fact evidence is sometimes admitted and sometimes excluded".

the five years preceding the date of the offence charged been convicted of theft or of handling stolen goods.

2.28 In short, on a charge of handling stolen goods, in order to prove that the defendant knew or believed the goods to be stolen, section 27(3) permits the prosecution to adduce in chief evidence of criminal disposition, in the form of evidence of prior possession of stolen goods or previous convictions.

The application of section 27(3)

2.29 Section 27(3) applies to all forms of handling[61] but its application is restricted by its terms to cases where handling is the only type of offence charged in the proceedings. The prosecution can only rely on the subsection in order to prove guilty knowledge or belief;[62] it cannot be used to prove possession of the goods in question. Moreover, the prosecution must adduce evidence of the actus reus of the offence before the provision can be relied upon to show guilty knowledge.[63]

2.30 Since the subsection allows the prosecution to prove facts that would not ordinarily be relevant at common law and would not therefore be admissible, the courts have held that the terms of the subsection must be strictly adhered to.[64] The Court of Appeal in *Bradley*[65] said that the section ought to be construed "with strict regard to its terms". This attitude has led to an extremely restrictive attitude towards the subsection. We discuss the provision in detail at paragraphs 4.13 – 4.23 below.

SECTION 1(2) OF THE OFFICIAL SECRETS ACT 1911

2.31 Section 1(2) provides:

> On a prosecution under this section,[66] it shall not be necessary to show that the accused person was guilty of any particular act tending to

---

[61] *Ball* [1983] 1 WLR 801.

[62] It cannot be used to assist the prosecution in proving dishonesty: *Duffas* (1994) 158 JP 224.

[63] The fact that the defendant denies that possession does not, of itself, prevent the prosecution relying on the section. However, where there are several counts, in some of which possession is denied and others in which the issue is guilty knowledge there must be a careful direction that the evidence adduced under s 27(3) is admitted only for the purpose of proving guilty knowledge, and not to prove the act of handling: see *Wilkins* (1974) 60 Cr App R 300.

[64] See, in particular, *Davies* [1953] 1 QB 489, 493, *per* Lord Goddard CJ.

[65] (1980) 70 Cr App R 200, 203, *per* Snow LJ.

[66] Section 1(1) of the Act, as amended by the Official Secrets Act 1920, ss 10, 11(2), Schedules 1 and 2, provides:
> If any person for any purpose prejudicial to the safety or interests of the State –
> (a) approaches, inspects, passes over or is in the neighbourhood of, or enters any prohibited place ... ; or (b) makes any sketch, plan, model, or note which is calculated to be or might be or is intended to be directly or indirectly useful to an enemy; or (c) obtains, collects, records, or publishes, or communicates to any other person any secret official code word or pass word, or any sketch, plan, model, article, or note, or other document or information which is calculated to be

show a purpose prejudicial to the safety or interests of the State, and, notwithstanding that no such act is proved against him, he may be convicted if, from the circumstances of the case, or his conduct, or his known character as proved, it appears that his purpose was a purpose prejudicial to the safety or interests of the State ...

2.32 In the consultation paper we noted that this section constitutes an exception to the general exclusionary rule at common law that evidence of a defendant's bad character may not be adduced as part of the prosecution case.[67] Therefore, the provision runs contrary to the usual principles of justice. Whether or not it represents a defect in the present law depends very much on whether it is viewed as a defensible special case. We discuss this provision at paragraphs 11.56 – 11.61 below.

Special cases where bad character evidence is inadmissible *in chief*

SPENT CONVICTIONS

2.33 The philosophy of the Rehabilitation of Offenders Act 1974[68] is that, once a conviction is "spent", the rehabilitated person should be treated in law as a person who has not been convicted of or charged with the offence. The Act does not apply to the use of convictions in criminal proceedings.[69] Nevertheless, a Practice Direction has been issued[70] under which "it is recommended that both court and counsel should give effect to the general intention of Parliament by never referring to a spent conviction [of a defendant or a witness] when such reference can be reasonably avoided".[71] To achieve this aim, no party may refer in open court to a spent conviction without the authority of the judge or magistrates, "which authority should not be given unless the interests of justice so require".[72]

2.34 The Practice Direction achieves much the same result as if criminal proceedings had not been expressly excluded from the scope of the Act. This has created what

---

or might be or is intended to be directly or indirectly useful to an enemy; he shall be guilty of [an offence].

[67] See para 3.5 and n 3 of the consultation paper.

[68] The 1974 Act was the result of the report *Living it Down* (1972) published by a committee set up by JUSTICE, the Howard League and the National Association for the Care and Resettlement of Offenders.

[69] Rehabilitation of Offenders Act 1974, s 7(2)(a).

[70] *Practice Direction (Crime: Spent Convictions)* [1975] 1 WLR 1065. See Appendix A of the consultation paper for the text of the Direction.

[71] *Practice Direction (Crime: Spent Convictions)* [1975] 1 WLR 1065, para 4.

[72] *Practice Direction (Crime: Spent Convictions)* [1975] 1 WLR 1065, para 6. A failure to obtain leave in respect of a defence witness may, but does not necessarily, lead to the conviction being set aside. See *Smallman* [1982] Crim LR 175, where the Court of Appeal stated that a breach of para 6 of the Practice Direction could not be a ground for upsetting a conviction which was otherwise perfectly proper. This is difficult to square with the Court of Appeal's further assertion that the Practice Direction made it *necessary* to seek leave to refer to spent convictions. It may be significant that in *Smallman* the trial judge strongly directed the jury to disregard any prejudice resulting from disclosure of the spent convictions.

is perhaps better described as a "constitutionally difficult area",[73] rather than as a defect in the present law.

2.35 One gap in the present law on spent convictions is that neither the Act nor the Practice Direction refer to formal cautions.[74] Since there is no concept of a caution becoming "spent", at least in theory (in practice they are kept on record for five years), it is still open to parties to refer to stale cautions with impunity in a situation where they could not refer to stale convictions.[75] A caution is not a conviction although it shares many of its features. It is not a decision of the court and may therefore be challenged.[76] Evidence of a formal caution can be excluded under section 78(1) of PACE.[77]

2.36 Where a conviction is spent and it is immaterial to the particular case, there is authority that a person who has no other convictions should be treated as of good character and entitled to receive a full good character direction.[78] It would seem likely that by way of analogy a "spent" caution for an offence which was immaterial should similarly not prejudice the defendant's good character.

2.37 Two views have been identified about the effect of a caution on character. On the one hand, the admission of the offence, which is a prerequisite to a caution, shows that the accused has not kept on the right side of the law, which one might have thought a necessary attribute of a person of good character. On the other hand, a person should not be said to lose his or her good character in the eyes of the law unless there has been a conviction by a court, and a caution should not be regarded as of equivalent effect.[79]

2.38 According to Professor Birch,[80] commenting on the case of *Martin*,[81] the state of the law is that a caution may prevent the full good character direction being given

---

[73] *Evans* (1992) 156 JP 539, 541F, *per* Lane LCJ; [1992] Crim LR 125.

[74] Where the decision is taken not to prosecute a suspect for an offence, the police have a discretion to issue a formal caution. Although records are kept of the administering of cautions, they do not rank as convictions. The Home Secretary has power to direct for what period of time cautions are to be kept. Should a cautioned person subsequently be convicted of an offence, the caution may be cited at the sentencing stage: see Home Office Circulars of 1990 and 1994 (1990/59 and 1994/18).

[75] See Anthony Edwards, "Cautions – Further Problems" [1997] Crim LR 534.

[76] *Abraham v Commissioner of the Police for the Metropolis* (2001) 98(5) LSG 37. The defendant contended that the acceptance of a formal caution should not prevent her from bringing a civil claim which denied the admission of guilt made in accepting the caution. The court allowed the appeal and held that the fundamental distinction between a formal caution and a criminal conviction was that the former was not brought about by any decision of a court and was not open to public view and scrutiny. The only challenge to a formal caution was by way of judicial review, which, in the circumstances, could not supply an adequate remedy. The caution was not the decision of a court and so was not res judicata.

[77] *Hayter v L* [1998] 1 WLR 854, which involved a private prosecution for the same offence.

[78] *Heath* (1994) *The Times*, 10 February 1994.

[79] Anthony Edwards, "Cautions – Further Problems" [1997] Crim LR 534.

[80] [2000] Crim LR 615.

[81] [2000] 2 Cr App R 42.

(the *Vye*[82] direction) but the more normal outcome will be that the direction is given in a modified form rather than withheld altogether. According to Lord Steyn in *Aziz*[83] the position prima facie is that both limbs of a good character direction should be given, but that ultimately a trial judge has a

> residual discretion to decline to give any character directions in the case of the defendant without previous convictions if the judge considers it an insult to common sense to give directions in accordance with *Vye*.

(II): Evidence adduced by the defendant

2.39 The defendant can adduce evidence of his or her own previous misconduct without restriction.

Evidence adduced against a co-accused

2.40 A defendant can adduce evidence of a co-defendant's bad character if it is relevant to the former's defence. If the evidence is relevant, the court has no discretion to exclude it, notwithstanding its prejudicial effect. The rationale is that a defendant should not be inhibited in the presentation of his or her defence. The test of relevance is strictly applied so that if the evidence is propensity evidence it must support the accused's defence.[84]

IS THERE A DISCRETION TO EXCLUDE DEFENCE EVIDENCE?

2.41 The existence of a discretion to exclude defence evidence is in some doubt. There are authorities which state that there is no such discretion, but some recent dicta raise the possibility that the issue has not been finally decided.[85]

2.42 The possibility of a discretion to exclude evidence which is prejudicial to a co-defendant was canvassed by Evans LJ in *Thompson, Sinclair and Maver*.[86] He noted that the only discretionary safeguard for a defendant who risks having prejudicial evidence adduced by the co-defendant is the "cumbersome device of separate trials".[87] He went on "This seems undesirable, and it might be preferable to allow a discretion where the prejudice is substantial and the evidence is of only limited benefit to the co-defendant".[88] He argued that under the current authorities, the protection for the co-accused lay in the strict application of relevance, as

---

[82] (1993) 97 Cr App R 134.

[83] (1995) 2 Cr App R 478, 488–489.

[84] *Neale* (1977) 65 Cr App R 304.

[85] See, eg, *Myers* [1997] 3 WLR 552, 571, where Lord Hope of Craighead expressed the view that "worthless" defence evidence could be excluded, although in that case, which concerned hearsay evidence, the House of Lords decided that there was no such discretion.

[86] [1995] 2 Cr App 589.

[87] [1995] 2 Cr App R 589, 597.

[88] *Ibid*, 596–597.

illustrated by *Bracewell*[89] and *Neale*,[90] and that the Court of Appeal in the former might have been referring to a discretion by saying that "There are obvious objections to putting a co-accused in the position of having to fight two quite different battles at the same time".[91] Evans LJ continued: "We should not like it to be thought that we have concluded that such a discretion can never exist, although the authorities make it difficult to hold that it does".[92]

(III): Adducing bad character evidence in cross-examination

2.43 Section 1 of the Criminal Evidence Act 1898, as amended, provides:

> Every person charged with an offence shall be a competent witness for the defence at every stage of the proceedings, whether the person so charged is charged solely or jointly with any other person. Provided as follows –
>
> (e) A person charged and being a witness in pursuance of this Act may be asked any question in cross-examination notwithstanding that it would tend to criminate him as to the offence charged:
>
> (f) A person charged and called as a witness in pursuance of this Act shall not be asked, and if asked shall not be required to answer, any question tending to show that he has committed or been convicted of or been charged with any offence other than that wherewith he is then charged, or is of bad character, unless –
>
> > (i) the proof that he has committed or been convicted of such other offence is admissible evidence to show that he is guilty of the offence wherewith he is then charged; or
> >
> > (ii) he has personally or by his advocate asked questions of the witnesses for the prosecution with a view to establish his own good character, or has given evidence of his good character, or the nature or conduct of the defence is such as to involve imputations on the character of the prosecutor or the witnesses for the prosecution, or the deceased victim of the alleged crime; or
> >
> > (iii) he has given evidence against any other person charged in the same proceedings.

2.44 In short, the defendant has a "shield" against cross-examination on his or her character (other than directly connected with the allegation for which he or she is

---

[89] (1979) 68 Cr App R 44.

[90] (1977) 65 Cr App R 304.

[91] (1979) 68 Cr App R 44, 51, *per* Ormrod LJ.

[92] [1995] 2 Cr App R 589, 597.

on trial) (section 1(f)), but risks losing this shield in the circumstances provided for by section 1(f)(i), (ii) and (iii).[93]

The meaning of section 1(f)

2.45 The rule does not prevent a defendant from voluntarily making revelations about his or her past, nor does it prevent defence counsel from asking questions leading to disclosure of previous convictions or bad character.

2.46 It has been recently confirmed that the prohibition is not limited to cross-examination which shows a defendant to have a criminal record but also covers cross-examination designed to show that a defendant is of bad character, in the sense of reputation and disposition.[94] The prohibition relates to all convictions, whether they occurred before or after the offence charged.[95]

2.47 The House of Lords has held that the word "charged" means "charged in court", not merely suspected or accused without subsequent prosecution, as "The most virtuous may be suspected, and an unproven accusation proves nothing".[96] This does not mean that questions about incidents giving rise to a suspicion cannot be the subject of comprehensive cross-examination: the courts use the doctrine of relevance to decide whether such questions may be put.[97]

The relationship between section 1(e) and section 1(f)

2.48 At first glance, section 1(e) appears to permit cross-examination of a kind which section 1(f) appears to prohibit. The House of Lords sought to resolve the apparent conflict between these subsections in *Jones v DPP*,[98] where a majority took the view that, in cases of conflict, the prohibition in section 1(f) defeats the permission in section 1(e). However, the majority judgments are complicated and not entirely consistent. Professor Sir John Smith proposes the simplest solution to the problem.[99] He argues that the existence of section 1(f)(i) leads to the conclusion that section 1(f) must prevail over section 1(e), since questions which may be put to the defendant under section 1(f)(i) are inevitably questions which "tend to criminate him as to the offence charged", so that if section 1(e) were dominant, section 1(f)(i) would be of no effect as there would be no shield to pierce.

---

[93] The paragraphs of s 1 of the 1898 Act are to be renumbered under para 1(7) of Sched 4 to the Youth Justice and Criminal Evidence Act 1999 which is not yet in force. Paras (a), (e), (f), and (g) will respectively be numbered as subsections (1), (2), (3) and (4) of s 1. Schedule 4 also amends the wording of s 1, updating the language of the section but not altering its substantive meaning.

[94] *Carter* (1997) 161 JP 207.

[95] *Wood* [1920] 2 KB 179. The date of the convictions might be a factor affecting the exercise of the judge's discretion to prevent cross-examination: *Coltress* (1978) 68 Cr App R 193.

[96] *Stirland v DPP* [1944] AC 315, 324, *per* Viscount Simon LC.

[97] *Maxwell v DPP* [1935] AC 309, 321; affirmed in *Stirland v DPP* [1944] AC 315.

[98] [1962] AC 635.

[99] J C Smith, *Criminal Evidence* (1995) p 180.

2.49 The matter was revisited in *Anderson*,[100] in which Lord Lane CJ (giving the judgment of the Court of Appeal) appears to have considered a question revealing an offence other than that charged as permissible if proof of the commission of that other offence "tended to connect the appellant with the offence charged". We take the view that *Blackstone*[101] is right to say that the correct interpretation of the majority decision in *Jones v DPP* is that such a question is permissible only if it falls within the terms of section 1(f)(i).

Section 1(f)(i)

2.50 It is this exception to the general prohibition against the cross-examination of the defendant on his or her bad character that permits cross-examination on similar fact evidence and evidence of previous misconduct which is an integral part of the offence.[102]

2.51 *Cross and Tapper*[103] points out that the practical effect of the provision is greatly reduced by the decision of the House of Lords in *Jones v DPP*.[104] In that case it was held that, where evidence of a previous offence has been adduced in chief, the accused may be cross-examined about it without reliance on the exception in section 1(f)(i). This was because the words "tending to show" meant "make known to the jury", and therefore the prohibition in section 1(f) did not apply. The paragraph remains of importance where no revelation has been made in chief; although the House of Lords in *Jones v DPP* held that the prosecution should adduce some evidence of such a matter in chief, so as to allow the defendant to challenge any supposed points of similarity between the two offences or to cross-examine the witnesses for the prosecution.[105] The decision in *Anderson*[106] "seems to erode the natural meaning of the words of the prohibition still further".[107] In this case, it was held that the prohibition did not apply where, although the prohibited matter had not itself been revealed in chief, the defence themselves revealed the commission of (another) crime, the justification being that no further prejudice would be caused to the defendant by the cross-examination.

---

[100] [1988] QB 678.

[101] At para F14.3.

[102] Eg, evidence of a previous conviction for a road traffic offence, in later proceedings for driving while disqualified.

[103] At p 397.

[104] [1962] AC 635.

[105] It may be that the prosecution is unwilling or unable to offer such evidence in chief, as in *Jones* itself.

[106] [1988] QB 678.

[107] *Cross and Tapper*, p 394.

2.52 Section 1(f)(i) refers only to evidence of *commission* or *conviction* of a crime, and not to *charges* or to misconduct falling short of crime. These omissions are unfortunate, since they may require the exclusion of highly probative evidence.[108]

The first limb of section 1(f)(ii): asserting good character

2.53 Where a defendant is of good character, the jury will be directed that this is relevant both to the likelihood of the defendant's guilt and, where applicable, to his or her credibility.[109]

2.54 The rationale of the exception in the first limb of section 1(f)(ii) is that

> if the prisoner by himself or his witnesses seeks to give evidence of his own good character, for the purpose of showing that it is unlikely that he committed the offence charged, he raises by way of defence an issue as to his good character so that he may fairly be cross-examined to show the contrary.[110]

WHAT IS AN ASSERTION OF GOOD CHARACTER?

2.55 The prosecution cannot invoke the first limb of section 1(f)(ii) merely because the defendant gives evidence which is relevant to the charge, and incidentally casts him or her in a good light.[111]

2.56 The shield is also not lost where the assertion of good character is elicited by the *prosecution's* cross-examination of a defence witness,[112] or is volunteered by such a witness,[113] or is made in opening the defence case but not in evidence.[114]

2.57 The courts have held that a defendant has given evidence of good character where he or she claims to have been earning an honest living for a considerable time,[115]

---

[108] See, eg, *Cokar* [1960] 2 QB 207. The prosecution were not permitted to cross-examine the defendant in order to show that he had formerly been acquitted of the same type of offence as in the present charge. They wished to show that, since he had used the same defence previously, he was lying when he said that he did not know such a defence existed. This was affirmed in *Pommell* [1999] Crim LR 578, where the defendant's appeal was successful on the grounds that cross-examination about his previous acquittal for possession of a prohibited weapon was wrongly permitted by the judge.

[109] *Vye* [1993] 1 WLR 471.

[110] *Maxwell v DPP* [1935] AC 309, 319, *per* Viscount Sankey LC.

[111] *Ellis* [1910] 2 KB 746.

[112] *Stronach* [1988] Crim LR 48.

[113] *Redd* [1923] 1 KB 104.

[114] *Ellis* [1910] 2 KB 746.

[115] *Powell* [1985] 1 WLR 1364.

to be a regular churchgoer[116] or to have performed kind or honest deeds (such as returning lost property to its owner) on a previous occasion.[117]

2.58 Difficulties arise where the accused seeks to suggest a favourable contrast between his or her character and the bad character of others who could have committed the offence.[118] *Cross and Tapper* states that where those others are not called, the question whether the defendant has lost the shield depends on "exactly how pointedly the contrast is made".[119] This principle poses difficulties in its application. In *Lee*[120] the accused was charged with theft from the house in which he was lodging, and did not lose the shield by pointing out that others with criminal records had access to the house. In *Bracewell*,[121] however, the defendant to a charge of murder in the course of burglary lost the shield by contrasting his own cool, non-violent professionalism with the inexperience of his companion.[122]

CHARACTER IS INDIVISIBLE

2.59 The character of the accused is regarded as indivisible:

> there is no such thing known to our procedure as putting half a prisoner's character in issue and leaving out the other half.[123]

Similarly, the accused cannot confine the inquiry to a particular period of time when his or her character was good.[124]

2.60 When the defence chooses to reveal some part of the accused's character which is not in any sense *good* character, the prosecution or a co-accused is, in general, not then entitled to add further evidence of bad character.[125] There are, however, two qualifications to this rule. First, there may be cases where a certain aspect of bad character is asserted for the purpose of suggesting a lack of disposition to commit the offence. The accused may, for example, seek to deny a charge of raping a woman by claiming to be homosexual,[126] or claim to be a highly professional

---

[115] *Ferguson* (1909) 2 Cr App R 250. But not merely by waving a Bible around while testifying: *Robinson* [2001] EWCA Crim 214.

[117] *Samuel* (1956) 40 Cr App R 8.

[118] *Ellis* [1910] 2 KB 746. Note that if those others are called as witnesses for the prosecution, the matter is governed by the second limb of s 1(f)(ii). See para 2.43 above.

[119] At p 431.

[120] [1976] 1 WLR 71.

[121] (1979) 68 Cr App R 44.

[122] Initially, evidence of B's violent disposition was held not to be relevant, but it became so when he made claims about not tending to be violent. This case could, alternatively, be explained as coming within s 1(f)(iii).

[123] *Winfield* (1940) 27 Cr App R 139, 141, *per* Humphreys J.

[124] *Shrimpton* (1851) 2 Den 319; 169 ER 521.

[125] *Thompson* [1966] 1 WLR 405.

[126] Cf *Redgrave* (1982) 74 Cr App R 10, where the accused sought to put in evidence of his heterosexual disposition (he was accused of importuning in a public lavatory). That evidence was rejected by the Court of Appeal as irrelevant.

burglar who would not be likely to commit the clumsy murder with which he is charged.[127] Such claims appear to put the defendant's character in issue. Second, an accused may not pretend to have made a clean breast of previous misconduct when he or she has not in fact done so.[128]

THE DISCRETION TO EXCLUDE

2.61 This issue more usually arises in relation to the second limb of section 1(f)(ii), but the existence of a discretion under this limb was recognised by the Court of Appeal in *Thompson*,[129] and *Marsh*,[130] although in neither case was the discretion exercised in the defendant's favour. More recently,[131] the Court of Appeal has held that the trial judge should have exercised his discretion to exclude previous convictions for offences similar to those charged. They were so overwhelmingly prejudicial as to outweigh any possible marginal relevance to the issue of credibility, and only the defendant's previous convictions for dissimilar dishonesty offences should have been admitted, since these would have been sufficient to deal with the issue of credibility.

COMMON LAW RULES

2.62 If an accused falsely asserts good character, the prosecution can respond by eliciting extrinsic evidence of bad character or previous convictions in rebuttal, although there is obviously no need to do so if the defendant admits these matters in cross-examination.[132] This is consistent with the modern rule which allows a prosecutor to adduce evidence in rebuttal where he or she could not reasonably have foreseen that the matter would arise.[133]

The second limb of section 1(f)(ii): casting imputations against prosecution witnesses

2.63 Where a defendant loses the shield under the second limb of section 1(f)(ii), it is sometimes said that his or her own bad character has become admissible on a "tit-for-tat" basis, because the essence of the provision is that the defendant has attacked the character of a prosecution witness, and so the defendant loses the protection of the shield. There are two main issues to be considered: first, the preconditions for the operation of this limb of section 1(f)(ii), and second, the difficult question of the exercise of the court's discretion.

---

[127] *Bracewell* (1979) 68 Cr App R 44; n 121 above.

[128] *Wattam* (1953) 36 Cr App R 72, 78, obiter, *per* Oliver J. In that case, the defendant to a charge of murder had given evidence that he was a thief and had spent time in Borstal. The Court of Criminal Appeal held that this was *not* equivalent to a defendant saying that he or she had been convicted of a crime once when in fact he or she has been convicted on several occasions.

[129] [1966] 1 WLR 405.

[130] [1994] Crim LR 52.

[131] *Davison-Jenkins* [1997] Crim LR 816.

[132] See, eg, *Lowery* [1974] AC 85.

[133] *Scott* (1984) 79 Cr App R 49.

THE PRE-CONDITIONS

2.64 As *Cross and Tapper* points out,[134] it is not possible to set out an exact definition of what amounts to an imputation, as much depends upon the detailed facts of each case. To trigger this limb of the subsection, the imputation must be related to the "character of the prosecutor or the witnesses for the prosecution or the deceased victim of the alleged crime".[135] It would seem from this wording that an attack upon the conduct of a living person not called as a witness does not endanger the shield.[136] However, it was held in the case of *Miller*[137] that a witness is a person with material evidence to give, and that such evidence could be given in a variety of ways. A witness is nonetheless a witness if dead, or beyond the seas or unfit to attend. Attacks on a witness who has made depositions which are read[138] would trigger the section. This must overrule *Westfall*[139] which holds that a "witness for the prosecution" within section 1(f)(ii) means a "witness called in the case". However, *Westfall* is not cited in *Miller*.

2.65 On a literal construction, this provision might lead to accused persons being liable to cross-examination on their criminal record whenever they assert their innocence or contend that the prosecution's evidence is false, because of the implied suggestion that at least one of the prosecution witnesses is guilty of perjury. This argument has had some judicial support.[140] However, it has been argued that "unless [this limb] is given some restricted meaning, a prisoner's bad character, if he had one, would emerge almost as a matter of course",[141] and that such revelation is "always damaging and often fatal to a defence".[142]

2.66 Thus, the word "imputation" is given a limited meaning. It has been held that an emphatic denial does not count as an imputation, even though it may take the form of the accused stating in cross-examination that a prosecution witness's evidence is a lie and the witness therefore a liar,[143] or of defence counsel making a clear suggestion of lies and drawing on inconsistencies in the witnesses' accounts

---

[134] At p 405.

[135] The reference to the deceased victim was inserted by s 31 of the Criminal Justice and Public Order Act 1994, as a result of an amendment proposed by Lord Ackner. It is not limited to cases of homicide, and would, on the face of it, apply to any case in which the victim has died: see R May, *Criminal Evidence* (4th ed 1999) p 141.

[136] *Westfall* (1912) 7 Cr App R 176.

[137] [1997] 2 Cr App R 178.

[138] In accordance with s 13(3) of the Criminal Justice Act 1925 or s 23 of the Criminal Justice Act 1988 (and presumably Sched 2 to the Criminal Investigations and Procedure Act 1996).

[139] (1912) 7 Cr App R 176.

[140] *Hudson* [1912] 2 KB 464, 470.

[141] *Cook* [1959] 2 QB 340, 345, *per* Devlin J.

[142] *Selvey v DPP* [1970] AC 304, 353D, *per* Lord Pearce.

[143] *Rouse* [1904] 1 KB 184. In *Selvey v DPP* [1970] AC 304, 339F, Viscount Dilhorne said that a rule had developed whereby "If what is said amounts in reality to no more than a denial of the charge, expressed, it may be, in emphatic language, it should not be regarded as coming within the section".

to lend the suggestion weight.[144] If, however, the defendant's denial goes beyond what is necessary to challenge the veracity of the accuser it will amount to an imputation.[145] The line between a mere denial and an accusation that a prosecution witness is lying or fabricating the evidence is very difficult to draw, and some of the authorities are difficult to reconcile.[146] This difficulty seems to have motivated the court in *Britzman*[147] to lay down guidelines for the exercise of the discretion to disallow cross-examination where the shield is technically lost.[148]

2.67 Not every allegation of misconduct or impropriety will amount to an imputation,[149] and what is considered to be an imputation may well vary from one generation to the next.[150]

SEXUAL CASES

2.68 In cases of rape, a defendant who alleges consent on the part of the victim does not, for the purpose of this limb, make "imputations on the character of the prosecution or witnesses for the prosecution".[151] It is not clear whether this is because rape is sui generis, justifying special rules[152] or because it would be unjust to put the defendant at risk of losing the shield by doing no more than deny one of the elements of the offence which the prosecution must prove.[153] The latter reasoning would apply equally to other offences. It is also possible to explain the cases on the basis that although an imputation is made, the discretion to prevent cross-examination is always exercised.[154]

2.69 A defendant's ability to make imputations about the complainant's sexual behaviour has been limited by the Youth Justice and Criminal Evidence Act 1999,

---

[144] *Desmond* [1999] Crim L R 313.

[145] *Rappolt* (1911) 6 Cr App R 156.

[146] Compare, for example, *Rouse* [1904] 1 KB 184 with *Rappolt* (1911) 6 Cr App R 156; and *Tanner* (1911) 6 Cr App R 117 with *Nelson* (1979) 68 Cr App R 12.

[147] [1983] 1 WLR 350, 355.

[148] See paras 2.71 – 2.76 below.

[149] Eg, it is questionable whether an imputation necessarily entails an allegation of unlawful or immoral conduct: see *Bishop* [1975] QB 274, 279.

[150] *Blackstone*, para F14.24.

[151] See especially *Selvey v DPP* [1970] AC 304; *Sheean* (1908) 21 Cox CC 561; *Turner* [1944] KB 463.

[152] *Cook* [1959] 2 QB 340, 347, *per* Devlin J. *Blackstone*, at para F14.26, submits that rape should not be treated as an offence sui generis. Professor J Temkin also argues that there is no reason that it should: "Rape and Criminal Justice at the Millennium" in *Feminist Perspectives on Criminal Law* (eds D Nicolson and L Bibbings) (2000) p 199.

[153] *Turner* [1944] KB 463, 469, *per* Humphreys J. See *Goodwin*, *The Times* 26 November 1993, where it was held that the mere denial of the existence of an incriminating fact does not amount to an imputation.

[154] Following *Cook* [1959] 2 QB 340, 347, *per* Devlin J.

sections 41–43.[155] These provisions are stricter than their earlier counterparts:[156] evidence may only be admitted with leave of the court, which may be given only where the exclusion of the evidence may lead to an unsafe conviction.[157] Evidence relating to the issue of consent cannot be adduced unless it is contemporaneous, or the behaviour is so similar to contemporaneous behaviour or behaviour described by the accused that it could be a pattern of sexual behaviour.[158] No question may be asked which has as its main purpose impugning the credibility of the complainant as a witness.[159] However, this protection does not extend to evidence relating to the issue of the defendant's belief in consent.

2.70 The limitations on the questions that may be asked of a complainant in sections 41–43 must, however, be read subject to the House of Lords case of *A (No 2)*.[160] Their Lordships held that a prior consensual sexual relationship between a complainant and the defendant might, in the circumstances of an individual case, be relevant to the issue of consent; that, although in giving effect to the defendant's rights under Article 6 account might also be taken of the interests of the complainant and of society in general, his right under Article 6(1) to a fair trial, assessed by reference to the overall fairness of the proceedings, was absolute and fundamental and would be infringed if he were denied the admission of relevant evidence where its absence led to his unsafe conviction.[161]

THE DISCRETION TO EXCLUDE

2.71 The trial judge or magistrate has a discretion under the second limb of section 1(f)(ii) to disallow cross-examination if the prejudicial value of the cross-examination exceeds its probative value. This may be used to disallow cross-examination altogether, or to disallow cross-examination on particular instances of previous misconduct.[162] The court will have to decide how to exercise its discretion on the particular facts of each case, and precedents are therefore of

---

[155] Which came into force on 4 December 2000: Youth Justice and Criminal Evidence Act 1999 (Commencement No 5) Order 2000 (SI 2000 No 3075).

[156] Sexual Offences (Amendment) Act 1976 s 2.

[157] The application should be made in advance of the trial and include much detail. The application procedure is set out in Crown Court Rules, r 23D, inserted by Crown Court (Amendment) (No 2) Rules 2000 SI 2000 No 2987. See Criminal Law Week (2000) 42/17 for a discussion on the application of the rules and whether the rules take the provision far further than the statute envisaged.

[158] Section 41(3).

[159] Section 41(4).

[160] [2001] UKHL 25.

[161] *A (No 2)* [2001] UKHL 25, para [46], *per* Lord Steyn. His Lordship put the question in these terms:

> …the test of admissibility is whether the evidence (and questioning in relation to it) is nevertheless so relevant to the issue of consent that to exclude it would endanger the fairness of the trial under article 6 of the Convention. If this test is satisfied the evidence should not be excluded.

[162] *Selvey v DPP* [1970] AC 304.

limited value, but there are factors which must be taken into account.[163] The principles are summarised by Ackner LJ in *Burke*.[164] They are essentially concerned with ensuring that the trial is fair to all concerned.

2.72 Before looking at the way in which the courts have exercised the discretion, it must be emphasised that the purpose of the cross-examination is to attack the defendant's credit as a witness, not to show that he or she has a disposition to commit the offence[165] – although in some cases it may incidentally have this effect. This is consistent with earlier judicial reasoning.[166]

Similarity of offences

2.73 It is now established that the mere fact that the accused's previous convictions are of a similar nature to the offence charged does not mean that the judge ought to exercise the discretion to exclude cross-examination on the defendant's record in the defendant's favour.[167] It was recently said that "there is no reason ... to distinguish between previous convictions of a like nature and previous convictions which are not of a like nature" for the purpose of the second limb.[168] The purpose of the cross-examination is to attack the defendant's creditworthiness as a witness and not to show disposition to commit an offence.[169] By way of contrast the Court of Appeal held in the more recent case of *Davison-Jenkins*[170] that the discretion ought to have been exercised in the defendant's favour to exclude previous convictions of a similar nature to those which were the subject of the current charge. This illustrates that judicial attitudes may differ on the exercise of the discretion to exclude cross-examination.

Where the convictions do not reveal dishonesty

2.74 There is some authority for the view that the discretion should be exercised so as to exclude a criminal record which does not involve dishonesty,[171] but it now

---

[163] Where irrelevant factors are taken into account, it may be held that the trial judge exercised his or her discretion incorrectly and the conviction quashed: *Showers* [1996] Crim LR 739.

[164] (1986) 82 Cr App R 156, 161, referring to *Selvey v DPP* [1970] AC 304, *Jenkins* (1945) 31 Cr App R 1, 15 and *Cook* [1959] 2 QB 340, 347–8.

[165] *McLeod* [1994] 1 WLR 1500, 1511H, *per* Gage J (reading a judgment prepared by Stuart-Smith LJ). This passage was cited with approval in *Fearon v DPP* (1995) 159 JP 649, 653E–G, *per* Leggatt LJ.

[166] Eg *Watts* (1983) 77 Cr App R 126.

[167] *McLeod* [1994] 1 WLR 1500, 1512G.

[168] *Fearon v DPP* (1995) 159 JP 649, 654B, *per* Leggatt LJ, with whom Buxton J agreed.

[169] *McLeod* [1994] 1 WLR 1500, 1511H.

[170] [1997] Crim LR 816.

[171] *Watts* (1983) 77 Cr App R 126. This fact was given as one reason for excluding the criminal record of the defendant, but this was a very unusual case.

seems clear that it may be right for the jury to know, in general terms, the character of a person making an imputation.[172]

Defence necessarily involving imputations

2.75 Difficulties occur where the defence necessarily involves making imputations. In *Selvey v DPP*[173] the House of Lords rejected the contention that the discretion ought to be exercised in favour of the accused where his or her defence necessarily involves the making of such imputations,[174] approving instead the approach of Devlin J in *Cook*.[175] The Court of Appeal in *Britzman*[176] sought to lay down guidelines for the exercise of discretion in this situation. They do not directly take account of the need of the accused person to mount a defence to a charge: rather, they address the practical meaning of the word "imputation". Essentially, the discretion should be exercised if there is "nothing more than a denial, however emphatic or offensively made, of an act or even a short series of acts amounting to one incident or in what was said to have been a short interview", as opposed to a "denial of evidence of a long period of detailed observation extending over hours".[177] Allowance should also be made for the possibility of mistake, misunderstanding and confusion, and for the fact that the defendant might be under strain, or led into making allegations during cross-examination.[178] Undue emphasis should not be placed upon the accused's choice of words. However, commentators have pointed out that "It cannot be pretended that such guidelines offer very substantial protection."[179]

---

[172] In *Fearon v DPP* (1995) 159 JP 649, 654C–D, Leggatt LJ, with whom Buxton J agreed, said that "The mere fact that the appellant had no previous convictions for dishonesty was no more than a factor for the justices to consider, as they did. But it did not constitute any bar to their permitting the cross-examination that they did permit." In *Powell* [1985] 1 WLR 1364, 1370D, the Court of Appeal criticised the decision in *Watts* for "paying too much attention ... to the question whether the previous offences did or did not involve dishonesty". Subsequently, *Powell* was approved on this point in *Owen* (1986) 83 Cr App R 100.

[173] [1970] AC 304.

[174] Cf *Flynn* [1963] 1 QB 729, 737, *per* Slade J, where the Court of Criminal Appeal held that "where ... the very nature of the defence necessarily involves an imputation, against a prosecution witness or witnesses, the discretion should, in the opinion of this court, *be as a general rule exercised in favour of the accused*, that is to say, evidence as to his bad character or criminal record should be excluded" (emphasis added).

[175] [1959] 2 QB 340, 347–8.

[176] [1983] 1 WLR 350.

[177] *Britzman* [1983] 1 WLR 350, 355D–E, *per* Lawton LJ.

[178] This last point was reconsidered in *Powell* [1985] 1 WLR 1364, 1370A–C, where the Court of Appeal approved the dictum of Devlin J in *Cook* [1959] 2 QB 340, 347. Devlin J held that the judge should ask himself whether the defendant has made a deliberate attack on a prosecution witness. If so, a judge "might well feel that he must withdraw the protection which he would desire to extend as far as possible to an accused who was endeavouring only to develop a line of defence."

[179] *Cross and Tapper*, p 441.

2.76 The Court of Appeal in *Britzman*[180] did not specifically discuss the issue of "necessary attacks". The House of Lords in *Selvey v DPP*[181] said there should be no *presumption* against allowing cross-examination in such cases. The Court of Appeal in *St Louis* has confirmed, however, that the discretion is available in this situation, and has said that a line should be drawn between "accusations going essentially to the credit of a police officer and suggestions made in cross-examination that are essential to [the defendant's] plea of 'not guilty'".[182] If the defence necessarily involves imputations the defendant can avoid cross-examination by declining to give evidence.[183]

Section 1(f)(iii): attacking a co-defendant

2.77 Cross-examination where one defendant has given evidence against another is justified on the grounds that, if evidence is adduced by D1 against a co-defendant (D2),[184] D2 may then show (by reference to D1's previous convictions) that his evidence should not be relied upon.[185] This may arise where the defendants put forward so-called "cut-throat" defences. For example, two parents are charged with the murder of their child. One or both of them must have been responsible for the death. Each denies guilt and maintains in evidence that the other was solely responsible. Both lose the shield at the behest of the other.

"HAS GIVEN EVIDENCE"

2.78 On a literal reading, section 1(f)(iii) applies only if the evidence against D2 is given by D1 in person. It seems to be implicit in some of the authorities on the first limb of section 1(f)(ii)[186] that the words "has given evidence" include calling a witness to give the evidence. It seems reasonable to assume that the words have the same meaning in section 1(f)(iii).[187]

2.79 Where, however, D1's advocate cross-examines D2 (or a prosecution witness) with a view to showing D2's guilt of the offence charged, it seems that this will *not*

---

[180] [1983] 1 WLR 350.

[181] [1970] AC 304.

[182] *St Louis and Case* (1984) 79 Cr App R 53, 60, *per* Purchas L J.

[183] *Butterwasser* [1948] 1 KB 4.

[184] We use this terminology throughout this section: D1 is the accused who attacks D2. Under s 1(f)(iii), D2 may then cross-examine D1 on his criminal record. For convenience, D1 is assumed to be male and D2 female.

[185] *Murdoch v Taylor* [1965] AC 574, 584E–F, *per* Lord Morris of Borth-y-Gest, and 590F, *per* Lord Donovan. The rule extends to the spent convictions of the co-defendant: *Corelli* unreported, 11 April 2001, CA.

[186] *Redd* [1923] 1 KB 104; *Winfield* (1939) 27 Cr App R 139.

[187] In *Mason, Lidgard and Herrington* [1996] Crim LR 325, the court seemed to assume that a witness could be cross-examined by counsel for one accused about the previous convictions of the other defendants (although the discretion was exercised against the cross-examination in this case). This was permissible regardless of the position under s 1(f)(iii).

render D1 liable to cross-examination – although there is some suggestion to the contrary.[188]

"AGAINST ANY OTHER PERSON CHARGED IN THE SAME PROCEEDINGS"

2.80 As a result of the decision of the House of Lords in *Murdoch v Taylor*,[189] it is now established that evidence "against" a co-defendant means evidence "which supports the prosecution's case in a material respect or which undermines the defence of the co-accused".[190] It is irrelevant whether the evidence is given with a hostile intent.[191]

2.81 The courts have laid down a number of factors to be considered in deciding whether evidence is evidence "against" a co-defendant.[192] In *Varley*[193] the House of Lords laid down guidelines for determining this issue. The evidence should be judged objectively and particular care should be taken where the co-defendant's defence may have been undermined: inconvenience or inconsistency is not sufficient, but direct contradiction may bring section 1(f)(iii) into play.[194] It has been held by the House of Lords that

> If, while ignoring anything trivial or casual, the positive evidence given by the witness would rationally have to be included in any survey or summary of the evidence in the case which, if accepted, would warrant the conviction of the [co-defendant] then the witness would have given evidence against such other person.[195]

2.82 It is immaterial whether D2 gives evidence. It is sufficient that D1 gives evidence which supports the prosecution case against D2 or undermines D2's defence. D2's defence may emerge either from evidence given or called by D2 or from statements made to the police.[196]

2.83 Where D1's evidence undermines both the prosecution's case against D2, *and* D2's defence, the shield will be lost if D2's defence is undermined *more* than the prosecution's case.[197] Thus in *Bruce*,[198] a defendant gave evidence which

---

[188] In *Bircham* [1972] Crim LR 430 it was suggested that in such a case D1 *would* be liable to cross-examination on his record. *Blackstone* disagrees: para F14.37.

[189] [1965] AC 574.

[190] *Ibid*, 592D, *per* Lord Donovan.

[191] *Ibid*, 591A, *per* Lord Donovan.

[192] See R May, *Criminal Evidence* (4th ed 1999) paras 7-72 – 7-77.

[193] [1982] 2 All ER 519, 522c-f, *per* Kilner Brown J.

[194] These guidelines should not be treated as equivalent to a statutory provision: see *Crawford* [1997] 1 WLR 1329, 1335C, *per* Lord Bingham CJ, where the Court of Appeal held, "The words used in the statute are simple and readily intelligible. There is, in our judgment, a danger in over-complicating what we feel sure was intended to be an easily applicable test."

[195] *Murdoch v Taylor* [1965] AC 574, 584B–C, *per* Lord Morris of Borth-y-Gest.

[196] *Adair* [1990] Crim LR 571.

[197] *Hatton* (1977) 64 Cr App R 88.

[198] [1975] 1 WLR 1252.

contradicted the evidence of one of his co-defendants, but which provided him with a *better* defence, thereby undermining the case for the prosecution. The Court of Appeal decided that the evidence was, on balance, in the co-defendant's favour, and held that the cross-examination of the defendant on his previous convictions should not have been permitted.[199]

2.84 Where two defendants are charged with an offence, and it is alleged that the commission of the offence was a joint venture, one defendant's denial of participation is to be considered as evidence against the other defendant only if the denial necessarily leads to the conclusion that the co-defendant committed the offence.[200] This conclusion need not follow, and more recent authority states that a co-defendant [D1] may lose the shield if his or her testimony leads to the conclusion that, "if [D1] did not participate, it *may* have been the other who did."[201] Similarly, a view of a joint venture which directly contradicts a view put forward by a co-defendant may be considered as evidence "against" him or her – it depends on how fundamental the conflict is.[202]

When section 1(f)(iii) is invoked

2.85 Unlike section 1(f)(ii), the judge has no discretion to prohibit D2's right to cross-examine D1 under section 1(f)(iii), provided such cross-examination is relevant.[203] The court has a discretion at common law to order separate trials to prevent the prejudice that might otherwise result from the absence of a discretion to prevent cross-examination by a co-accused on the accused's previous misconduct.[204]

2.86 The court has discretion to prevent cross-examination if the *prosecution* seeks to cross-examine an accused under section 1(f)(iii) on the grounds that he or she has given evidence against a co-accused.[205] In exercising the discretion the court has a duty to secure a fair trial, and, to this end, the prejudicial effect of evidence establishing the accused's bad character should not outweigh the probative value of such evidence as tending to show that he or she is guilty of the crime alleged.[206]

---

[199] It is doubtful whether the co-defendant was in fact provided with a better defence, since the fact that his story was contradicted would be bound to show him in a bad light.

[200] *Davis* (1974) 60 Cr App R 157.

[201] *Rigot* [2000] 7 Archbold News 2. The commentary in Criminal Law Week (CLW/00 32/4) states that further refinement can be expected so that the shield is only lost where D1's evidence presents the fact-finders with a choice – either both accused committed the crime or one of them did – but not where D1's evidence merely raises the possibility that D2 was solely responsible.

[202] *Davis* (1974) 60 Cr App R 157. In *Kirkpatrick* [1998] Crim LR 63, the defendant's evidence was inconsistent with the co-accused's version of events, but it did not amount to undermining the co-accused's defence.

[203] *Murdoch v Taylor* [1965] AC 574, applied by the Court of Appeal in *Varley* [1982] 2 All ER 519.

[204] *Varley* [1982] 2 All ER 519, 522g-j, *per* Kilner Brown J.

[205] *Seigley* (1911) 6 Cr App R 106, *per* Hamilton J.

[206] *Murdoch v Taylor* [1965] AC 574, 593D, obiter, *per* Lord Donovan.

The court also has a discretion to refuse to allow D2 to cross-examine D1 where D1 has given evidence against D3.[207]

2.87 It is incumbent upon the judge to warn the jury that previous convictions revealed in cross-examination of a defendant are relevant only to his or her credibility, and are not indicative of guilt;[208] but distinguishing between the various purposes of cross-examination in the case of a defendant is extremely difficult.

SEVERANCE OF DEFENDANTS

2.88 Both the Crown Court and magistrates' courts have a discretion to order separate trials.[209] The courts will not readily sever defendants properly joined. This is illustrated by the case of *Thompson, Sinclair and Maver*.[210] One of the defendants, S, was permitted to adduce evidence of incriminating admissions allegedly made by the other two defendants, T and M. This was not admissible as evidence against T and M, and was prejudicial to them, but it was relevant and admissible on S's defence. The Court of Appeal held that the trial judge had been correct not to sever. Evans LJ said: "Severance could only be justified if there was undue prejudice to the appellants from the admission of evidence relevant to Sinclair's defence but not to theirs". He went on to conclude that the prejudice was not sufficient to justify separate trials.

Section 1(f)(iii) and separate trials

2.89 As stated above, the court has a discretion to order separate trials where the exercise of a defendant's rights under section 1(f)(iii) would lead to injustice. The courts have, however, shown a marked reluctance to order severance. In *Hoggins*[211] two defendants accused each other of the murder for which they were on trial. They appealed against conviction on the basis that the judge should have ordered separate trials. Lawton LJ held that this was only one factor to take into account:

> The factor of the public interest in the proper administration of justice is a very powerful factor indeed, and in the majority of cases where men are charged jointly, it is clearly in the interests of justice and the ascertainment of truth that all the men so charged should be tried together.[212]

2.90 In a similar vein, the Court of Appeal has said:

> The truth of the matter is that this was a case where two experienced criminals metaphorically cut each other's throats in the course of their

---

[207] *Lovett* [1973] 1 WLR 241. Cf *Russell* [1971] 1 QB 151.

[208] *Hoggins* [1967] 1 WLR 1223.

[209] Indictments Act 1915, s 5(3). See, eg, *Grondowski and Malinowski* [1946] KB 369.

[210] [1995] 2 Cr App R 589.

[211] [1967] 1 WLR 1223.

[212] [1967] 1 WLR 1223, 1226C–D.

respective defences. If separate trials had been ordered, one or other or both might have succeeded in preventing a just result.[213]

SEVERANCE OF COUNTS/INFORMATIONS

2.91 The present law is contained in statute, secondary legislation and case law.[214] In brief, under the current law, counts may be properly joined on an indictment if the counts are "founded on the same facts, or form or are part of a series of offences of the same or a similar character",[215] but a judge has a discretion to order that properly-joined counts be tried separately.[216] The House of Lords recently confirmed in *Christou*[217] that, once counts have been properly joined, it is a matter for the discretion of the judge whether they should be severed.

2.92 The preceding case law was not consistent.[218] At one stage it was thought that there might be a separate rule where the counts on the indictment were of sexual offences, namely that in such cases there was a rule that unless the evidence satisfied the similar fact test and was admissible on each count then the indictment should be severed. It is now clear that there is no such special rule but that the matter is always one for the trial judge's discretion, having regard to fairness both from the point of view of the defendant and of the prosecution, and to all relevant factors, including those set out in the judgment of Lord Taylor CJ in *Christou*.

2.93 The case law applicable to summary trials achieves a similar result to that in the Crown Court: informations may be tried together if a joint trial would not risk injustice to the defendant and the facts are sufficiently closely connected. The court should ask both parties whether either has an objection to all the informations being heard together. If all parties consent to a joint trial then the magistrates should accede to their wishes. Lack of consent by either party is not a bar if, in the justices' view, a joint trial would not risk injustice to the defendant, and the facts are sufficiently closely connected.[219]

2.94 The case of *Chief Constable of Norfolk v Clayton*[220] made it clear that the decision should be made by the magistrates concerning whether informations should be tried separately. Lord Roskill reviewed the development of practice in magistrates'

---

[213] *Varley* [1982] 2 All ER 519, 522h–j, *per* Kilner Brown J.

[214] It is described in more detail at paras 2.92 – 2.103 of the consultation paper.

[215] Indictment Rules 1971, r 9.

[216] Indictments Act 1915, s 5(3).

[217] [1997] AC 117, 129C–F, in which Lord Taylor CJ confirmed the scope of judicial discretion and gave a non-exhaustive list of factors a judge ought to consider in the correct exercise of his or her discretion.

[218] Contrast *Brooks* (1991) 92 Cr App R 36, and *Cannan* (1990) 92 Cr App R 16.

[219] See *Stone's Justices' Manual* (2000) para 1–428.

[220] [1983] 2 AC 473.

courts and stated[221] that he saw no reason why the practice in magistrates' court should not be analogous to that in the Crown Court. The House stated:[222]

> ... if justices ask themselves, before finally ruling, the single question – what is the fairest thing to do in all the circumstances in the interests of everyone concerned? – they are unlikely to err in their conclusion, for the aim of the judicial process is to secure a fair trial.

2.95 This approach was confirmed in *R v Camberwell Green Stipendiary Magistrates, ex parte Martin*:[223] the test is no stricter in the magistrates' court than on indictment.

---

[221] *Ibid*, 491G–492E.

[222] *Ibid*, 492F.

[223] [2001] ACD 40.

PART III
THE EUROPEAN CONVENTION ON HUMAN RIGHTS

3.1 It has long been a principle of English law that the defendant should receive a fair trial. Article 6 of the Convention seeks to uphold the same principle. Article 6 reads:

> (1) In the determination of his civil rights and obligations or of any criminal charge against him, everyone is entitled to a fair and public hearing within a reasonable time by an independent and impartial tribunal established by law. ...
>
> (2) Everyone charged with a criminal offence shall be presumed innocent until proved guilty according to law.
>
> (3) Everyone charged with a criminal offence has the following minimum rights: ...
>
>> (d) to examine or have examined witnesses against him and to obtain the attendance and examination of witnesses on his behalf under the same conditions as witnesses against him ...

THE STRUCTURE OF ARTICLE 6

3.2 Article 6 contains guarantees or rights on three levels of specificity. First, it *explicitly* spells out a number of specific rights or guarantees. Those in paragraph (1) apply to both civil and criminal proceedings. Those in paragraphs (2) and (3) relate only to criminal matters. Second, the first sentence of paragraph (1) spells out the general right to a "fair hearing". From it have been developed in the case law of the Court certain other *specific* rights which are said to be *implicit* in the formulation. They include the right to an oral hearing in person,[1] and equality of arms.[2] Third, the general statement in the first sentence operates as an additional open-ended, *residual guarantee*. This general right to a fair hearing can be directly applied, even where it is not possible to point to a violation of one of the specific rights, whether explicit or implied.[3]

3.3 The specific rights spelt out might be regarded as examples or manifestations of the general right to a fair hearing,[4] but they do not necessarily exhaust it. This point is often made particularly with reference to the paragraph (3) guarantees. In such cases or where evidential matters are considered (see paragraph 3.4 below), the Strasbourg Court adopts what Harris et al describe as a "trial as a whole" basis, in which the Court makes a general assessment of the fairness of the trial,

---

[1] *Ekbatani v Sweden* (1988) 13 EHRR 504.

[2] *Borgers v Belgium* (1993) 15 EHRR 92.

[3] *Barbera, Messegue and Jabardo v Spain* (1989) 11 EHRR 360.

[4] As stated, eg, in *Van Mechelen and Others v The Netherlands* (1998) 25 EHRR 647.

taking all the circumstances into account.[5] This approach can work to the benefit of the accused where a number of features cumulatively undercut the fairness of the hearing,[6] or it can work to the benefit of the state.[7]

ARTICLE 6 AND RULES OF EVIDENCE

3.4 Because of the wide variation in systems of criminal procedure and evidence within the member states of the Council of Europe, the Court has adopted the principle that it is a matter primarily for the member state to determine questions of admissibility of evidence.[8] The result is that the Court looks at the circumstances as a whole to determine whether the hearing has in fact been fair. Harris et al describe the position as follows:

> In practice, the Strasbourg authorities ... allow states a wide margin of appreciation as to the manner of [national courts'] operation, for example in the rules of evidence they use. A consequence of this ... point is that in certain contexts the provisions of article 6 are as much obligations of result as of conduct, with national courts being allowed to follow whatever particular rules they choose as long as the end result can be seen to be a fair trial.[9]

3.5 Whilst the use of a particular rule of evidence may cause a trial to be unfair on the facts in any system, the Strasbourg Court and Commission have not, however, established that any particular rule of evidence about bad character evidence is impermissible.[10]

3.6 In this context, it is perhaps worth drawing attention to Article 6(3)(d). This particular explicit guarantee has echoes in the principle of "equality of arms" which has been read into Article 6.[11] Taken together, we assume these principles would militate against rules of evidence which placed a defendant at a disadvantage, especially with regard to the examination of witnesses. In English

---

[5] See Harris, O'Boyle and Warbrick, *Law of the European Convention on Human Rights* (1995) pp 202–203; Van Dijk and Van Hoof, *Theory and Practice of the European Convention on Human Rights* (3rd ed 1998) pp 428–430. For cases see for instance *Barbera, Messegue and Jabardo v Spain* (1999) 11 EHRR 360.

[6] As in *Barbera, Messegue and Jabardo v Spain* (1999) 11 EHRR 360.

[7] As in *Stanford v UK, The Times* 8 March 1994 (although the Court also considered that the state's obligations were not engaged where the failure to object to the fact that the defendant in a trial could not properly hear the proceedings was a tactical decision taken by counsel).

[8] See for instance *Van Mechelen and Others v The Netherlands* (1998) 25 EHRR 647; *Barbera, Messegue and Jabardo v Spain* (1999) 11 EHRR 360; *Kostovski v The Netherlands* (1990) 12 EHRR 434; *Windisch v Austria* (1991) 13 EHRR 281; *Saidi v France* (1994) 17 EHRR 251; *Doorson v The Netherlands* (1996) 22 EHRR 330; *Ferrantelli and Sontangelo v Italy* (1997) 23 EHRR 288; *Schenk v Switzerland* (1991) 13 EHRR 242 (unlawfully obtained evidence is not excluded as a matter of principle).

[9] Harris, O'Boyle and Warbrick, *Law of the European Convention on Human Rights* (1995) p 164.

[10] For a comprehensive survey of the law in this area, see A H Robertson and J G Merrills, *Human Rights in Europe* (3rd ed 1993) pp 85–124.

[11] *Kaufman v Belgium* (1986) 50 DR 98; *Neumeister v Austria (No 1)* (1979–80) 1 EHRR 91.

law, complainants in sexual cases are protected against certain questions.[12] The same protection does not extend to a witness for the defence. In *A* on this point Lord Hope said,

> The rights listed in article 6(3) include the accused's right to examine or have examined witnesses against him and to obtain the attendance and examination of witnesses on his behalf under the same conditions as witnesses against him: see paragraph (d). There is no doubt that Parliament, by placing restrictions on the questions that may be asked and the evidence that may be adduced by or on behalf of the accused was entering upon a very sensitive area.
>
> But article 6 does not give the accused an absolute and unqualified right to put whatever questions he chooses to the witnesses. As this is not one of the rights which are set out in absolute terms in the article it is open, in principle, to modification or restriction so long as this is not incompatible with the absolute right to a fair trial in article 6(1).[13]

Thus, the 6(3)(d) point is subsumed within the fair trial question.

THE FAIRNESS OF THE ADMISSION OF PREVIOUS CONVICTIONS *PER SE*

3.7 In a number of Continental systems, lists of previous convictions are routinely added to the case file, which forms the basis of the prosecution and becomes evidence. That this is capable of being fair *per se* is clearly not contestable at Strasbourg. In the consultation paper we expressed the provisional view[14] that the Convention did not have any especial relevance to this project. In support of this conclusion we referred to a decision of the Strasbourg Commission[15] in which it was said that, since many member states provide for the disclosure of previous convictions in their criminal procedure, it was not prepared to hold that such a procedure was in violation of any provision of Article 6.

3.8 One respondent commented this was a decision of the Commission only, and since this was a case decided more than 30 years ago, "that make[s] it a very uncertain pointer towards current views." We do not agree. In numerous cases involving Article 6, it is clear from the recital of the facts that previous convictions have been before the court, and indeed have influenced the judgment.[16] Further, in these cases the previous convictions are admitted as evidence of guilt, not merely credit. Moreover, it is important to note that in the *Denmark* case, the trial was before a jury, and "lay judges" (exact status unknown) sat in the *Austria* case, so it cannot be argued that Continental systems are to be distinguished because they have professional fact-finders.

---

[12] See para 2.69 above.

[13] *A* [2001] UKHL 25, paras [90–91].

[14] At para 1.12.

[15] *X v Denmark* Yearbook (1965) vol 8, p 370. See also *X v Austria* Yearbook (1966) vol 9, p 550.

[16] For instance, *Unterpertinger v Austria* (1991) 13 EHRR 175, para 20; *Kostovski v The Netherlands* (1990) 12 EHRR 434, para 18.

LOSS OF SHIELD BY CASTING IMPUTATIONS

3.9 It follows from the above discussion that, with all the caveats mentioned above, the *fact* of the revelation of previous convictions will not result in a breach of the Convention.

3.10 It is undoubtedly the case that, by virtue of the second limb of section 1(f)(ii) of the Criminal Evidence Act 1898, a defendant may fear revelation of his or her criminal record as a consequence of the way the defence is conducted.[17] An argument might be raised that the distortion of a defence as a result of the defendant's *fear* of losing the shield amounted to a violation of the right to a fair trial. If it were to do so, it would have to arise under the residual guarantee discussed in paragraph 3.2.

3.11 The particular want of fairness to which this argument might be addressed is what the Court has described as the requirement of fairness in Article 6 in placing the tribunal "under a duty to conduct a proper examination of the submissions, arguments and evidence adduced by the parties, without prejudice to its assessment of whether they are relevant to its decision".[18] As Van Dijk and Van Hoof emphasise, the Strasbourg authorities have deliberately avoided giving a list of abstract criteria: "The proceedings as a whole may, for instance, create the picture that the accused has had insufficient possibilities to conduct an optimal defence, although none of the explicitly granted minimum guarantees has been violated."[19] Thus, the argument might run, the distortion of a defence by fear of losing one's shield could be described as something which detracts from the possibility of conducting an optimal defence.

3.12 In our judgment, such an argument would be highly unlikely to succeed save in highly individual circumstances. One cannot get away from the jurisprudence supporting the fairness of reliance on previous convictions at trial. Although a defendant in the position described is, in a sense, being "forced" to distort the defence, he or she is only doing so to avoid a consequence that the Strasbourg Court would not regard as in itself unfair. The distortion is a tactical decision to take advantage of a state of affairs (the fact-finder's ignorance of the previous convictions) which is significantly more to the advantage of the defendant than would be adherence to the minimum requirements of fairness.[20] Weight is added

---

[17] See para 4.37 below. In the research conducted for the Royal Commission it appeared this fear was operative in a significant proportion of defended cases: M Zander and P Henderson, Research Study No 19 (1993) for the Report of the Royal Commission, para 4.6.8.

[18] *Kraska v Switzerland* (1994) 18 EHRR 188, para 30.

[19] Van Dijk and Van Hoof, *Theory and Practice of the European Convention on Human Rights* (3rd ed 1998) p 429.

[20] In *Stanford v UK, The Times* 8 March 1994, the Court considered that the state's obligations were not engaged where the applicant's counsel could have objected, but chose not to, to the fact that the applicant, in the dock in a court said to have problems with its acoustic properties, could not hear proceedings. It was a tactical decision motivated by a desire to avoid the appearance of intimidation if the defendant was moved nearer to the vulnerable witnesses.

to this point when one considers that it is, under the Convention, considered fair for previous convictions to be taken into account by a fact-finder in directly determining guilt. The utmost, in theory, that loss of the shield can expose the defendant to is the undermining of his or her credit.

3.13 Nevertheless, the approach of looking at the nature of the trial as a whole cannot exclude the possibility that in a particular, unusual, case, the facts might be such that the Strasbourg Court, or the English courts applying the Convention, would find a violation of Article 6. It does not seem possible, on this issue, to go further than this very speculative conclusion.

VICTIMS OF CRIME AND THE CONVENTION

3.14 Most of the case law of the Strasbourg Court on issues of criminal procedure has arisen from the parts of the Convention which provide guarantees for defendants. However, victims of crimes have human rights as well, and if a country's rules of criminal law, procedure or evidence are ineffective to protect such victims, this deficiency sometimes enables them to complain that their rights under the Convention have been infringed.

3.15 In *X and Y v The Netherlands*,[21] for example, the Strasbourg Court upheld a complaint by a mentally handicapped woman that, in effect, Dutch criminal procedure was not adequate to protect her. At the age of 16, she had sexual intercourse forced upon her by the son-in-law of the director of the privately-run home for mentally incapacitated children where she lived. As Dutch law then stood, this man could not be prosecuted, because the offence which he had apparently committed could only be prosecuted where the victim had made a formal complaint, and the girl was considered too seriously handicapped to do this. In consequence, the Netherlands were held to be in breach of Article 8(1) of the Convention.[22] This provision, said the Court, required the contracting States to provide their citizens with effective protection against being sexually abused, which, in the context of Dutch law as a whole, meant the possibility of criminal sanctions.

3.16 One area in which an infringement of a person's Convention rights might arise is where a person who is a witness in a criminal trial has his or her bad character exposed in public. A lack of protection might impinge in two ways. It might lead to a breach of the witness' Article 8 rights or, if it deters the victim from pursuing a prosecution, it might lead to a complaint under Article 3 or, more likely, Article 8. In *MK v Austria*, the Commission said that

> the interests of witnesses and victims are in principle protected by the Convention, in particular Article 8, which imply that Contracting States should organise their criminal proceedings in such a way that those interests are not unjustifiably imperilled. Against this background, principles of fair trial also require that in appropriate

---

[21] (1986) 8 EHRR 235.

[22] Article 8(1) provides: "Everyone has the right to respect for his private and family life, his home and his correspondence."

cases the interests of the defence be balanced against those of witnesses or victims called to testify.[23]

3.17 There has been no consideration of the rights of witnesses in cases on Article 8 itself. There has, however, been some reference to witness rights in the context of other Articles, which may impact on Article 8.

3.18 The Strasbourg organs have, to an extent, sought to balance the right to a fair trial against the rights of witnesses. Thus far the instances of conflict of interests have been focused on witnesses being in actual danger, for example from reprisals or identification.[24] Article 8 has been considered in the context of Article 6 in *Doorson v The Netherlands*. The Court held:

> It is true that Article 6 does not explicitly require the interests of witnesses in general ... to be taken into consideration. However, their life, liberty or security of person may be at stake, as may interests coming generally within the ambit of Article 8 of the Convention. Such interests of witnesses and victims are in principle protected by other, substantive provisions of the Convention, which imply that Contracting States should organise their criminal proceedings in such a way that those interests are not unjustifiably imperilled. Against this background, principles of fair trial also require that in appropriate cases the interests of the defence are balanced against those of witnesses or victims called upon to testify.[25]

3.19 Clearly this does not amount to an explicit indication of what the Court might make of a case where it was argued that the defendant's right to a fair trial had been subordinated to a right or interest of another person. The key word in the above judgment upon which the court might focus may be "unjustifiably". What is justifiable will depend very much on the features of an individual case.

3.20 The balancing of a witness's interests against a defendant's rights has been considered at the highest level in the English courts, following the incorporation of the Convention into English law, and we now turn to deal with the way the courts have approached the question.

---

[23] *MK v Austria* (1997) 24 EHRR CD 59, 60–61.

[24] See Keir Starmer, *European Human Rights Law* (1999) para 9.36.

[25] (1996) 22 EHRR 330, para 3(c). In *Van Mechelen v The Netherlands* (1998) 25 EHRR 647 the court applied the *Doorson* balancing test, and thereby held that the national courts had given too much weight to the rights of police witnesses by granting them anonymity such that the defendants' rights under Article 6 had not been sufficiently respected. At paragraph 56 the court stated:

> Although their interests – and indeed those of their families – also deserve protection under the Convention, it must be recognised that their position is to some extent different from that of a disinterested witness or a victim. They owe a general duty of obedience to the State's executive authorities and usually have links with the prosecution; for these reasons alone their use as anonymous witnesses should be resorted to only in exceptional circumstances.

THE EFFECT OF INCORPORATION

3.21 At the time of the consultation paper the Convention was not incorporated into English law – it now has been.[26] The approach which will be followed where a provision of English law which governs the admissibility of evidence raises an Article 6 issue has recently been set out by the House of Lords in the case of *A*.[27]

3.22 The facts were that the complainant began a sexual relationship with the defendant's friend and she visited him at the flat which he was then sharing with the defendant. On the evening of 13 June 2000 the complainant and the friend had sexual intercourse at the flat when the defendant was not there. Later, when the defendant returned, the three of them went for a picnic. The two men drank whisky and beer. When they got back to the flat the friend collapsed and was taken to hospital. Later, in the early hours of 14 June 2000, the defendant and the complainant left the flat to go to the hospital. The prosecution's case was that as they walked along the route selected by the defendant, he fell down. When the complainant tried to help him, he pulled her to the ground and had sexual intercourse with her. The complainant said that it was rape. The defendant said that it was part of a continuing sexual relationship that they had been having.

3.23 The issue for the court was whether evidence of the sexual relationship which the defendant claimed had existed between him and the complainant was admissible. The first question is whether the evidence is admissible under ordinary principles of construction. If it is not, the second question is whether it would be compatible with the defendant's right to a fair trial under Article 6(1) to exclude the evidence.

3.24 The courts have held that, "while the right to a fair trial is absolute in its terms and the public interest can never be invoked to deny that right to anybody under any circumstances, the rights which [the court] has read into article 6 are neither absolute nor inflexible."[28] Where one of those rights which have been read into Article 6[29] conflicts with another public interest, a court thus has to assess whether the right balance has been struck between the competing interests. Lord Steyn has explained that "The only balancing permitted is in respect of what the concept of a fair trial entails: here account may be taken of the familiar triangulation of interests of the accused, the victim and society. In this context proportionality has a role to play."[30] Lord Steyn approved the description of the task given by Lord Lester of Herne Hill QC:

> The first question the courts must ask is: does the legislation interfere with a Convention right? At that stage, the purpose or intent of the legislation will play a secondary role, for it will be seldom, if ever, that Parliament will have intended to legislate in breach of the Convention. It is at the second stage, when the Government seeks to justify the

---

[26] Human Rights Act 1998, which came into force on 2 October 2000.

[27] [2001] UKHL 25.

[28] *Brown v Stott* [2001] 2 WLR 817, 851a, *per* Lord Hope of Craighead.

[29] See para 3.2 above.

[30] *A* [2001] UKHL 25, para [38].

interference with a Convention right, under one of the exception clauses, that legislative purpose or intent becomes relevant. It is at that stage the principle of proportionality will be applied.[31]

The distinctive nature of Article 6

3.25 It has been held by the Strasbourg Court that interference with the right to a fair trial has to pass a stricter test than interference with other rights and freedoms:

> Having regard to the place that the right to a fair administration of justice holds in a democratic society, any measures restricting the rights of the defence should be strictly necessary.[32]

3.26 This principle has also been recognised domestically:

> ... difficult choices may have to be made by the executive or the legislature between the rights of the individual and the needs of society. In some circumstances it will be appropriate for the courts to recognise that there is an area of judgment within which the judiciary will defer, on democratic grounds, to the considered opinion of the elected body or person whose act or decision is said to be incompatible with the Convention. ... It will be easier for [this discretionary area of judgment] to be recognised where the Convention itself requires a balance to be struck, much less so where the right is stated in terms which are unqualified. It will be easier for it to be recognised where the issues involve questions of social or economic policy, much less so where the rights are of high constitutional importance or are of a kind where the courts are especially well placed to assess the need for protection.[33]

3.27 The seriousness of the crime alleged will not justify greater intrusion on fundamental rights:

> ... the general requirements of fairness contained in Article 6, including the right not to incriminate oneself, "apply to criminal proceedings in respect of all types of criminal offences without distinction from the most simple to the most complex".[34]

3.28 While it is true that the rights which go to make up the right to a fair trial in Article 6(1) are not inflexible, they may not be so eroded, for the sake of some

---

[31] "The Act of the Possible: Interpreting Statutes under the Human Rights Act" [1998] EHRLR 665, 674. Lord Steyn also commended Bertha Wilson J, "The Making of a Constitution: Approaches to Judicial Interpretation" (1988) PL 370, 371–372; and David Feldman, "Proportionality and The Human Rights Act 1998" in *The Principle of Proportionality in the Laws of Europe* (1999) pp 117, 122–123.

[32] *Van Mechelen and Others v The Netherlands* [1998] 25 EHRR 647, para 58.

[33] *R v DPP ex p Kebilene* [2000] 2 AC 326, 381, *per* Lord Hope.

[34] *Saunders v UK* (1997) 23 EHRR 313, para 74; cited with approval in *Heaney and McGuinness v Ireland* [2001] Crim LR 481; application no 34720/97, 21 December 2000, para 57.

other public interest, as to extinguish "the very essence" of Article 6(1).[35] As Harris et al explain (see paragraph 3.4 above) Article 6 is result-focused. The ultimate question must be whether the right is still effective.[36]

HRA, section 3

3.29 If a court concludes that the legislature has apparently gone too far in diminishing a part of a defendant's right to a fair trial in order to achieve some other goal, it must then consider whether the provision in question can be interpreted compatibly with the Convention by praying in aid HRA section 3(1). This reads:

> So far as it is possible to do so, primary legislation and subordinate legislation must be read and given effect in a way which is compatible with the Convention rights.

3.30 As Lord Steyn has said,

> the interpretative obligation under section 3 of the 1998 Act is a strong one. ... It is an emphatic adjuration ... Section 3 places a duty on the court to strive to find a possible interpretation compatible with Convention rights. Under ordinary methods of interpretation a court may depart from the language of the statute to avoid absurd consequences: section 3 goes much further.[37]

3.31 A court must, if it is possible to do so, read and give effect to legislation in a way which is compatible with the Convention rights even if an otherwise binding pre-HRA judicial decision exists which would require that the legislation be applied in an incompatible way. If it is not possible to interpret the provision in question compatibly, a declaration of incompatibility must be made.[38] The rule does not, however, affect the validity of primary legislation which cannot be interpreted

---

[35] *Heaney and McGuinness v Ireland* [2001] Crim LR 481; application no 34720/97, 21 December 2000, para 58. In that case, at para 55, it was decided that the privilege against self-incrimination had effectively been extinguished:

> ... the Court finds that the "degree of compulsion", imposed on the applicants by the application of section 52 of the 1939 Act with a view to compelling them to provide information relating to charges against them under that Act, in effect, destroyed the very essence of their privilege against self-incrimination and their right to remain silent.

[36] This point is also emphasised by D Friedman, "Defending the Essence Of The Right: Judicial Discretion and the Human Rights Act 1998" [2001] Archbold News (4) 6, 8:

> ... even if the *purpose* behind legislation is deemed to be valid in terms of protecting the wider interests of the community, a court is required to consider whether the *effect* of the legislation nevertheless produces invalid results from the point of fundamental rights and freedoms.

Friedman cites the Canadian case of *Big M Drug Mart Ltd* (1985) 18 DLR (4th) 321 as an example of this approach.

[37] *A* [2001] UKHL 25, para [44].

[38] HRA 1998, s 4.

compatibly with the Convention,[39] nor the validity of incompatible secondary legislation where primary legislation prevents the removal of the incompatibility.[40]

Reading down

3.32 Section 3 might be used not only to interpret legislation but to restrict its scope, by reading it as subject to certain limits. This technique seems most apt in situations where the legislation permits a public authority, including a court, to do something which, in some circumstances, would be a violation of the Convention, but, in other circumstances, would not.[41] The technique is sometimes known as "reading down".[42]

Reading in

3.33 A statutory provision which apparently conflicts with Article 6 may be saved by the technique of "reading in". To what extent will a court be prepared to read words into a provision in order to make it compatible with the Convention? On the one hand Lord Steyn has held:

> In accordance with the will of Parliament as reflected in section 3 it will sometimes be necessary to adopt an interpretation which linguistically may appear strained. The techniques to be used will not only involve the reading down of express language in a statute but also the implication of provisions.[43]

In the same decision, however, Lord Hope held, "I would find it very difficult to accept that it was permissible under section 3 of the Human Rights Act 1998 to read in to section 41(3)(c) [of the Youth Justice and Criminal Evidence Act 1999] a provision to the effect that evidence or questioning which was required to ensure a fair trial under article 6 of the Convention should not be treated as inadmissible. ... the rule [in section 3(1)] is only a rule of interpretation. It does not entitle the judges to act as legislators."[44] Lord Hope did not, unlike the other

---

[39] HRA 1998, s 3(2)(b). See *R v Sec of State for Home Department, ex p Simms* [2000] 2 AC 115, 131, *per* Lord Hoffmann.

[40] HRA 1998, s 3(2)(c).

[41] An example from New Zealand is *Ministry of Transport v Noort* [1992] 3 NZLR 260, which concerned the right to seek legal advice by telephone before submitting to a compulsory blood or breath test. It was held that, notwithstanding the lack of provision in the Transport Act, the Act could be read as subject to the right, under the Bill of Rights, of an arrested person to consult a lawyer without delay. See Lord Cooke of Thorndon, "The British Embracement of Human Rights" [1999] EHRLR 243, 249–50.

[42] The Lord Chancellor has also given some support to the view that the scope of the powers granted by primary legislation can be pared down so that they do not allow Convention rights to be transgressed. See Lord Irvine of Lairg LC, "The Development of Human Rights in Britain under an Incorporated Convention on Human Rights" [1998] PL 221 at 228–229. A helpful discussion of the application of s 3 of the HRA, including the possible relevance of the techniques of "reading in" and "reading down", is provided in Clayton and Tomlinson's *The Law of Human Rights* (2000) vol 1, paras 4.04 – 4.38.

[43] *A* [2001] UKHL 25, para [44].

[44] *A* [2001] UKHL 25, para [108]. We note also that the Home Secretary stated before the enactment of the HRA that it was not the Government's intention that the courts "should

Law Lords, consider it necessary to have recourse to section 3 for the resolution of the question before their Lordships.

3.34 Lord Steyn was content to conclude that it is "possible under section 3 to read section 41 ... as subject to the implied provision that evidence or questioning which is required to ensure a fair trial under article 6 of the Convention should not be treated as inadmissible".[45] Lords Clyde, Hutton and Slynn took a similar line to Lord Steyn,[46] whereas Lord Hope's conclusion was

> In the present case it seems to me that the entire structure of section 41 contradicts the idea that it is possible to read into it a new provision which would entitle the court to give leave whenever it was of the opinion that this was required to ensure a fair trial. ... Section 41(2) *forbids* the exercise of such a discretion *unless* the court is satisfied as to the matters which that subsection identifies. It seems to me that it would not be possible, without contradicting the plain intention of Parliament, to read in a provision which would enable the court to exercise a wider discretion than that permitted by section 41(2).[47]

3.35 Their Lordships all concurred with Lord Steyn, however, in the test to be applied in the case of this statutory provision:

> The effect of the decision today is that under section 41(3)(c) of the 1999 Act, construed where necessary by applying the interpretative obligation under section 3 of the Human Rights Act 1998, and due regard always being paid to the importance of seeking to protect the complainant from indignity and from humiliating questions, the test of admissibility is whether the evidence (and questioning in relation to it) is nevertheless so relevant to the issue of consent that to exclude it would endanger the fairness of the trial under article 6 of the convention. If this test is satisfied the evidence should not be excluded.[48]

Conclusion

3.36 A rule which made evidence admissible or inadmissible, such that it appeared that a defendant had not had or could not have a fair trial, or that one of the rights of the defendant which is a constituent part of the right to a fair trial had been breached, would threaten to bring English law into conflict with the Convention. In that circumstance, a court would strive to interpret the rule such that the defendant's right to a fair trial was upheld. If the rule was contained in a statute, section 3 of the HRA would oblige the court to interpret the provision compatibly in so far as it was possible. It is not, however, settled to what extent words may be implied into a statutory provision in order to achieve that result.

---

contort the meaning of words to produce implausible or incredible meanings": *Hansard* (HC) 3 June 1998, vol 313, col 422.

[45] *A* [2001] UKHL 25, para [45].

[46] *Ibid*, paras [136] and [13] respectively.

[47] *Ibid*, para [109].

[48] *Ibid* para [46].

PART IV
DEFECTS OF THE PRESENT LAW

4.1 In this Part we review the problems in the current law. We summarise the principal defects, and then describe the problems in detail.

THE PRINCIPAL DEFECTS

Evidence adduced as part of the prosecution case in chief

"similar fact"

- There is still confusion about the law on "similar fact evidence". The test for the admissibility of this kind of evidence does not, in our view, give clear enough guidance on how it is to be applied.

background evidence

- If evidence is admitted as "background" evidence its value does not have to be assessed in the light of its prejudicial effect (as it would if it were "similar fact evidence") and yet it may be very prejudicial. Moreover, it is not clear what counts as "background" evidence.

Theft Act 1968, section 27(3)

- This provision is neither justified nor useful.

Evidence adduced in the course of cross-examination

- The statutory rules are supposed to have the effect that only bad character evidence which goes to credibility is admitted in cross-examination of a defendant who "loses the shield", but the courts can and do admit evidence which does not relate to credibility.

- The rule that bad character evidence on the "tit-for-tat" basis may only be adduced in cross-examination means that witnesses are inadequately protected from irrelevant cross-examination on their character.

- The fear of "losing the shield," which should deter a defendant from making gratuitous attacks, does not bite where that defendant does not testify, or has no criminal record to be revealed. This puts a premium on tactical decisions and distorts the process.

- Defendants may be inhibited from putting their true defence on the central set of facts for fear of their character going in.

- The statute does not preclude evidence of the defendant's bad character being admitted even where its prejudice outweighs its relevance to the defendant's credibility.

- There is no power to prevent the record of a defendant being admitted where that defendant has undermined the defence of a co-accused. Unfairness can result.

THE PROBLEMS IN DETAIL (I): EVIDENCE IN CHIEF

Lack of clarity in the "similar fact evidence" rules

4.2 It is hard for parties and courts to establish exactly what the law is in this area. When the CLRC looked at it in 1972, they said it was "far the most difficult of all the topics which we have discussed"[1] and, despite the decision in *DPP v P*, it is still very problematic. This area of the law is ripe for codification which would bring greater clarity, certainty and accessibility.

4.3 The test in the leading authority, *DPP v P* is too vague. The test was formulated as follows:

> ... the essential feature of evidence which is to be admitted is that its probative force ... is sufficiently great to make it just to admit the evidence, notwithstanding that it is prejudicial to the accused in tending to show that he was guilty of another crime.[2]

4.4 To state that the evidence is admissible when it is "just" to do so, does not settle the question of how the probative value ought to relate to the prejudicial effect in order for it to be admitted.[3] There are a number of possibilities. Some of them are quantitative, weighing the probative value against the prejudicial effect by reference to a quantitative benchmark such as *on balance*; or *substantially*[4] or *clearly* outweighing or that it would be "an affront to common sense"[5] to exclude the evidence. Another approach might be qualitative, that is to say placing a burden on one party or the other and/or by being more specific about the way in which the concept of doing justice feeds in to the decision. Thus there might be a presumption of inclusion or exclusion. The test might require the interests of justice to be served marginally or absolutely. For example it may be sufficient that it *may be* in the interests of justice for the evidence to be admitted, or it may be that the interests of justice must *require* the evidence to be admitted. In the absence of such clarification different judges may be adopting completely different approaches to the question whether it is just to admit the evidence having regard to probative value and prejudice.

4.5 In a matter requiring the exercise of judgment in an individual case, it is impossible for a test based on what is just to be so precise that there is no room for argument in individual cases, but we do think that there is scope for more guidance. For example, there is no indication of the factors that are relevant in

---

[1] CLRC, Evidence Report (1972) para 70.

[2] *DPP v P* [1991] 2 AC 447, 460E–F.

[3] As Professor Birch says: "...the truth is that we do not know what we are looking for". See her commentary on *Channing* [1994] Crim LR 924, 926.

[4] As in the Australian Evidence Act 1995 (Cth), s 101(2).

[5] *Boardman* [1975] AC 421, 454A, *per* Lord Hailsham of St Marylebone, approving Lord Simon of Glaisdale's use of that phrase in *Kilbourne* [1973] AC 729, 759D.

assessing the probative value of similar fact evidence (such as *dis*similarities in the evidence),[6] or in assessing its likely prejudicial effect.

4.6 Until recently, the common law did not adequately cover cases where identity is in dispute. It was arguable that Lord Mackay preserved the requirement of "striking similarity" for cases where identity is in dispute by his dicta in *DPP v P*. However, the recent decision of *John W*[7] has limited the scope of those dicta to cases where the *only* evidence to show identity is the similarity between the offence charged and another offence which the defendant can be proved to have committed.

Evidence of propensity admitted as similar fact evidence

4.7 In the consultation paper[8] we agreed with *Blackstone* that the demarcation between what is permitted and what is prohibited is a matter of degree: "the evidence must be shown to be of very specific significance to the issue before the court. Viewed in this way 'mere' evidence of propensity is simply another way of describing evidence which does not sufficiently specifically prove guilt."[9] Nevertheless, recent authority indicates that "propensity reasoning" continues to cause difficulties.

4.8 The Court of Appeal decision of *B(RA)*[10] illustrates the problem. The defendant was charged with the indecent assault of his two grandsons. His defence was to deny that there had ever been any sort of indecency. He appealed against his conviction on the ground that evidence of his possession of homosexual pornographic magazines ought not to have been admitted. The appeal was allowed. It was held that, given that the thrust of his defence was a general denial, the possession of the pornography was not probative of anything save propensity and that, following the decision in *Wright*,[11] this "is not a proper basis to render [it] admissible".[12] The Court of Appeal in *Wright* had attempted, in the spirit of *Makin*,[13] to determine the admissibility of evidence according to the legal category into which the evidence falls, irrespective of its probative value. It is an authority

---

[6] In *Johnson* [1995] Crim LR 53 the Court of Appeal allowed an appeal because the similarities between the present charge and the previous misconduct were taken into account but the clear dissimilarities were ignored.

[7] [1998] 2 Cr App R 289.

[8] At para 2.54.

[9] *Blackstone*, para F12.8.

[10] [1997] 2 Cr App R 88.

[11] (1990) 90 Cr App R 325, which was not cited to the trial judge. Note that *Wright* pre-dates *DPP v P* and one might therefore have expected the approach in *Wright* to have been subsumed within the general principle set out in *DPP v P*. In *Wright* the prosecution case was that W, a headmaster of a school, had for his last two years at the school engaged in homosexual activities with the pupils. The evidence in question was a booklet and a video, both of which tended to show a sexual interest in males, especially young males, on the part of whoever they belonged to. W denied that they were anything to do with him.

[12] [1997] 2 Cr App R 88, 93C, *per* Rose LJ.

[13] See para 2.15 above.

which, according to Lord Justice Rose in *B(RA)*, "ought to be more widely known".[14]

4.9 We consider it both unfortunate and significant that counsel for the prosecution in *B(RA)* conceded without argument[15] that *Wright* did not require reconsideration in the light of the House of Lords decision in *DPP v P*. It may well be the case that, in the particular circumstances of *B(RA)*, the evidence did lack sufficient probative value, but to suggest that, in the absence of a specific defence, propensity evidence can *never* be advanced, must surely be open to doubt.

4.10 In the consultation paper[16] we rejected the notion of a "forbidden chain of reasoning" and concluded that the admissibility of similar fact evidence should not depend on the purpose for which it is adduced. Only one respondent expressed reservations about this proposal. They said that "it [is] difficult to conceive of circumstances in which propensity alone could be sufficiently probative to warrant admission". Nevertheless, they did accept that "it could become sufficiently relevant if combined with other features of the case" and therefore their analysis is not markedly different from our own.

Background evidence

4.11 In a recent line of cases, evidence which is prejudicial, and which might be expected to be required to fall within the similar fact category before it is admitted, has been held to escape the test in *DPP v P* because it is "background evidence". Background evidence is admitted because it is "so closely entwined and involved with the evidence directly relating to the facts in issue that it would amount to distortion to attempt to edit it out".[17] This approach can, however, be used to smuggle in similar fact evidence which would otherwise be inadmissible.[18] The current law is not altogether clear on when evidence counts as background evidence, and when it does not. We have identified four "indicators" which may enable evidence to avoid the normal exclusionary rule.[19]

4.12 To add to the confusion, there is authority in which it is said that *DPP v P* applies to evidence which is admissible because it is part of the essential background, which conflates res gestae, background evidence, and evidence which would normally fall within the test in *DPP v P* into one.[20] On the other hand, in *Butler*,[21]

---

[14] [1997] 2 Cr App R 88, 90D. This would be, according to Professor Birch in her commentary on the case, "a retrograde step"; see [1997] Crim LR 441.

[15] [1997] 2 Cr App R 88, 92B.

[16] At para 2.54, 10.14 and Part XVI, provisional proposal 14.

[17] *Cross and Tapper*, p 343.

[18] *Cross and Tapper*, p 343. See also para 10.2 below.

[19] See para 10.1 below. The case law is discussed in some detail at paras 2.70 – 2.84 in the consultation paper.

[20] In *Underwood* [1999] Crim LR 227 evidence of violence on a different occasion, evidence that the defendant prevailed upon the victim, his girlfriend, to have an abortion, and evidence about his knowledge of the effect of violence upon her given that she had a

(in which the case of *Underwood* was not cited) it was held that counsel should assist the judge by agreeing an account of the background events so as not to distract the jury from consideration of the central events, and failing such agreement there should be a full analysis of the situation in the absence of the jury.

Section 27(3) of the Theft Act 1968

The justification for section 27(3)

4.13 On a charge of handling stolen goods, section 27(3) of the Theft Act 1968 permits the prosecution to adduce in chief evidence of criminal disposition, in the form of evidence of prior possession of stolen goods (section 27(3)(a)) or previous convictions (section 27(3)(b)) in order to prove that the defendant knew or believed the goods to be stolen.[22] Guilty knowledge in handling cases is notoriously difficult to prove, and this is undoubtedly relied on as a justification for the subsection.[23] People do from time to time acquire or deal with stolen goods without knowing or believing them to be stolen, and this possibility can make it difficult for the fact-finders to know whether a defence of lack of knowledge or belief might be true in the case before them. Their doubts in such cases can be resolved if they learn that the accused had dealt with other stolen property in the past, or has previous convictions for handling or theft.

4.14 There can be no doubt that the risk of wrongful convictions is increased by virtue of this provision.[24] Clearly, however, this is a risk which the legislature has decided must be taken if habitual or professional receivers are to be prosecuted effectively. The extent of the risk taken by the legislature is shown by the fact that subsection 27(3) permits the prosecution to adduce evidence, under paragraph (a), of a crime with which the defendant has never been charged, let alone convicted.

4.15 We are not convinced that the difficulty of proving knowledge or belief justifies the existence of this statutory exception to the general rule prohibiting bad character evidence being adduced in chief. As we said in the consultation paper,[25] there are many other instances where the mental element of an offence may be difficult to prove and previous misconduct might be of assistance.

4.16 One of the principal reasons why section 27(3) was felt to be necessary was that, until recently, no inference could be drawn against a defendant who refused to answer questions put by the police or to give evidence. We believe that in two respects the Criminal Justice and Public Order Act 1994 renders this justification

---

stroke was all said to be part of the "essential background" to the relationship but also said to be admitted applying *DPP v P*.

[21] [1999] Crim LR 835.

[22] See paras 2.27 – 2.30 above.

[23] See *Cross and Tapper*, p 378.

[24] A point made by the authors of *Andrews and Hirst on Criminal Evidence* (3rd ed 1997) para 15–056.

[25] At para 14.13.

far less compelling. First, by virtue of the provisions concerning silence in interview a judge can, in certain circumstances, comment on the failure of a defendant when questioned by the police either to mention facts on which subsequent reliance is placed or to explain the presence of objects or belongings found.[26] Second, as we argued in the consultation paper,[27] the possibility of drawing adverse inferences from silence at trial[28] means that a defendant will be more likely to testify than was previously the case: this will give the prosecution the opportunity of cross-examining the defendant on whether or not he or she knew or believed the goods to be stolen.

The defects of section 27(3)

4.17 Aside from the question whether it is now justified, there are problems with the application of the subsection itself. Under paragraph (a) all that is admissible is the bare fact "that the defendant was on a previous occasion found to be in possession of stolen goods" – no conviction for handling or theft need be proved. According to Mustill LJ in *Wood* "the only relevance of the fact is that the previous occasion would have served as a warning to be more careful in future".[29] The fact-finders will not, therefore, hear any details of the earlier transaction, and will have no evidence as to whether the defendant's earlier possession was that of a guilty handler or an unfortunate person who had acted honestly.[30] There is, of course, an alternative argument which has been described in the following terms: "given [the defendant's] previous skirmishes with the courts, he will have been more careful and the reason that once again he has stolen goods in his possession is because he is genuinely more likely *not* to have known that they were dishonestly come by".[31]

4.18 Although paragraph (b) used to be similarly construed,[32] the House of Lords held in *Hacker*[33] that it necessitates evidence being given of what the indictment for the earlier offence reveals about the nature of the goods stolen or handled.[34] In that

---

[26] See s 34 (accused's failure to mention facts when charged or questioned) and s 36 (accused's failure or refusal to account for objects in his or her possession etc).

[27] At para 3.12.

[28] Section 35.

[29] [1987] 1 WLR 779, 784E. This rationale cannot be universally correct because the section permits the admission of evidence of *any* prior possession, including one later than the present alleged offence.

[30] *Wood* [1987] 1 WLR 779.

[31] See R Munday, "The Admissibility of Evidence of Criminal Propensity in Common Law Jurisdictions" (1989) 19 VUWLR 223, 231, n 35 (emphasis in original).

[32] See *Fowler* (1988) 86 Cr App R 219.

[33] [1994] 1 WLR 1659.

[34] The reasoning was that paragraph (b) had to be read together with s 73(2) of PACE, which defines the phrase "certificate of conviction", in the case of a conviction on indictment, as "a certificate ... giving the substance and effect (omitting the formal parts) of the indictment and of the conviction". A certificate of a summary conviction consists of "a copy of the conviction" signed by the clerk of the convicting court. The certificate must record the nature of the goods stolen or handled, and *Hacker* shows that "the whole certificate ... is admissible".

case the charge was of handling the bodyshell of a Ford Escort RS Turbo motor car, and the evidence of the previous handling conviction revealed that it had also related to a Ford RS Turbo. The prosecution was not restricted, as the defence had contended it should be, to the bare fact, time and place of the earlier conviction.

4.19 The courts have assumed a discretion to exclude such evidence if there is a danger of undue prejudice.[35] This discretion is exercised where there is a danger of the jury regarding the evidence as relevant on the issue of possession.[36] The judge should admit the evidence only if the demands of justice warrant its admission.[37] This means that the judge has a duty to exclude it if, in the circumstances of the case, it can be of only minimal assistance to the jury.[38]

4.20 The section has been widely criticised:[39] its width means that "in their perfectly proper concern for the liberty of the individual, the courts may have made something of a nonsense of the provision".[40] The courts have given an extremely restrictive interpretation to these provisions whilst, at the same time, developing a wide discretion to exclude their application. In addition to this, the subsection contains a number of other particular defects.

4.21 In the first place, the subsection relates not only to *previous* misconduct, but also to misconduct *after* the time of the alleged offence.[41] Second, paragraph (a) allows evidence to be given of any act of handling even though no charge has been brought. This is likely to lead to disputes as to whether the defendant *was* in possession of stolen goods on a previous occasion. Further, paragraph (a) applies only if the goods were stolen not more than 12 months before the alleged handling: it is irrelevant when the alleged handler dealt with those goods. This can lead to bizarre results.[42]

4.22 Finally, prosecutors have said to us that it is almost impossible for them to be confident that the court will permit them to adduce evidence under this

---

[35] See *Herron* [1966] 2 All ER 26, 30B–C. For a recent example, see *Irwin* [1997] 1 CLY 1110.

[36] *Perry* [1984] Crim LR 680.

[37] *Rasini, The Times* March 20 1986.

[38] *Knott* [1973] Crim LR 36. But in *Canton* 2 June 1992, CA No 90/5242/X3 the Court of Appeal emphasised the importance of the judge's ascertaining the circumstances of the conviction rendered admissible by paragraph (b) so that he or she may assess its relevance and probative value; E Griew, *The Theft Acts* (7th ed 1995) p 255 n 18a.

[39] See, eg, R Munday, "Handling the Evidential Exception" [1988] Crim LR 345. The CLRC has recommended that the subsection be repealed: Evidence Report, para 101(vi). Interestingly, A T H Smith, *Property Offences* (1994) para 30-65, n 65, points out that similar provisions were not incorporated into the Victorian Crimes Act 1973 when the Theft Act 1968 was adopted, following a recommendation by the Chief Justice's Law Reform Committee that they were unfair to defendants.

[40] A T H Smith, *Property Offences* (1994) para 30-64.

[41] The subsection states that the handling to be relied on must have occurred "not earlier" than twelve months before the offence charged; see *Davies* [1972] Crim LR 431.

[42] See J Parry, *Offences against Property* (1989) para 4.67.

subsection. The Court of Appeal has given a clear indication that prosecutors should be discouraged from seeking to introduce evidence just because it is technically admissible under the subsection.[43] In exercising their discretion the courts are mindful that "to let in evidence of circumstances from which the existence of guilty knowledge on the prior occasion could be inferred would be such a striking inroad into the general rule which excludes evidence of prior unconnected offences that one would need clear words in the statute to justify it, and section 27(3) is quite silent".[44] This, prosecutors say, makes it difficult for them to decide whether to institute a prosecution. Indeed, it appears to be uncommon for prosecutors to seek to invoke the subsection, possibly because they do not think they will be successful.

4.23 In summary, the subsection is faulty, not needed, and not justified. We consider what respondents said about it, and whether it should be repealed, at paragraphs 11.53 – 55 below.

THE PROBLEMS IN DETAIL (II): CROSS-EXAMINATION OF THE DEFENDANT

4.24 The admissibility of evidence of the accused's bad character in cross-examination is governed by section 1 of the 1898 Act.[45] Below, we attempt to catalogue and clarify the defects of the provisions.

Section 1(f)(i)

4.25 Section 1(f)(i) provides an exception to the general prohibition against the cross-examination of the defendant on his or her bad character. This exception allows the defendant to be asked about misconduct which has already been admitted in chief as part of the prosecution case.[46] The subsection is defective because it refers only to evidence of the *commission* of the crime or evidence of a *conviction*, not to *charges* or to misconduct falling short of crime. If it is accepted that there is a sound principled basis for this provision these omissions are unfortunate, since they may require the exclusion of highly probative evidence.[47]

---

[43] *Rasini*, The Times 20 March 1986.

[44] *Wood* [1987] 1 WLR 779, 784E–F, *per* Mustill LJ.

[45] We describe the present law briefly in Part II above where sections 1(e) and 1(f) are set out.

[46] Eg, "similar fact evidence", or evidence of a previous conviction for a road traffic offence in later proceedings for driving while disqualified.

[47] Eg, in *Cokar* [1960] 2 QB 207 the defendant was charged with breaking and entering with intent to steal. His defence was that he had entered the house in question in order to have a rest. The prosecution alleged that C feigned being asleep to avoid conviction but he claimed not to know that such conduct would not be an offence. In order to rebut this claim, the prosecution was permitted to ask him about a previous occasion on which he had been acquitted of the same offence. It was held that these questions, though relevant, should not have been allowed. Lord Parker CJ held, at p 210, " ...it seems to this Court quite impossible, under exception (i), to question a man in regard to a charge in respect of which he was acquitted."

In *Pommell* 16 October 1998, CA No: 97/5655/W2 the Court of Appeal commented, obiter, that

The first limb of section 1(f)(ii): assertions of good character

4.26 If the defendant's character is such that the court will not treat him or her as a person of good character then there is a risk of losing the shield under the first limb of section 1(f)(ii) if the defendant claims to be of good character. This subsection gives rise to the following problems.

(i) The doctrine that character is indivisible

4.27 A significant problem with the present law is the notion that a person's character is indivisible, so that an accused cannot assert one part of his or her character which happens to be good without risking the exposure of another part which may be bad.[48] The psychological research does not support this doctrine,[49] it is inconsistent with the civil law of defamation,[50] two Australian law reform bodies have recommended the abolition of this rule,[51] and the Evidence Act 1995 (Cth) has now implemented that recommendation.[52] With some exceptions, mock juries and magistrates have shown that they recognise that there is no necessary connection between different character traits.[53] We discuss respondents' comments on this doctrine at paragraphs 13.22 – 13.28 below.

(ii) The use that can be made of bad character evidence

4.28 Under the current law, evidence admitted under the first limb of section 1(f)(ii) cannot go directly to the issue of guilt but is to be used as relevant only to the defendant's general truthfulness.[54] This may, of course, be difficult for fact-finders to do. If it is effectively impossible for the jury to treat the evidence as only relevant to credibility, then, as a matter of judicial discretion, the bad character should not be admitted at all.[55] Four respondents complained that it is illogical and unjust that if a defendant is of good character then the fact-finders will be told that character is relevant to propensity and to truthfulness, but if it is shown under this provision that the defendant is of bad character then the fact-finders must be told that this is irrelevant to his or her propensity to commit the crime.

The last sentence [of Lord Parker's] seems to rule out any questions in cross-examination in any circumstances in respect of events leading to a charge of which a man has been acquitted. If that is the effect of the Act it may appear surprising.

Pommell is also reported at [1999] Crim LR 576 (but this quotation from the judgment does not appear there).

[48] *Winfield* (1939) 27 Cr App R 139. See para 2.59 above.

[49] See paras 6.23 – 6.34 of the consultation paper.

[50] *Plato Films v Speidel* [1961] AC 1090, 1102, *per* Lord Devlin.

[51] ALRC, *Evidence* (1987) Report No 38, paras 177–178; New South Wales Law Reform Commission, *Working Paper on Evidence of Disposition* (1978) p 122, Draft Bill clause 111(5)(e).

[52] Section 110(3). The Evidence Act 1995 (New South Wales) was drafted in similar terms.

[53] See n 87 below.

[54] *Maxwell v DPP* [1935] AC 309, 321, *per* Lord Sankey LC; *Richardson and Longman* [1969] 1 QB 299, 310C and 311B–C, *per* Edmund Davies LJ.

[55] *Davison-Jenkins* [1997] Crim LR 816.

4.29 Judge Rivlin QC pointed out that there is a disparity between the treatment of prosecution witnesses and the treatment of defendants in this regard. He argued that where a prosecution witness's bad character is relevant to propensity, there is no pretence that it is relevant only to credibility.

(iii) It is unclear what kinds of assertions will trigger the loss of the shield

4.30 A further problem is that at present it is unclear what kinds of claim made in what ways will trigger the loss of the shield.[56] For example, it is not clear from the case law whether the section encompasses "the mere repetition in court of words claiming a good character uttered upon arrest",[57] or a claim made in a letter "probably intended to be read only in mitigation of sentence".[58]

4.31 Nor is it clear whether a defendant asserts good character for the purposes of the subsection by claiming (truthfully) to be, for example, a solicitor or a church warden.[59] The CLRC was concerned about defendants giving evidence which indirectly gave the (false) impression that they were of good character. In the recent case of *Carter*,[60] Sedley J, giving the judgment of the Court of Appeal, was of the opinion that:

> When the appellant gave evidence on his own behalf he made sufficient assertions about his own experience (as a farmer, a qualified electrician and a car dealer, when the fact was that much of his life had been spent in prison for similar offences) to make it arguable that he had "put his character in" …

(iv) Previous convictions of other possible culprits

4.32 An anomaly may arise where the defendant seeks to suggest a favourable contrast with other possible culprits, such as by adducing evidence that they have previous convictions for offences similar to that charged.[61] Where those other people do not give evidence, there is no question of the defendant making "imputations" against "witnesses" and so the shield is not lost under the second limb of section 1(f)(ii), but if they did happen to be prosecution witnesses, the imputation would cost the defendant the shield. *Cross and Tapper* states that where these witnesses are not called, the question whether the defendant has lost the shield depends on "exactly how pointedly the contrast is made".[62] One view is that there is an implication that

---

[56] See *Cross and Tapper*, p 405.

[57] *Solomon* (1909) 2 Cr App R 80.

[58] *Parker* (1925) 18 Cr App R 14.

[59] The courts have held that a defendant has given evidence of good character where he or she claims to have been earning an honest living for a considerable time (*Powell* [1985] 1 WLR 1364), to be a regular churchgoer (*Ferguson* (1909) 2 Cr App R 250), or to have performed kind or honest deeds on a previous occasion (*Samuel* (1956) 40 Cr App R 8).

[60] (1997) 161 JP 207, 208.

[61] *Ellis* [1910] 2 KB 746.

[62] *Cross and Tapper*, p 399.

the other person is more likely than the defendant to have committed the offence. If the defendant also has such convictions, this implication could be misleading, but it will remain uncorrected. Another view is that no such implication is entailed, in which case the jury is not misled.[63] However, it is difficult to see what purpose an accused can have in adducing evidence of another's previous misconduct, other than to show that he or she is more likely to have committed the offence than the accused.

The second limb of section 1(f)(ii): imputations against prosecution witnesses and deceased victims

Summary

4.33   The whole foundation of the second limb of section 1(f)(ii) is flawed. The rule can lead to harsh results, especially for the defendant who effectively has no choice but to make the imputation. The desire to avoid these harsh results has led the courts to rely on a wide-ranging discretion to mitigate its effects. This leads to uncertainty, as does lack of clarity over what counts as an imputation. We believe that this is particularly unsatisfactory in an area where the law should be as clear as possible. On the other hand, section 1(f)(ii) often fails to achieve one of its purposes, both because defendants succeed in making covert imputations without losing the shield, and because non-testifying defendants escape the consequences. This puts a premium on tactics and manipulating the "rules of the game".

(i)   No exception for necessary imputations

4.34   The second limb of section 1(f)(ii) provides that a defendant may be cross-examined on other offences where "the nature or conduct of the defence is such as to involve imputations on the character of the prosecutor or the witnesses for the prosecution or the deceased victim of the alleged crime". The fact that a defence cannot be advanced *without* making an imputation does not mean that the court will refuse to allow cross-examination on previous offences.

4.35   The Court of Criminal Appeal in *Hudson* held

> We think that the words of the section, "unless the nature or conduct of the defence is such as to involve imputations," etc, must receive their ordinary and natural interpretation, and that it is not legitimate to qualify them by adding or inserting the words "unnecessarily," or

---

[63]   Consider the facts of *Lee* [1976] 1 WLR 71. The accused was alleged to have taken some money and a ring from a person living in the same house. He denied taking them, part of his case being that at least two persons with convictions for dishonesty had also had access to the house. The Court of Appeal held that cross-examination of a prosecution witness to the effect that the two persons had such convictions did not result in the loss of the shield, for "it is not implicit in an accusation of dishonesty that the accuser himself is an honest man" (at p 73F, *per* Orr LJ). But it is difficult to see what purpose the accused might have had in adducing evidence of the others' criminal records, if not to make it appear that they were more likely than the accused to have committed the crime.

"unjustifiably," or "for purposes other than that of developing the defence," or other similar words.[64]

In *Stirland*[65] the House of Lords sought to provide guidance on whether the shield was only lost under the second limb of section 1(f)(ii) where the imputation was not necessary to the defendant's defence. Their Lordships interpreted the rule as meaning that "an accused is not to be regarded as depriving himself of the protection [of section 1(f)] because the proper conduct of his defence *necessitates* the making of injurious reflections on the prosecutor or his witnesses."[66] However, the House of Lords held in *Selvey*[67] that the court has a discretion to restrict the cross-examination permitted by section 1(f)(ii), but rejected the contention that this discretion ought to be exercised in favour of the accused where his or her defence necessarily involves the making of such imputations,[68] and the point must be regarded as settled.

4.36 The Court of Appeal in *Britzman*[69] laid down guidelines for the exercise of the discretion in this situation, but the guidelines do not directly take account of the need of an accused to mount a defence to the charge.

4.37 The lack of an exception for necessary imputations may deter the defendant from testifying,[70] and a defendant might not put forward his or her defence, however

---

[64] [1912] 2 KB 464, 470–71, *per* Lord Alverston CJ.

[65] *Stirland v DPP* [1944] AC 315.

[66] *Ibid*, 327 (emphasis added). Following *Miller* [1997] Crim LR 217, the shield will be lost where an imputation is made against a person with material evidence to give, even if he or she is not called as a witness in the proceedings. It now seems that there is no difference between a prosecution witness who testifies, or a deceased victim, or a declarant whose evidence is read in accordance with s 13(3) of the Criminal Justice Act 1925, s 23 of the Criminal Justice Act 1988 or s 9 of the Criminal Justice Act 1967. The interpretation of the phrase "witnesses for the prosecution" may be questionable (see R Munday, (1997) 161 JP 379, 381 and the commentary of Professor Birch at [1997] Crim LR 217 at p 218), but at least one anomaly has been removed.

[67] [1970] AC 304, with the proviso that there is a discretion regarding emphatic denials, and an exception for rape cases, so a defendant may allege consent to intercourse without exposing himself to cross-examination.

[68] See also, eg, *Jenkins* (1946) 31 Cr App R 1, 13–14; and *Cook* (1959) 43 Cr App R 138.

[69] [1983] 1 WLR 350.

[70] This danger was appreciated during the Second Reading of the 1898 Bill in the House of Commons. Mr Atherley Jones MP said,

> if it happened by chance that, although I was innocent of the particular offence which was the subject of the charge which was brought against me, I was a man of indifferent character and I had been in previous years convicted of a similar offence, then nothing in the world would induce me, short of compulsion, to go into the witness box and submit to cross-examination.

Hansard (HC) 25 April 1898, vol 56, col 1035.

In the research conducted for the Royal Commission, 28% of defence counsel thought their clients' defences had been inhibited by the statutory provision: M Zander and P Henderson, *Crown Court Study* (1993) Research Study No 19 for the Report of the Royal Commission, para 4.6.8.

true, if it is likely that the shield will be lost. As the Magistrates' Association wrote, "The imputation might be necessary for the defence. The defence ought not to be inhibited from making the imputation just because D has a criminal record". If the witness' bad character is relevant, the defendant should not have to risk losing the shield by drawing the court's attention to it.[71]

4.38 Several respondents argued that the lack of an exception for "necessary" defences is a defect in the current law. As one experienced magistrate wrote:

> Suppose that the imputations are in fact accurate, correct, true ... However true the imputations, however good the defence, the record going before the jury will almost inevitably be damaging to the accused and prejudice his chances of acquittal ... The defence are inhibited. The defence may feel unable to conduct the defence as vigorously as they would like for fear of the record going in. It may seem too dangerous for the defence to attack corrupt prosecution witnesses. So the jury are led to believe that those corrupt prosecution witnesses are honest and truthful and reliable.

4.39 As we said in the consultation paper,[72] a defendant who denies a confession attributed to him by the police faces three unattractive options:

(a) deny the confession from the witness-box, be cross-examined on his convictions and run the gauntlet of prejudice;

(b) testify but not contest the confession, and accept that a verdict of guilty will most probably follow; or

(c) get his or her counsel to deny the confession, refrain from testifying and thus rob the denial of any force.[73]

4.40 Section 35(3) of the Criminal Justice and Public Order Act 1994 now creates a pressure to give evidence by permitting the fact-finders to draw adverse inferences

---

[71] The Court of Appeal has suggested that the onus should perhaps fall on the prosecution to put evidence of their witness' character before the fact-finders and not leave it to the defence: *Hickey and Robinson* 30 July 1997, CA No 96/5131/S1/2/3/5. This avoids the situation in *Taylor and Goodman* [1999] 2 Cr App R 163 discussed below at para 4.42. But see also para 4.67 for the inconsistency of prosecution practice.

[72] At para 12.41 (footnotes omitted).

[73] This quandary is set out by A Zuckerman in *The Principles of Criminal Evidence* (1989) at p 265. In a recent case, counsel described the defendant as being "between a rock and a hard place" in deciding whether to give evidence himself in support of his defence, as his criminal record was highly prejudicial: *Dempster* [2001] EWCA Crim 571, para [40].

from a failure to do so.[74] It is expected that fact-finders will be able to draw adverse inferences in almost every case where the accused fails to testify.[75]

4.41 In *Taylor*[76] it was held that the defendant could not avoid the possibility of inferences being drawn under the section by arguing that the failure to testify was based on the fear that his previous convictions might be disclosed. It was observed that the defendant would already have been given the mandatory warning under section 35(2), in the presence of the jury, of the risk that he would be running by not testifying. If he then chose not to testify on the basis that evidence of past discreditable conduct would prejudice the jury, it would be difficult for the judge, when directing the jury that they should not draw inferences, to give reasons. He could not give reasons, lest he create the prejudice which the defendant set out to escape.[77]

4.42 The case of *Taylor and Goodman* serves as an example. A prosecution witness, M, had originally been a co-accused with the appellants to charges of conspiracy to rob and of having a firearm with intent to commit an indictable offence (robbery). He changed his plea to guilty and became a witness for the Crown. M had convictions including one offence of assault occasioning actual bodily harm, and, more significantly, two of conspiracy to rob. When M was called as a witness, the prosecution did not tell the jury of his record. Defence counsel did not ask M about his record, for fear that the bad records of their clients would go in. The Court of Appeal commented, "We acknowledge, and indeed emphasise, that it was most unfortunate, for whatever reason, that the jury was not given the full picture of [M]'s previous record. We think the jury should have had that information."[78]

4.43 One respondent disagreed that there should be any exception for necessary imputations. He argued that where a defendant "attacks" a prosecution witness, the defendant assumes the status of a witness. In this capacity "it is only fair that the witness who vilifies that other should have his own credibility tested, subject always to the discretion of the judge". The South Eastern Circuit took the same

---

[74] Four respondents thought more defendants were testifying. In the Home Office Study on the right of silence, the researchers note that "Virtually all respondents … agreed that fewer defendants are declining to testify since the introduction of the provisions" but "There are no centrally collected statistics on the numbers and proportions of defendants testifying to support or refute these perceptions." T Bucke, R Street, and D Brown, *The Right of Silence: the Impact of the Criminal Justice and Public Order Act 1994* (2000) Home Office Research Study 199, pp 52–53.

[75] In *Cowan* [1996] 1 Cr App R 1, the Court of Appeal held that there would need to be some evidential basis or some exceptional factors in a case to justify *not* drawing an adverse inference. The court did not accept that the fact that the accused had attacked prosecution witnesses and had a criminal record could constitute such a factor; otherwise a defendant with a criminal record would be in a better position than one without, which would be "a bizarre result" (at p 6B, *per* Lord Taylor CJ).

[76] *Taylor* [1999] Crim LR 77.

[77] T Bucke, R Street, and D Brown, *The Right of Silence: the Impact of the Criminal Justice and Public Order Act 1994* (2000) Home Office Research Study 199, p 15.

[78] [1999] 2 Cr App R 163, 173E, *per* Judge LJ.

view, arguing that it was necessary that the jury know of the defendant's previous misconduct in order to assess the credibility of the defendant's story. We agree, to the extent that the defendant's previous misconduct is in fact relevant to his or her credibility, but do not agree that all previous misconduct should therefore be admissible.

(ii) Over-reliance on judicial discretion

4.44 The court has an overall discretion to disallow cross-examination even where there has been a breach of section 1(f)(ii) if the prejudicial effect of the cross-examination exceeds its probative value.[79] It is not permissible for the discretion to be exercised in the defendant's favour merely on the basis that the previous convictions which would be revealed are of a similar nature to the offence charged,[80] nor, as we point out above, on the basis that the defence could not be put without making imputations. In practice, however, the discretion can be exercised in the defendant's favour where the suggestions made are essential to the defendant's plea of not guilty[81] or where there "is nothing more than a denial, however emphatic or offensively made, of an act or even a short series of acts amounting to one incident or in what was said to have been a short interview",[82] or where the evidence is overwhelming.[83]

4.45 The width of this discretion has two main consequences. First, its effect is that the statutory rule is comprehensively undermined by the discretion. This is an unusual and unsatisfactory instance of the discretionary tail wagging the dog.

4.46 Second, it is not easy for defence advocates to predict what may or may not be put to prosecution witnesses in cross-examination without running the risk that their clients' records would be revealed.[84] This is not so much a problem in the Crown Court because the advocate can ask the judge for a ruling without prejudicing the defendant's case, but this is not practicable in magistrates' courts[85] because simply asking for an indication from the Bench reveals to them that the defendant has a record which may be significant.

---

[79] *Powell* [1985] 1 WLR 1364. See also *Murdoch v Taylor* [1965] AC 574, 592G, *per* Lord Donovan; *Selvey v DPP* [1970] AC 304; and *Thompson* [1966] 1 WLR 405.

[80] *McLeod* [1994] 1 WLR 1500, 1512G.

[81] *St Louis* (1984) 79 Cr App R 53.

[82] *Britzman* [1983] 1 WLR 350, 355D, *per* Lawton LJ.

[83] *Britzman* [1983] 1 WLR 350, 355G.

[84] It will be recalled that, in the Crown Court study conducted by the Royal Commission, 28% of defence counsel believed that their clients' defences were inhibited by this provision; see n 70 above.

[85] In 1999 (the latest year for which figures are available for magistrates' courts and the Crown Court) 77,000 people appeared for trial at the Crown Court, while 1,884,000 people were proceeded against in magistrates' courts. Ie, approximately 96% of people who face trial do so in a magistrates' court. Criminal Statistics England and Wales (2000) Cm 5001.

(iii) The foundations for the second limb of section 1(f)(ii) are unsound

4.47 Three justifications for the admission of bad character evidence under this limb may be advanced: credibility, fairness and deterring attacks on the characters of prosecution witnesses.

(A) CREDIBILITY

4.48 It has been said that: "the jury is entitled to know the credit of the man on whose word the witness's character is being impugned."[86] The impact of this knowledge may be subject to doubt. The psychological research shows that previous misconduct evidence may not be very, or at all, relevant to the defendant's truthfulness.[87] In fact, of far more significance than a general tendency are the motivations in the individual case.[88]

4.49 In some cases, moreover, the imputations on the prosecution witness do not relate to his or her credibility, and it may follow that the purpose of putting the defendant's character in also has nothing to do with credibility. For example, in an assault case, the defendant might wish to put previous convictions for violence to the complainant with a view to showing that the complainant started the fight. If the defendant has a similar background, then it may be that it should be admitted, but it will have more to do with the defendant's propensity than with his credibility.

4.50 A case where this occurred in a way which was unfair to the defendant was *S*.[89] Each of the Court of Appeal judges took the view that

> it was not reliable to assume that because a man was a regular robber he was to be disbelieved when he said that he did not commit a sexual attack on a 14 year old girl. These two activities are so vastly different that one is reluctant to import the one into the other.[90]

The trial judge, however, must have reached a different view because he had allowed the defendant's record to be admitted on the ground that the defendant had made imputations against the complainant, thus losing the shield under the

---

[86] *Cook* [1959] 2 QB 340, 348, *per* Devlin J.

[87] This would seem to be the view taken by the participants in the research conducted by Dr Lloyd-Bostock. They were told that the defendant had a previous conviction for handling, or for an assault. The mock jurors did not say that they found him to be a less credible witness. Only if they were told that the defendant had a previous conviction for an indecent assault on a child were the mock jurors likely to say that they found him to be a less credible witness: see Appendix D to the consultation paper, paras D.37 – D.41. Conversely, the magistrates who took part in the subsequent study found a defendant with a previous conviction for a serious assault a less credible witness, whilst other convictions had a less significant impact on their assessment of credibility: see Appendix A below.

[88] A cross-examining advocate will test a witness's specific credibility in the case by pointing to: inconsistency with other evidence, inconsistency with a previous statement by that witness, bias, the possibility that the witness will profit from a conviction, or the possibility that the witness has been pressurised into giving particular testimony.

[89] *S* 98/1296/X4.

[90] *S* 98/1296/X4 at p 6 of the transcript, *per* Schiemann LJ.

second limb of section 1(f)(ii). The conviction depended on the jury's view as to who was telling the truth. It was quashed. The doctrine of the indivisibility of character[91] must have played a part here: given this doctrine, once the shield was lost, it was open to the prosecution to adduce any evidence of bad character, subject to the judge's discretion to exclude it. The reason for admitting the evidence (for the light it would shed on the defendant's credibility) was lost sight of.

(B) FAIRNESS

4.51 Some would argue that if the defendant attacks the characters of prosecution witnesses then it is *fair* that the defendant should lose the special protection given by the shield against cross-examination on bad character.[92] It is difficult to see how it can be fair to promote a verdict which may be reached on the basis of evidence which is more prejudicial than probative. The CLRC wrote in 1972 that

> if relevant evidence is excluded during the case for the prosecution because it may be too prejudicial to the accused, it does not become any less prejudicial because the accused attacks the witnesses for the prosecution.[93]

4.52 The dangers which a defendant faces when evidence of bad character is admitted do not, indeed, decrease simply because the defendant has cast imputations. Although the probative value of the bad character evidence may in some cases be such that it is nevertheless fair to admit it, this criticism of the statutory provision has considerable force. This argument was commented on by one respondent, who wrote: "There is clearly on the one hand an illogicality in this provision because the effect of the evidence and the prejudice to the accused has not altered; but on the other hand it may be an inescapable consequence of the trial system, where the only way of seeking to address the balance of fairness when the defendant attacks prosecution witnesses is by the use of the admittedly blunt device of the introduction of his bad character". Another respondent called the tit-for-tat rule a "disgrace" and said: "Tit-for-tat suggests some element of equality; but in reality the accused can be penalised for daring to dispute and contradict the evidence against him".

(C) DETERRING ATTACKS ON PROSECUTION WITNESSES

4.53 The third justification for the defendant losing the shield where he or she makes imputations against prosecution witnesses or deceased victims is that the defendant is thereby deterred from making such imputations.

---

[91] See para 4.27 above.

[92] Eg, in *Taylor and Goodman* [1999] 2 Cr App R 163 (see para 4.42 above), Goodman made serious imputations against prosecution witnesses. His own record showed that he was a professional armed robber. The judge considered that "fairness required" that Goodman's record should go in. The charges were conspiracy to rob and possession of a firearm with intent to commit robbery.

[93] CLRC, Evidence Report, para 123(i).

4.54 The reasons for seeking to protect witnesses were summarised by counsel in *Bishop*[94] before the Court of Appeal. They are as follows:

(a) there is a disincentive for witnesses to come forward and give evidence if they are aware that they themselves will be attacked;

(b) the jury may be prejudiced against the witness by what they hear, and be tempted to reach a verdict on a non-rational basis; and

(c) the defendant will be tempted to make untrue allegations about the prosecution witnesses.

There is also a public interest in protecting those who cannot be present to defend themselves from irrelevant or untrue attacks on their character.

4.55 Three respondents thought that prosecution witnesses should be protected to a greater extent than is currently the case. Professor McEwan said that cross-examination was too often

> unnecessarily long-winded, grilling witnesses on the most minute details which have no bearing on the reliability of the description of the main event, all in the hope of producing self-contradiction which can be pounced on. Others are too often hostile and designed to cause loss of composure ... Fear of disclosure of criminal record will not deter invidious cross-examination. It is also wrong to use the threat of a fairly arbitrary kind of punishment against someone on trial. Either a criminal record is relevant or not. We should instead be looking closely at the ways to control unacceptable cross-examination.[95]

4.56 We also think the law is inadequate in this regard. We believe that our recommendations in Parts VIII and IX go a considerable way to improving it.[96] We do not think that the second limb of section 1(f)(ii) is the best way of securing protection from irrelevant and unfair cross-examination.

4.57 Although prosecution witnesses, amongst others, do need to be protected against irrelevant or untrue imputations, and the law, rightly in our view, should seek to discourage such imputations, the accused is in need from protection from wrongful conviction. A minority of the CLRC believed that the sanction of losing the shield is too severe: "the sanction should not be one which may well make it more likely that he will be convicted of the offence".[97]

4.58 Even if this sanction were fair, it is not effective. It offers no protection to *defence* witnesses, and does not protect any witnesses where either the defendant is of good character or does not testify.

4.59 Further, as the CLRC pointed out,

---

[94] [1975] QB 274, 279.

[95] Jenny McEwan, "Law Commission Dodges the Nettles in Consultation Paper No. 141" [1997] Crim LR 93, 102.

[96] See paras 8.32, 9.41 and 9.42.

[97] CLRC, Evidence Report, para 123(i).

The present rule also makes possible a particular abuse where there are two accused, A and B, and A has a bad record and B none. B makes the attack on the witnesses for the prosecution for the benefit of both A and himself, but A cannot be cross-examined on his record. We should have liked to find a way of preventing this abuse ... .[98]

(iv) Non-testifying defendants

4.60 Under the current law, a defendant who attacks prosecution witnesses through his or her advocate, does not lose the shield under section 1(f)(ii) unless he or she testifies. This is the rule in *Butterwasser*.[99] The justification for this is that a non-testifying defendant does not put his or her credibility in issue.[100]

4.61 This is a contentious issue, and opinions were divided about whether the rule in *Butterwasser* needs to be changed. Forty-one respondents addressed the point. We put forward three options for reform, the first of which (A) was no change in the existing law. The others were (B) the Royal Commission approach, namely that a defendant's previous misconduct can be adduced whenever imputations are made against prosecution witnesses, and (C) allowing previous misconduct to be adduced if the nature of the defence is such as to put the defendant's credibility in issue.

4.62 Eight respondents argued that the rule in *Butterwasser* should be retained. Paul Roberts, Reader in Criminal Justice at the University of Nottingham, was one of four respondents who argued that where a defendant does not testify, his or her credibility cannot be in issue. He said:

> ... the defendant's credibility cannot be in issue unless he chooses to become a witness in the trial! As Lord Goddard CJ made pellucidly clear in *Butterwasser* itself, when defence counsel cross-examines a prosecution witness to credit, it is the prosecution witness's credibility that is put in issue, not the defendant's.[101]

4.63 The other respondents who favoured the retention of the current position did so either on the basis that the Criminal Justice and Public Order Act 1994 makes it more difficult for a defendant to hide behind silence, and so it is less likely that defendants would choose not to testify simply in order to be able to attack prosecution witnesses, or on the basis that if a defendant does not give evidence, any attack on a witness's credit is of no weight anyway, unless the witness admits the matter or the defendant calls evidence to prove it (in which case the witness can be cross-examined on it). In either event, change is not warranted.

---

[98] CLRC, Evidence Report, para 131.

[99] [1948] 1 KB 4.

[100] *Butterwasser* [1948] 1 KB 4, 7, *per* Lord Goddard CJ.

[101] Paul Roberts, "All the Usual Suspects: A Critical Appraisal of Law Commission Consultation Paper No 141" [1997] Crim LR 75, 89. See also Paul Roberts, "Evidence of Previous Misconduct" [1997] Crim LR 369.

4.64 The remaining thirty-three respondents thought the law in this area ought to be reformed. Twenty-one of these respondents thought that evidence of the defendant's previous misconduct should be adduced *whenever* imputations are made against prosecution witnesses. It seems likely that these respondents thought that credibility *is* in issue, even if the accused does not testify, although only two said so expressly. Eleven respondents argued that the defendant's previous misconduct should be adduced if the nature of the imputations was such as to put the defendant's credibility in issue.

4.65 We do not agree that a defendant's credibility can only be in issue if he or she gives evidence in person. The traditional view seems to ignore the reality that a defendant *may* put his or her credibility in issue even without testifying: it depends on whether a particular version of events is being put forward as the case for the defence. Where this occurs, the fact-finders will inevitably assess the credibility of the prosecution witness in relation to the credibility of the defendant in deciding whose version of events to believe. We note that in *Woodward and Dobson*[102] the court held that the defendants were entitled not only to a propensity direction but also to a direction about the significance of their good characters on their credibility (following *Vye*)[103] because, although neither testified at trial, out-of-court answers in interviews had been admitted in evidence.

(v) A temptation to fabricate

4.66 The current law could be construed as presenting a temptation to investigating officers to break the rules in the knowledge that if the accused alleges in court that this has happened, his or her previous convictions are likely to be admitted, thus making a conviction more likely.[104] However likely or unlikely in practice, the fact that such a temptation can present itself must be viewed as a defect of the present law.

(vi) Inconsistent prosecution practice

4.67 Another matter to consider, although not strictly a defect of the statute, is inconsistent prosecution practice in relation to the introduction of evidence of bad character of prosecution witnesses. Our attention has been drawn[105] to a "growing practice" among prosecutors of voluntarily disclosing the bad character of any witnesses it proposes to rely on. The purpose of such disclosure is "apparently to reveal the prosecution in a better light than where the evidence is subsequently extracted by the defence by way of cross-examination". The result is that some defendants do not have to risk losing the shield because they will not have to raise the issue of the character of a prosecution witness. The problem is that the present practice is entirely voluntary, and can therefore lead to unfairness in that

---

[102] [1996] Crim LR 207.

[103] [1993] 1 WLR 471.

[104] See para 12.13 of the consultation paper and see generally J D Heydon, "Can the Accused Attack the Prosecution?" (1974) 7 Syd LR 166, 167. This point is also made by Latham CJ in *Curwood* (1944) 69 CLR 561, 577.

[105] See (1997) 161 JP 378.

defendants are being treated differently. Further, it diminishes the protection to witnesses by assuming that certain issues will be raised when they might not have been.

(vii) Lack of clarity

4.68 It is unclear in general what *sort* of allegation will amount to an imputation,[106] and also *how* the allegation has to be made to count as an imputation. Where cross-examination is disallowed, it is not always clear whether this is a result of the exercise of the judge's discretion to exclude cross-examination where an imputation has been made, or whether it is because no imputation has in fact been made. This is particularly the case as regards "emphatic denials". In *Britzman*,[107] it was held that a denial which entails that a prosecution witness is lying is an imputation, not merely an emphatic denial,[108] while in *Desmond*[109] it was held that where defence counsel made a clear suggestion of lies and drew on inconsistencies in the witnesses' accounts to lend the suggestion weight, this did not amount to an imputation. The Crown Prosecution Service argued that this uncertainty comprised one of the reasons why reform was necessary.[110]

4.69 It is also not clear whether a co-accused is entitled to cross-examine an accused on his or her record if the accused has lost the shield under the second limb. It was suggested in *Lovett*[111] that there were cases where cross-examination by a co-accused under the second limb of section 1(f)(ii) might be appropriate. At that time a co-defendant could not take advantage of section 1(f)(iii), which permits cross-examination on a co-accused's record in certain circumstances, unless charged with the same *offence*,[112] and it was recognised that if cross-examination were not appropriate then it might be prevented as a matter of discretion. Doubt

---

[106] See, eg, *Courtney* [1995] Crim LR 63, in which the Court of Appeal upheld the trial judge's decision that an allegation that a Customs officer had asked the accused's mother to have a quiet word with him and persuade him to admit the offence, constituted an imputation.

[107] [1983] 1 WLR 350.

[108] Cf the House of Lords in *Selvey v DPP* which seemed to assume that an emphatic denial would not be an imputation.

[109] [1999] Crim L R 313.

[110] It might seem surprising that this point can still be the subject of litigation, but there is clearly room for argument. Eg, in *Taylor and Goodman* [1999] 2 Cr App R 163 the appellants argued that their records should not have been admitted under the second limb of section 1(f)(ii) because the cross-examination of the police and the accomplice were no more than vigorous denials, the judge at trial having decided otherwise. The Court of Appeal approved the trial judge's decision in this regard.

[111] [1973] 1 WLR 241.

[112] The effect of the Criminal Evidence Act 1979 is that the co-defendant need only be "charged in the same proceedings". The amendment reversed the effect of the decision of the House of Lords in *Metropolitan Police Commissioner v Hills* [1980] AC 26, in which it was held that the words "same offence" meant the same in all material respects, so that where two defendants were tried together but not for the same offence, the provision did not apply. See also P Mirfield, "The Meaning of 'the same offence' under Section 1(f)(iii)" [1978] Crim LR 725.

was cast on this latter proposition by *Rowson*,[113] which emphasised the general principle that a defendant must always be free to elicit evidence which advances his or her case; but this case was not directly concerned with section 1(f), and arguably leaves the *Lovett* discretion untouched as an exception to that principle.[114]

Section 1(f)(iii): cross-examination of a co-accused

4.70 Under section 1(f)(iii) of the 1898 Act, a defendant is liable to cross-examination on previous misconduct if "he has given evidence against any other person charged in the same proceedings".[115]

(i) Lack of judicial discretion

4.71 The principal criticism of section 1(f)(iii) is that the court has no discretion to prevent loss of the shield where D1 gives evidence against D2.[116] This might result in unfairness. Lord Pearce, in his dissenting speech in *Murdoch v Taylor*, gave two examples of situations calling for the exercise of a judicial discretion:

> The first is where [D2's] counsel has deliberately led [D1] into the trap, or has, for the purpose of bringing in his bad record, put questions to him in cross-examination which will compel him, for the sake of his own innocence, to give answers that will clash with the story of the other defendant, or compel him to bring to the forefront implications which would otherwise have been unnoticed or immaterial. The second type of situation is where the clash between the two stories is both inevitable and trivial, and yet the damage by the introduction of a bad record (perhaps many years previous) will in the circumstances be unfairly prejudicial.[117]

4.72 Professor Ian Dennis has suggested[118] that there is another situation which calls for a discretion to be available, an example of which occurred in *Varley*.[119] D2 is the

---

[113] [1986] QB 174.

[114] See *Blackstone*, para F14.36. Cf *Phipson on Evidence*, (15th ed 2000, ed M N Howard, P Crane, D A Hochberg, R Bagshaw, P Mirfield, K Grevling and C Hollander) para 18–48, where it is argued that the effect of *Rowson* is to confer a general *right* of cross-examination in such circumstances (excluding even the *Selvey* discretion to prevent cross-examination), but that the discretion recognised in *Lovett* ought to be preserved.

[115] In *Murdoch v Taylor* [1965] AC 574, 592D, Lord Donovan defined "evidence against" as meaning "evidence which supports the prosecutor's case in a material respect or which undermines the defence of a co-accused". Lord Bingham CJ cited this dictum with approval in the Court of Appeal in *Crawford (Charisse)* [1997] 1 WLR 1329, 1333G, adding that the essential question, put at its simplest, was whether the evidence given by the defendant in the witness box, if accepted, damaged in a significant way the defence of the co-defendant.

[116] Following the House of Lords' decision in *Murdoch v Taylor* [1965] AC 574. The court does have a discretion where it is the *prosecution* that seeks to cross-examine an accused under s 1(f)(iii) on the grounds that he or she has given evidence against a co-accused: *Seigley* (1911) 6 Cr App R 106, *per* Hamilton J. The court also has a discretion to refuse to allow D3 to cross-examine D1 where D1 has given evidence against D2: *Lovett* [1973] 1 WLR 241. Cf *Russell* [1971] 1 QB 151.

[117] [1965] AC 574, 587E–F.

[118] I H Dennis, "Evidence Against a Co-Accused" (1983) 36 CLP 177, 183.

first to testify, and inculpates D1. D1 faces a dilemma. If he remains silent, he may appear to have no answer to the allegation, and the jury may be invited to draw appropriate inferences from his silence.[120] If he testifies, he will have to contradict D2's evidence, thus giving evidence against her and losing the shield.[121]

4.73 It has been said that: "It is difficult to shake off the impression that the House of Lords, by opting for an inflexible rule under section 1(f)(iii), has promoted fairness to the co-accused at the expense of fairness for the accused quite unnecessarily."[122] The reason for this inflexibility is that nothing should be done to impede a defendant in the conduct of his or her defence.[123] An alternative explanation is that judges must not be seen to pick and choose between co-accused, since the "fairness" shown to one may produce an appearance of unfairness to another.[124]

4.74 The traditional approach has given precedence to the interests of the defendant seeking to admit the bad character evidence over those of the defendant who would be prejudiced by it, and this is the effect of the ruling in *Murdoch v Taylor*.[125] An experienced practitioner argued that *in the capacity of a prosecution witness*, it is only fair that the attacking defendant loses the shield. He said: "In the practical world of the hard fights in contested criminal cases with, in so very many instances, much hard lying taking place, it is improvident to put a premium upon the invention of cunning false stories giving rise to immunity from credit being properly tested". This argument is also made by the CLRC,[126] but it entirely overlooks the prejudicial impact the revelation of a criminal record can have on a defendant's case.[127]

4.75 We see much force in the argument that one defendant should be entitled to adduce properly relevant evidence without regard to the adverse effect that it has on the case of another defendant. On the other hand we also see the force in the suggestion that all persons who give evidence should be free to do so without

---

[119] [1982] 2 All ER 519.

[120] Criminal Justice and Public Order Act 1994, s 35(3).

[121] The problem becomes more acute when D2 has few or trivial convictions compared with D1. In such a case, D2 "has everything to gain and very little to lose by incriminating [D1] up to the hilt and making the trap as tight as possible"; I H Dennis, "Evidence Against a Co-Accused" (1983) 36 CLP 177, 183.

[122] R Pattenden, *Judicial Discretion and Criminal Litigation* (2nd ed 1990) p 259.

[123] Lord Donovan explained this in *Murdoch v Taylor* [1965] AC 574, 593D–E:

> [The accused] seeks to defend himself; to say to the jury that the man who is giving evidence against him is unworthy of belief; and to support that assertion by proof of bad character. The right to do this cannot, in my opinion, be fettered in any way.

[124] R Munday, "The Wilder Permutations of s 1(f) of the Criminal Evidence Act 1898" (1987) 7 LS 137, 144.

[125] [1965] AC 574.

[126] CLRC, Evidence Report, para 132.

[127] See I H Dennis, "Evidence Against a Co-Accused" (1983) 36 CLP 177, 184.

having irrelevant or marginal or barely relevant evidence of past misdeeds dragged into the public arena. Thus whilst it should not be a matter of balancing competing interests, it may be more satisfactorily approached by imposing generally a raised standard of relevance on bad character evidence which does not fall within the central facts of the case, and to require this standard to be satisfied before one party may adduce evidence of, or cross-examine about, the misconduct of another person on other occasions.[128]

(ii) Defendants may be inhibited in their defence or may be deterred from testifying

4.76 Although D2 may be inhibited in her defence if she is not permitted to adduce evidence of D1's bad character, D1 may be inhibited in his defence if he automatically loses the shield through undermining the other's defence.[129] Where D1's defence cannot be put forward *without* giving evidence "against" D2, it is at least arguable that it is inappropriate automatically to penalise him for what is unavoidable. Worse still, the fear of loss of the shield might inhibit defendants with bad character from testifying at all.

4.77 One practitioner disagreed that the current law was problematic. He said: "The defendant to be cross-examined, who knows what his defence is in advance and therefore knows the dangers to which he exposes himself as a witness, can always make [an] application [for a separate trial] before the trial starts". He acknowledges that this may not succeed, but maintains that this discretion to order separate trials is adequate. It seems to us that the discretion to order separate trials is something of a blunt instrument for correcting possible unfairness, and it is preferable to exclude evidence of trivial relevance in the first place.

(iii) The court may be misled

4.78 A problem can arise where one defendant (D2) gives evidence, but this does not amount to "evidence against" D1, with the result that D2's record does not go in. D1 then gives evidence against D2, and D1's record is admitted. D2's record may be worse than D1's, and a jury or magistrates will be left with a misleading picture about the relative creditworthiness of the two accused. This may happen irrespective of the order in which the two defendants give evidence.[130] For example, the second defendant to give evidence may do so without implicating the one who has already given evidence (and been cross-examined on his character),

---

[128] See Part XIV below.

[129] This point was referred to in the consultation paper: see paras 13.9 and 13.45.

[130] The order in which the two accused give evidence depends, in the Crown Court, on the order in which they are named in the indictment. *Stone's Justices' Manual* (2001) para 2-61 suggests that in the magistrates' court, the practice on trial on indictment should be followed so that, in the absence of agreement, the defendants should proceed in the order in which they appear on the court register.

thus retaining the shield.[131] In both situations the result is that the jury or magistrates only hear about one defendant's character although the other defendant's character is as bad or worse.

The hearsay exception for reputation

4.79 Evidence of reputation is hearsay evidence, admissible as an exception to the hearsay rule.[132] In the Hearsay Report we retained the common law exception for reputation on the ground that (like some other common law exceptions) "they fulfil useful functions and we are not aware that they cause any difficulties".[133] This general statement applies only weakly if at all to the common law exception of reputation and we doubt the exception is much relied on.

THE NEED FOR CHANGE

4.80 The law on "similar fact evidence" has merited criticism from the Royal Commission on Criminal Justice, which described it as "difficult to comprehend, embodied as it is in a series of judgments that are not always readily reconcilable".[134] The principal governing statute in this area of law, the 1898 Act, has been described by a former Lord Chief Justice as "a nightmare of construction".[135] In 1998 Schiemann LJ said that section 1 of the 1898 Act "has troubled the criminal courts ever since it was enacted at the end of the last century."[136]

4.81 Many more respondents to the consultation paper welcomed reform than wanted to keep the law unchanged. It did not, of course, follow that those who thought change is needed necessarily supported the provisional proposals, and more than one respondent sounded the cautionary note of Swinton Thomas LJ: "whereas the law should be amended, we must be sure before doing so, that we are putting something better in its place". We believe that our recommendations will, if adopted, bring about change for the better.

4.82 As can be seen from all the problems identified in this Part, many are matters of substance, but some also arise from the fact that the law has to be disinterred from so many sources. Thus part of the solution is to bring together all the rules into one place. This Commission has long advocated the advantages of

---

[131] Consider also the situation postulated by *Cross and Tapper*, p 415, in which two people charged in the same proceedings each give evidence against the other, but they both have criminal records and neither invokes s 1(f)(ii).

[132] *Rowton* (1865) 10 Cox CC 25. Richard May, *Criminal Evidence* (4th ed 1999) paras 7-07 – 7-13 gives a succinct account of the current law, and the defects of it.

[133] Evidence in Criminal Proceedings: Hearsay and Related Topics (1997) Law Com No 245, para 8.132.

[134] Report of the Royal Commission, ch 8, para 30.

[135] *Anderson* [1988] QB 678, 686E, *per* Lord Lane CJ.

[136] *S* 98/1296/X4, at p 3 of the transcript.

codification of criminal law and procedure, including the law of evidence.[137] The recent Government paper "Criminal Justice: the Way Ahead"[138] provides support for our position and proposes a "consolidated, modernised core criminal code to improve public confidence and make for shorter, simpler trials". One element of such a proposed code would be the rules of evidence.[139]

4.83 Codification cannot remove all uncertainties and difficulties at a stroke. No code can purport to second guess every situation which will be presented to a court for decision. What it can do and what we, in our recommendations, try to achieve, is to provide a clear, consistent and principled structure to support and guide parties, decision-takers and advisers whilst giving the courts the freedom to do justice in each case.

4.84 It can be seen from all the defects set out above that the law is not satisfactory as it stands. We conclude that the law is in need of reform, and **we recommend that all the rules on the admissibility of bad character evidence in criminal proceedings be contained in a single statute, and that the common law rules (including the hearsay exception for evidence of reputation) be abolished.**

---

[137] We have expressed these views more than once before: see our Twenty-Seventh Annual Report (1993) Law Com No 210, para 2.15; our Twenty-Eighth Annual Report (1994) Law Com No 223, para 2.27; and Evidence in Criminal Proceedings: Hearsay and Related Topics (1997) Law Com No 245, para 1.6. Our views are supported by Professor Andrew Ashworth, *Principles of Criminal Law* (3rd ed 1999) p 6.

[138] (2001) Cm 5074.

[139] (2001) Cm 5074, para 3.27.

PART V
GENERAL PRINCIPLES

5.1 In Parts II and IV we have sought to describe the present law on evidence of bad character in all its uncertainty and complexity and to highlight the numerous defects which we and others have identified. We believe that it is necessary to try to produce a single statutory framework dealing with this particularly difficult problem which approaches it as a reflection of first principles. We therefore endeavour in this Part to formulate a series of guiding principles which will inform the overall scheme we propose, the details of which we flesh out in succeeding Parts. We believe that these principles can and should be set out in a series of short propositions.

5.2 The rules of evidence should so far as is consistent with fairness be simple, accessible and readily understood.

5.3 They should be capable of being applied predictably and consistently by the courts but be sufficiently flexible to cater for the infinite variety of factual situations to which they will apply.

5.4 Where arbiters of law are called on to decide questions of admissibility, as they must be from time to time, the rules of evidence must give clear guidance on the proper approach to the decision so that its correctness may be judged on appeal.

5.5 Where a court decides questions of admissibility of evidence, reasons for the decision must be given.

5.6 Fact-finders are, prima facie, entitled to have placed before them all the relevant evidence which is available.

5.7 Relevant, in this context, means having some probative value on a matter in issue in the proceedings.

5.8 Such probative value may be direct, in the sense of bearing upon the matters in issue, or indirect in the sense of bearing upon the truthfulness of a witness's account of matters in issue.

5.9 The rules for the admission of evidence should be such that they preclude fact-finders being unnecessarily misled or left in the dark.

5.10 The rules for the admission of evidence should be such that they avoid deterring people who have relevant evidence to give from giving it.

5.11 Any person, whether a defendant, a witness, or otherwise involved, may only have their bad character referred to in evidence if it is relevant for the fact-finders to be aware of it for the performance of their task.

5.12 In any particular case certain instances of previous misconduct may be relevant and certain other instances of the same person's conduct may not. Where it is sought to adduce evidence of bad character it may only be admitted to the extent that it is relevant to the matters in issue in the proceedings.

5.13 A defendant may only be convicted on what he or she is proved to have done, and not merely on his or her character or past conduct on an occasion other than that the subject of the charge.

5.14 Evidence of a defendant's misconduct other than that of the offence charged may be of value on a number of bases:

(1) It is such an integral element of the offence charged that the trial would be impossible without the evidence of that previous misconduct being led.

(2) It is so much a part of the factual background that the fact-finders would be misled by incomplete evidence, or the case would be incomprehensible to them were it not to be adduced in evidence.

In these two instances the evidence may be of value even though it does not go to the issue whether the defendant committed the offence currently alleged.

(3) It demonstrates the defendant's propensity to commit the particular crime charged because he or she has in the past committed the same or a similar type of offence or offences.

(4) It may assist the fact-finders to judge which of contending accounts they accept by assessing the respective credibility of those putting forward or supporting such accounts.

(5) It is required to prevent the fact-finders being at risk of being misled by something said or done by or on behalf of the defendant in the course of the trial.

5.15 Evidence of bad character may be admissible as between co-defendants where it is relevant on a matter in issue between them or where it concerns the credibility of one defendant, the nature or conduct of whose defence is such as to undermine the defence of the other.

5.16 Some types of evidence, such as of identification and confessions, are intrinsically so potentially powerful in their operation on the minds of fact-finders that they cannot safely be left to weigh such evidence without special rules and guidance.

5.17 Rules of law require that evidence of this type need not be admitted despite its potential probative value, which the fact-finder might otherwise be expected to weigh.

5.18 Evidence of the defendant's bad character is one such category of evidence. Where it is introduced it is capable of being prejudicial and hindering rather than aiding the fact-finders in the proper performance of their function in that:

(1) they may give it weight out of all proportion to any reasonable view of its significance; and/or

(2) the nature of the misconduct may so poison their minds against the defendant as to cause them to convict in circumstances where the other evidence would not have persuaded them to do so.

5.19 The concerns referred to above require that, unless evidence of previous misconduct is of substantial, as opposed to marginal, probative value in respect of a matter in issue in the proceedings, it should not be admitted as evidence.

5.20 People who are not defendants but are witnesses or otherwise involved are entitled not to have their bad character adduced in evidence unless

(1) it is relevant on the bases identified in paragraph 5.14(1) or (2) above; or

(2) it is of substantial, as opposed to marginal, probative value in relation to a matter in issue in the proceedings.

5.21 Whether evidence is of substantial probative value is a question of law to be determined by the arbiters of such questions, namely the judge in the Crown Court and the magistrates in the magistrates' courts. In so doing they should have regard to all relevant matters including (i) the nature of each instance of bad character sought to be admitted, (ii) the number of such instances, (iii) when they occurred, (iv) the nature and extent of any similarity or dissimilarity to the matter in issue to which it is claimed it is of substantial probative value, and (v) in cases where the issue is *who* committed the crime and evidence of other offences is tendered on that issue, the extent to which the evidence suggests that the same person committed all of them.

5.22 Where evidence of a defendant's bad character *is* of substantial probative value and is therefore capable of being admitted, it may only be admitted as evidence if the interests of justice so require, having had regard to its probative value and the risk that it would operate prejudicially in either of the ways described in paragraph 5.18 above.

5.23 Whether the interests of justice require evidence of a defendant's bad character to be admitted is a question of law to be determined by the arbiters of such questions. In so doing they should have regard to all matters, including each of the matters referred to in paragraphs 5.21 and 5.18 above, relevant to weighing, respectively, the probative value of, and the risk of the prejudicial effect of, such evidence.

5.24 It is for fact-finders to weigh the probative value of the evidence but they are entitled to be given guidance, as a matter of law, on how to approach certain types of evidence.

5.25 Wherever evidence of bad character is introduced in evidence the fact-finders must not use it prejudicially, must be aware of the risk of so doing and should remind themselves, or should be reminded, of this risk.

PART VI
THE GENERAL APPROACH: THE OPTIONS

6.1 In the consultation paper we set out six general approaches. They were:

> option 1: adduce the defendant's criminal record at the start of every trial;[1]
>
> option 2: adduce the defendant's record of sex offences in sex cases;[2]
>
> option 3: allow evidence of the defendant's previous misconduct to be adduced *only* where it is an ingredient of the offence charged;[3]
>
> option 4: a single inclusionary rule with an exception for evidence whose likely prejudicial effect outweighs its probative value;[4]
>
> option 5: an exclusionary rule with a single exception for evidence whose probative value outweighs its likely prejudicial effect;[5]
>
> option 6: an exclusionary rule with separate exceptions for evidence admissible in chief and for evidence subsequently becoming admissible.[6]

6.2 Most respondents agreed with our provisional preference for option 6, although not necessarily without reservation. A substantial minority favoured option 1. Some favoured a more limited version of this option, namely the automatic disclosure of offences *similar* to that charged. This is a kind of halfway house between options 1 and 2, and we now include it as option 1a. There was little support for any of the other options. A few respondents thought that none of the options we identified would be an improvement on the present position.

OPTION 1: ADDUCE THE DEFENDANT'S CRIMINAL RECORD AT THE START OF EVERY TRIAL

6.3 Option 1 had by far the most supporters, after our preferred option, and we therefore reconsider the main arguments for and against this option.

Arguments in favour of option 1

6.4 Arguments put forward for introducing the defendant's record as a matter of course are: that to do so would simplify trials, get rid of the injustices and anomalies created by the present rules, it would be less prejudicial than the revelation of previous offences in cross-examination, that the record is relevant, and that the fact-finders will know anyway that the defendant has one.

---

[1] Paras 9.4 – 9.23.
[2] Paras 9.24 – 9.38.
[3] Paras 9.39 – 9.57.
[4] Paras 9.58 – 9.69.
[5] Paras 9.70 – 9.71.
[6] Paras 9.72 – 9.73.

Simplicity

6.5 Option 1 appealed to some because of its apparent simplicity. In the consultation paper we said:

> A further argument is that, given the tortuous nature of section 1 of the 1898 Act and the uncertainties of the similar fact rules, the course of a trial would be more predictable if a criminal record were put in automatically.[7]

6.6 We certainly agree with respondents who criticise the current law for its complexity; indeed, we made this criticism ourselves more than once. However, in our view, the apparent simplicity of option 1 would, in practice, turn out to be illusory, because, assuming that only the bare record of offences was initially disclosed, it would still have to be determined whether the fact-finders should hear *details* of the previous misconduct. It is generally agreed, for example, that such details should sometimes be admitted as part of the prosecution's case. Automatic disclosure of the bare record alone would do nothing to solve the problem of when the details should also be admitted. The only way to ensure simplicity would be by automatically disclosing not just the bare record but the details too; and, given that some or all of the previous convictions may have no relevance whatever to the issues in the case, this would be a waste of time which would puzzle the jury if it did not irretrievably prejudice them against the defendant.

6.7 Even if it were true that option 1 would simplify the law, we would not accept that simplicity should be achieved at the expense of justice; and, for reasons discussed below,[8] we do not think option 1 would be just.

Removal of injustices and anomalies in the current law

6.8 An attraction of option 1 for some was that it would get rid of some of the perceived injustices in the present law – for example, the sometimes capricious effects of section 1(f) of the 1898 Act. We agree that option 1 would rectify many of these defects in the existing law. It is by no means the only option that would do so. This is, therefore, not a reason *per se* for preferring it to alternatives which would address many of the same defects.

Avoiding the prejudicial effect of revealing the defendant's record in cross-examination

6.9 More than one respondent referred to the prejudicial effect in a jury trial of the *way* in which a defendant's record is introduced. If admitted in cross-examination under the 1898 Act, it has more impact than if it were routinely read out at the beginning of the trial, because it is perceived as relevant information which the defendant has tried to keep from the fact-finders. Defence advocates often try to take the sting out of the record by introducing it in the defendant's examination in

---

[7] Paras 9.10 – 9.11.

[8] Paras 6.30 – 6.52 below.

chief, in a "cards on the table" gesture. Some respondents thought this factor pointed towards option 1, because the dramatic effect would not persist. We agree that the manner of introduction of the record is a factor to consider. We do not agree that this is a good argument for automatic disclosure in cases where, under the present law, the record would not be admissible at all.

The relevance of the record

6.10 A number of respondents cited, as a reason for preferring option 1, the relevance of a criminal record to the question of the defendant's guilt. This argument is, in our view, crucial to the case for option 1. In the consultation paper we tried to assess whether, and if so how, previous offences really are relevant for this purpose.

RELEVANCE TO THE DEFENDANT'S PROPENSITY TO ACT IN THE MANNER ALLEGED

6.11 Clearly, in some cases a defendant's previous convictions may show a propensity to act in the way in which he or she is now alleged to have acted, and may thus help the fact-finders determine whether he or she did act in that way. However, we argued in the consultation paper that

> the bare bones of a criminal record do not give adequate information from which fact-finders may reasonably make an assessment of whether the accused is likely to have repeated past behaviour. If the record is admitted automatically, evidence of little or no probative value is admitted.[9]

This argument was based on our understanding of the psychological research, which we summarised as indicating that

> Past behaviour can be probative on the question whether the defendant is likely to have acted in the way alleged, but the probative value of a single previous instance can be easily over-estimated. The research supports the present approach, that past misbehaviour can be admitted where there are close and unusual similarities between the past and the present situations.[10]

6.12 Nearly all of the respondents who expressly commented on this conclusion agreed with it.[11] None of those who commented on it – not even those who thought we had underestimated the relevance of previous misconduct – supported option 1. We therefore cannot tell whether the supporters of that option would dispute the factual conclusions suggested by the research, and if so on what basis, or whether they think that evidence of previous offences should be admitted automatically

---

[9] Para 9.16.

[10] Para 6.93.

[11] Professors McEwan and Murphy thought that the consultation paper failed to recognise the particular probative value of evidence of certain kinds of disposition. See para 6.58 below.

even though we are right in thinking that the relevance of such evidence is usually limited.

6.13 Option 1 involves placing all previous convictions before fact-finders regardless of whether the previous offences had any similarity with those currently charged and of how long ago those offences may have been committed. We should be very surprised indeed were it to be supposed that a single offence of indecent assault, committed twenty years previously could have any relevance to the question whether a person had committed an offence of theft.

RELEVANCE TO THE DEFENDANT'S PROPENSITY TO LIE

6.14 One of the defendant's propensities which may be in issue is his or her propensity to lie. The current law assumes that a person's character as a whole is relevant to his or her *general* tendency to be truthful in a courtroom. In the light of our interpretation of the psychological research, in the consultation paper we doubted this. It does not appear to be generally true that a person who acts dishonestly in one situation is likely to do so in another. A fortiori, misconduct which does *not* involve dishonesty is unlikely to indicate a tendency to lie on oath. Conversely, the more similar the circumstances, the more likely it is that the defendant will act in the same way. We therefore provisionally concluded that

(1) the instances of previous misconduct most relevant to credibility are convictions for perjury;

(2) convictions for dishonesty may be relevant in some circumstances;

(3) behaviour not involving dishonesty is unlikely to be relevant to credibility;

but we do not think it appropriate to prescribe in a statute which kinds of conviction are and are not probative.[12]

6.15 Most of the respondents who commented on this conclusion agreed with it, though some thought that *all* convictions are relevant to credibility, while others thought that they are rarely relevant in this way. In this connection the example posed above is apposite. If the person had pleaded guilty to the single offence of indecent assault of which he was convicted twenty years previously it would be surprising in the extreme were that bare history to have any relevance whatsoever to the question of his credibility when giving evidence denying a charge of theft now.

6.16 In our view there is more to the issue whether a witness should be believed than his or her *general* credibility – that is, the extent to which the witness is the sort of person who can in general be trusted to tell the truth. Of far more significance is what in the consultation paper we called the witness's *specific* credibility – that is, the extent to which, in the circumstances of the individual case, the witness appears to have a *reason* to lie. Such reasons might include a grudge against the defendant, the hope that the witness will profit from a conviction, or the existence

---

[12] Para 6.63.

of pressure to give particular testimony.[13] As a magistrate of 17 years' experience put it, "Any witness is likely to divert from the truth if it is in his/her interest to do so." Previous misconduct *may* be relevant to a witness's general credibility; but, since little significance can in any event be attached to that credibility or the lack of it, the witness's bad character is generally of little value in determining the issues in the case.

6.17 If we are right in concluding that it is not difficult to envisage circumstances in which a person's previous convictions have no conceivable relevance to his or her guilt, either on the basis of propensity or credibility, then option 1 necessarily involves admitting non relevant evidence, presumably on the basis that, if it has no relevance, then no harm is done anyway. As the research to which we refer below indicates, that is by no means a sound conclusion. The prejudice attached to the fact of conviction, particularly for certain types of offence, is such as to give the lie to the assertion that fact-finders, even experienced ones, can be relied on to disregard irrelevant, though prejudicial, evidence. Thereby the risk is run that the fact-finders will convict where they are not persuaded of the defendant's guilt on the relevant evidence to the requisite standard, because they are influenced by irrelevant evidence which they should have disregarded. The defendant may thus be convicted, not on the basis of what he or she has done, but on the basis of one aspect of his or her character.

The fact-finders know anyway

6.18 A criticism often made of the current rules is that they do not acknowledge the reality, namely that the fact-finders will usually realise that the defendant is of bad character in any event. In the consultation paper we acknowledged that

> Any lay magistrate or jury with a week's experience knows that if the court is not told that the defendant is of good character then he or she must have a criminal record; so, the argument runs, it might as well be put in.[14]

6.19 Several respondents supported this argument. Michael McMullan, formerly the resident judge at Wood Green Crown Court, argued not only that a substantial percentage of jurors will assume the defendant to be of bad character if they are not told otherwise, but that that percentage is likely to increase as knowledge of the legal rules becomes more widespread; and that it would be better to tell jurors the truth than to proceed on the increasingly unrealistic assumption that they will not work it out for themselves.

> The present system may actually generate speculation about such convictions or, worst of all, suggest that there is an element of charade about the trial generally and that nods and winks are expected to play some part. A regime of complete openness is not possible in anything so intricate as a jury trial (improperly obtained confessions, for

---

[13] On the distinction between general and specific credibility see A Zuckerman, *The Principles of Criminal Evidence* (1989) p 248.

[14] Para 9.7.

instance, must be excluded) but, if we wish to retain trial by jury, the jurors should not be allowed to become demoralized or cynical. Where possible open procedures are best; the jury should be trusted and feel they are trusted. ... [T]here is no point in deciding that the convictions should be kept away from the jury unless an effective and fair means of doing so can be devised.[15]

One member of the public who had served on a jury wrote: "many of us felt that we were witnessing a 'legal game' rather than a search for 'the truth'."

IS THIS TRUE?

6.20 The first question is whether it is in fact true that the fact-finders know anyway. In the two research studies which she undertook for us,[16] Dr Sally Lloyd-Bostock found that, if given no information about the defendant's character, a majority of lay fact-finders will tend to assume that he or she has at least one previous conviction; but a substantial minority will assume that he or she has none.[17] Perhaps surprisingly, there was no significant difference in this respect between the study of simulated juries and that of real lay magistrates.

6.21 A member of this Commission wrote an article for "The Magistrate" inviting readers to let us know whether they assume that a defendant who does not claim to be of good character must have a criminal record.[18] Nine magistrates responded. They were unanimous that a defendant's bad character was not discussed in the retiring room, but not unanimous as to the assumptions made. Some thought it obvious that such a defendant must have a criminal record; others said the question did not cross their minds; others said they would not make such an assumption where the defendant was unrepresented, or represented by an inexperienced advocate. It is as well that they do not all make this assumption: research cited by Dr Penny Darbyshire shows that a defendant's good character is not always put before the justices, even where the defendant is represented.[19] We would not accept that if justices are told nothing about the defendant's character they will necessarily assume that he or she must be of bad character, or even that that assumption would necessarily be correct.

6.22 The position is somewhat different in the Crown Court, since the judge will almost certainly have ascertained whether the defendant is of good character and will remind a defence advocate who forgets to adduce evidence of that fact. While

---

[15] Michael McMullan, "The Wool Pulled Over the Jury's Eyes is Wearing Thin" (2000) 164 JPN 599, 600–601.

[16] The research relating to mock juries was summarised as Appendix D to the consultation paper and is referred to as "the Jury Study". The research relating to magistrates is published at [2000] Crim LR 734, and summarised at Appendix A below.

[17] See para A.20 below.

[18] Stephen Silber QC, "Previous convictions?" Oct 1996 The Magistrate 182.

[19] Penny Darbyshire, "Previous Misconduct and Magistrates' Courts – Some Tales from the Real World" [1997] Crim LR 105, 109–110. Dr Darbyshire refers to M McConville, J Hodgson, L Bridges and A Pavlovic, *Standing Accused* (1994) p 216, and J Vennard, *Contested Trials in Magistrates' Courts* Home Office Research Study No 71 (1982).

Dr Lloyd-Bostock's research suggests that by no means all jurors will infer that the defendant has a record unless they are told otherwise, it seems likely that most juries will include individual jurors who will draw that inference and may voice it; and that, where it is drawn, it will be correct. We therefore agree that, in the Crown Court at least, there is a problem which needs to be addressed. The question is whether this consideration points inexorably to option 1.

IS OPTION 1 THE ONLY SOLUTION?

6.23 We agree that it is unsatisfactory for jurors to be left with neither information on the subject of the defendant's character nor guidance on what to make of the absence of such information. The point at which we part company with the argument is where it is suggested that the jury should therefore be given information on the subject in every case, by disclosing the defendant's record at the start of each trial, *rather than* guidance on how to deal with its absence. It seems to us that the proposed solution goes much further than is necessary to meet the difficulty. The difficulty, in essence, is that there is information which jurors would be likely to regard as relevant but which is withheld from them, and which they are likely to realise is being withheld from them. The defendant's record is by no means the only information in relation to which this difficulty can arise. Indeed, the Judicial Studies Board recommends that the following direction be given where the judge thinks it may be of assistance in the particular case:

> You must decide this case only on the evidence which has been placed before you. There will be no more. You are entitled to draw inferences, that is come to common sense conclusions based on the evidence which you accept, but you may not speculate about what evidence there might have been or allow yourselves to be drawn into speculation.

6.24 It seems to us that, in appropriate cases, this direction might usefully be extended along the following lines:

> One matter on which you have not heard evidence is whether the defendant has committed offences before. You might from that be tempted to infer that he or she has. There are good reasons for your not being told about any previous convictions that he or she may have. If fairness both to the prosecution and the defence required you to be told, you would have been. As it is, however, there is no evidence on the matter. It therefore has no bearing on your verdict, and you must not speculate about it.

Where (in the Crown Court) no mention of good character has been made, we assume that this will be because the defendant does have a criminal record. It therefore seems reasonable to direct the jury in terms which, while not expressly confirming that fact (which would be inconsistent with the judge's role), nevertheless confront the likelihood that the jury will be aware of it. Moreover, since the purpose of such a direction would be to protect the defendant, it would not be appropriate to give it without the agreement of the defence. The defence could, if it so wished, insist that no mention of character should be made.

6.25 Arguably this would not go far enough. Michael McMullan points out that

> Competent defence advocates often prefer not to leave the jury to make guesses about what the defendant has been up to in the past, if the convictions are innocuous. But if the number of previous convictions is large, includes unpopular crimes, or some are relevant to the offence being tried, the defence will probably prefer not to reveal them. If this pattern became general, the sophisticated juror could infer not only that there *are* convictions but also that everyone is keeping quiet about them because their *nature* is, in some sort, damaging to the defendant. "If the convictions didn't matter", they may learn to say to themselves, "we would be told what they are". Innocence cannot be so easily preserved.[20]

6.26 This danger might still exist even if the jury were expressly warned not to draw inferences from the absence of evidence as to character. In our view, however, the availability of such a direction would probably lead to a reduction in the frequency with which defence advocates chose to adduce evidence of their clients' records. Some advocates might feel that the purpose of doing this, namely to head off uninformed and damaging speculation, could be more safely achieved by invoking the new direction. It is true that, if permitted to do so (and we do not suggest that it should cease to be permissible), advocates might continue to adduce details of the defendant's record where it is clearly irrelevant and the ensuing prejudice is likely to be negligible. However, we think that this would be done far less often than at present, and this would in turn make jurors less ready to draw inferences from an advocate's failure to do it. If a direction along the lines we suggest were available at the defence's request, we think that it would largely meet the concern. Thus option 1 is not the only solution to the problem.

IS OPTION 1 THE BEST SOLUTION?

6.27 There is a significant difference between the fact-finders' guessing that a defendant probably has a record and their knowing exactly how many convictions he or she has and for what crimes. The inevitability of the former therefore does not in itself justify the latter. Option 1 has a number of disadvantages, to which we will shortly turn. Does it have any advantages, in this respect, over the alternatives?

6.28 At present the defence can choose between (a) disclosing the record and (b) not mentioning it, and thus risking adverse speculation by the fact-finders. If our proposed new direction were available, the defence in a jury trial would have a further option, namely (c) invoking that direction. Why should it be fairer to the defendant to deprive the defendant of options (b) and (c), by making it mandatory for the record to be revealed at the outset? As far as we can see, the only circumstances in which this might be fairer are, first, where the defence advocate miscalculates the risk, and, second, where the defendant is of good character but the defence advocate fails to mention that fact – a situation which is only likely to arise in the magistrates' court anyway.[21] In both cases, some

---

[20] Michael McMullan, "The Wool Pulled Over the Jury's Eyes is Wearing Thin" (2000) 164 JPN 599, 600.

[21] See n 19 above.

defendants may in fact benefit from having the record revealed rather than having the fact-finders speculate; but others, and probably many more others, will suffer from the prejudicial effect of having their record revealed.

6.29 While we accept that the risk of speculation is a good argument for a change in the present practice, we do not accept that it is a compelling argument for option 1.

Arguments against option 1

6.30 A number of considerations militate against option 1. It would involve the admission of irrelevant material, and material which (even if relevant) is highly prejudicial; the likelihood that defendants may find the need to explain away or minimise the impact of their previous misconduct would make for longer trials, and risk distracting the fact-finders from the real issues in the case; and it might result in the criminal justice system as a whole becoming (or at least being perceived as) less fair.[22]

Irrelevance

6.31 If the defendant's criminal record were automatically disclosed without the need to demonstrate its relevance, it would not be clear what use the fact-finders were expected to make of it. As Sir John Nutting QC pointed out, "if the convictions are simply read out at the beginning of the prosecution case as part of the background, there is a real risk that they will float vaguely in some evidential limbo, to find an uncertain level of significance in the jury's deliberations."

6.32 Moreover, even the respondents who supported option 1 did not suggest that the defendant's record is always relevant. Sometimes it clearly is not; and in such cases we must ask what purpose would be served by introducing it. Having heard it, the fact-finders would then have to ignore it. This might not matter greatly if the irrelevant material were not prejudicial; but very often it will be.

The risk of prejudice

6.33 In the consultation paper[23] we distinguished two kinds of prejudice – "reasoning prejudice", the tendency to give bad character evidence undue weight in determining whether the defendant is guilty as charged, and "moral prejudice", the tendency to convict through distaste for the defendant without being truly satisfied that he or she is guilty as charged at all.[24] Moral prejudice is particularly

---

[22] Both the ALRC and the New Zealand Law Commission have reviewed this area of the law, and both concluded that an accused should be protected by special rules about evidence of propensity/tendency and truthfulness/credibility. See the ALRC *Evidence* (1987) Report No 38, and NZLC, *Evidence: Reform of the Law* (1999) Report 55.

[23] Paras 7.7 – 7.15.

[24] Both terms are taken from A Palmer, "The Scope of the Similar Fact Rule" (1994) 16 Adel LR 161, 169. The Jury Study found that if the defendant had a previous conviction for an indecent assault on a child, the mock jurors were not only more likely to convict him, but were also more likely to believe that he would commit other offences in the future, was more deserving of punishment and was more likely to lie on oath. See Appendix D to the consultation paper.

likely where the evidence of bad character discloses crimes for which the accused has not been punished. We thought there was a danger that bad character evidence could give rise to both these kinds of prejudice.[25] We said that "in the absence of convincing evidence that fact-finders will *not* be affected by prejudice, our provisional view ... is that proposals should err on the side of caution", and regarded this as a serious objection to option 1.[26]

6.34 The respondents who considered this provisional conclusion were almost equally divided on it. Supporters of option 1 thought the danger of prejudice was overstated. Some did not address the danger at all. Many asserted that the Commission, and society generally, should "trust the jury".[27]

6.35 Several respondents thought it patronising of us to think that jurors will be susceptible to prejudice. On the other hand, Phillips LJ wrote "Why do we assume that the jury will give it more weight than it deserves? Perhaps because we feel that we should risk doing so ourselves – that human nature carries with it the risk that such evidence will carry greater prejudice than its probative weight merits." We think it is legitimate to expect the training and experience which magistrates and judges have to reduce their susceptibility to prejudice. We recognise, however, that it is impossible to know how successful the training and experience is in this respect.[28]

6.36 Some argued that we must trust juries because we have them. We are unpersuaded by this argument. It seems to us that the crucial question is whether there is any *foundation* for such trust. The best way of determining this is through empirical research; yet few of the respondents who argued for greater openness referred to the empirical studies discussed in the consultation paper.

THE RESEARCH

6.37 Dr Lloyd-Bostock's research on the effect of bad character evidence on mock jurors, which we summarised in the consultation paper, found that a conviction

---

[25] See para 7.36.

[26] Para 9.19.

[27] Several respondents explicitly endorsed the views of David Pannick QC expressed in his article, "Juries can cope with a defendant's form" *The Times* 8 October 1996. More recently, though, he has written, "[The Government's] proposal that juries should be told about defendants' previous convictions is wrong in principle and flawed in practice. ... It does not make sense to give a dog a bad name." *The Times* 17 July 2001.

[28] At paras 9.13 – 9.14 of the consultation paper we referred to studies which cast doubt on the ability of judges to be immune to prejudice. One of these is a study of 35 Dutch cases where Roderick Munday concludes that, in 13 of the cases, the judges' decisions had been "critically affected" by the defendant's criminal records: "Comparative Law and English Law's Character Evidence Rules" (1993) 13 OJLS 589, 597. In the same study reference is made to an experiment which showed that the order in which information is presented to trained judges affected the likelihood of conviction, which was higher where the record was disclosed earlier. We note that, in France, where the defendant's record does form part of material on which the verdict is founded, a trained judge sits *with* the lay fact-finders. Both fact-finders and judge deliberate on guilt and sentence (see pp 593–594). See also A Zuckerman, *The Principles of Criminal Evidence* (1989) p 245.

was more likely to result if the jury were told that the defendant had *either* a recent conviction for an offence similar to that charged *or* one for indecent assault on a child (irrespective of the offence charged). The former tendency may well be explicable on the basis that it is entirely rational to attach probative weight to a recent similar conviction. However, it is hard to see any rational basis for the latter phenomenon, which would appear to be based on prejudice alone.[29]

6.38 This conclusion seems to be supported by the experience of respondents. Even those who had faith in juries found that that faith deserted them when it came to sexual offences. One QC wrote that "it is insulting to juries to assume they cannot be trusted properly to evaluate the worth of previous convictions"; yet he was unsurprised by the results of the Jury Study, explaining that "Any criminal hack could have told you that he was terrified of letting his client's character in *whatever the nature of the offence* where it included [a conviction for indecent assault on a child]."

6.39 Several respondents emphasised the limitations of the research. The most frequent observation was that a mock jury is no substitute for the real thing, and that the results should therefore be treated with circumspection. We acknowledged and emphasised the limitations of the research in the consultation paper,[30] and accept that studies on real jurors might produce different results. However, given that such research as has been done does reveal a risk of prejudice, we do not accept that we would be justified in asserting that there is no risk of prejudice to real defendants in real trials: we could only do that on the basis of research into real juries.

6.40 Moreover, the results of the Jury Study can now be compared with Dr Lloyd-Bostock's more recent research, which, being concerned with real magistrates, is not open to the same objection. It was found that magistrates tend to regard a defendant with a previous conviction for indecent assault on a child as more likely to commit not only an indecent assault on a woman (which is understandable) but also an offence of violence.[31] A previous conviction for a section 18 assault, on the other hand, was perceived as increasing the likelihood that the defendant would commit not only another offence of violence but also an offence of dishonesty.[32] These findings are not easy to reconcile with the view that lay justices (and, by inference, real jurors) are not susceptible to prejudice.

6.41 While we recognise the limitations of the research so far carried out, it would in our view be irresponsible to disregard its findings altogether. Unless and until further research demonstrates that the prejudicial effect on lay fact-finders is

---

[29] There was a further tendency to regard a defendant as *less* likely to have committed the offence charged if he had a recent conviction for a *dissimilar* offence (unless it was for indecent assault on a child). This may be explicable, but strongly suggests an element of irrationality in the reasoning process.

[30] Paras D.54 – D.59.

[31] By contrast with the mock jurors, however, the magistrates did not regard such a defendant as more likely to commit an offence of dishonesty.

[32] But not a sexual offence.

acceptably small, we believe that the wisest course is to maintain a general rule against the disclosure of the defendant's criminal record.

6.42 We also believe that the research provides a strong counter-argument to the argument that the fact-finders might as well be told of the defendant's record because they will guess that he or she has one anyway.[33] It appears that both mock jurors' and magistrates' perceptions of a defendant are adversely influenced by the knowledge that he or she has a conviction for specific *kinds* of offence (though it seems that the kind of offence giving rise to this effect may vary between jurors and magistrates). This tends to confirm our suspicion that it is easier for fact-finders to ignore a vague perception that "this defendant almost certainly has a record" than to ignore specific knowledge that the defendant has, for example, three convictions for burglary, one for indecent assault and one for resisting arrest.

MINIMISING THE PREJUDICIAL EFFECT OF AUTOMATIC DISCLOSURE

6.43 Some respondents acknowledged that the disclosure of the defendant's record involves a risk of prejudice, and suggested ways of minimising that risk.

6.44 Some thought that option 1, which would involve reading out the record at the start of the trial, would in itself be less prejudicial than disclosure of the record at a later stage. In our view this will depend on the manner in which such later disclosure occurs. We agree that it can be particularly prejudicial if it occurs in cross-examination of the defendant, because of the inevitable suspicion that the defence has tried to conceal relevant information. In Dr Lloyd-Bostock's research, however, this did not occur. The information about the defendant's record was first given to the participants in a voice-over commentary as he entered the witness-box, and repeated in the summing-up (with an appropriate direction on the relevance of that information).[34] Yet the findings suggest strongly that the disclosure of the information affected the fact-finders' approach in ways which are hard to explain on any rational basis. We doubt that it would have made much difference if the voice-over commentary had mentioned the defendant's record at the very beginning of the trial.

6.45 A few respondents who favoured disclosure of the record thought that, in a jury trial, prejudice could be avoided by an appropriate direction from the judge. In the consultation paper we considered the effectiveness of judicial directions and the available research.[35] We concluded:

> We are uncertain whether juries adequately understand or carry out directions given to them by judges on the use they are to make of evidence of previous misconduct. In the absence of convincing

---

[33] See paras 6.18 – 6.22 above.

[34] The videos of a jury trial were used in the research on magistrates as well as that on mock jurors. This did not appear to cause the participants any difficulty.

[35] See paras 7.16 – 7.20 of the consultation paper.

evidence that fact-finders will not be affected by prejudice, our view is that the rules of evidence should err on the side of caution.[36]

Nothing has been brought to our attention to change this view.

The perceived risk of prejudice

6.46 Even if magistrates and jurors are in fact able to ignore irrelevant information, and to withstand the prejudicial effects of bad character evidence, it is very unlikely that the defendant will be convinced that they have done so and may not feel that justice is being done. The Magistrates' Association made this point, stating,

> The defendant is likely to be very resentful if his previous record goes in, feeling that he is being tried and convicted on his record, for which he has already paid the price. Therefore the occasions upon which that record goes in, according to law, should in principle be confined or restricted as much as possible, in order to maintain confidence in the system.

We agree.

Longer trials

6.47 Whatever rules were devised about the use to which the defendant's record could be put by the prosecution, the defence might well wish to call evidence to show that that misconduct was in fact irrelevant, to put it in a more favourable light, or even to prove that the defendant had been wrongly convicted. Once the record had been disclosed, it would clearly be unfair to prevent the defence from doing this. As a result, not only would trials not be simplified as much as option 1's supporters would hope: their length could actually increase. As JUSTICE put it, "Any change to an *automatic* inclusion of past convictions would ... have the consequence of taking up a great deal of court time in defendants explaining past behaviour in evidence, in the context of a trial about something else entirely."

6.48 It may be (as Lord Justice Schiemann suggested) that this danger could be avoided in part by adopting a more flexible version of option 1 under which it would be up to the prosecution to decide whether to disclose the record. This solution would have disadvantages of its own – for example, practice would inevitably vary from one prosecutor to another – but, even if it worked, it would not meet the other objections to option 1. It would still allow the admission of prejudicial evidence with little or no relevance to the issues in the case.

Distraction

6.49 Another practical disadvantage of option 1 is that, even if the defence did not adduce evidence about the offences disclosed, the fact-finders' attention would still be distracted from the real issues in the trial. Lord Justice Schiemann, although favouring option 1, acknowledged that this could be a justification for limiting the admissibility of bad character evidence:

---

[36] Para 7.37.

> I accept reasons of convenience point towards the exclusion of some facts because their investigation is likely to make it more difficult for everyone to keep their eye on the ball. That may provide a rough and ready reason for excluding convictions in relation to matters which happened "x" years ago.
>
> It may also provide a rough and ready reason for excluding allegations of past misconduct which has not resulted in a conviction. ...

The fairness of the criminal justice system

6.50 In the consultation paper we concluded that "There is a danger that unfairness to those with criminal records would be built into the criminal justice system if previous convictions were freely admitted".[37] We pointed out that

> once someone has a record, he or she is more likely to be questioned than if he or she had no record; if at the trial a previous conviction is admitted and is for a similar offence to the current charge, a conviction is more likely to follow;[38] the record gets longer and so he or she is even more likely to be questioned when there is next a crime of that type committed in that locality. There is thus a cumulative effect,[39] which could make it difficult for someone with a criminal record to be acquitted.[40]

Most of those who commented on this argument agreed.

6.51 We went on to argue that

> People with criminal records would be particularly vulnerable to conviction on fabricated evidence where other people know their modus operandi, if it is known that evidence of all similar crimes will automatically be admitted;[41] finally, as McHugh J put it: "law enforcement officers might be tempted to rely on a suspect's antecedents rather than investigating the facts of the matter".[42]

Some respondents thought our fear of malpractice by law enforcement officers was exaggerated or did not correspond with their experience,[43] though Sir John Nutting QC referred to "well documented" instances of such conduct.[44]

---

[37] Para 7.38.

[38] See Appendix D to the consultation paper.

[39] As described by, eg, C Tapper, "Proof and Prejudice" in E Campbell and L Waller (eds) *Well and Truly Tried* (1982) p 207.

[40] Para 7.23.

[41] D McBarnett, *Conviction* (1983) p 113.

[42] Para 7.24. The quotation from McHugh J was taken from *Pfennig (No 2)* (1995) 127 ALR 99, 136.

[43] H M Customs & Excise pointed out that since the consultation paper was published, s 23(1)(a) of the Criminal Procedure and Investigations Act 1996 has created a statutory duty on police officers to pursue all reasonable lines of enquiry.

6.52 Even if this fear is not justified (and we do not think it can be discounted) we think our concerns about the cumulative effect to which we referred remain valid. We suspect that public confidence in the system would decrease if bad character evidence was admitted which was more prejudicial than probative, and that that lack of confidence would be to some extent justified.

Conclusion

6.53 In our view option 1 would involve the admission of prejudicial and irrelevant evidence for no very clear purpose, with potentially damaging consequences to the administration of justice and public confidence in it. We reject this option.

OPTION 1A: ADDUCE THE DEFENDANT'S RECORD OF *SIMILAR* OFFENCES AT THE START OF EVERY TRIAL

6.54 The research suggests, unsurprisingly, that past offences are more likely to be regarded as relevant where they are similar to that charged. A few respondents thought that convictions for such offences, but only those, should be automatically revealed. One favoured admitting all previous convictions for similar offences, subject to a discretion to exclude them in exceptional circumstances if it would be unfair to admit them.

6.55 A practical difficulty with this suggestion is that it is often difficult to classify offences according to their supposedly similar features. For example, it may not be as straightforward as at first appears to determine which offences are "offences of dishonesty". Some drugs offences will necessarily involve an element of dishonesty, such as the illegal importation of a controlled drug;[45] but many offences commonly thought of as dishonesty offences do not in law require proof of dishonesty.[46] Producing workable rules for determining when the defendant's record should be automatically disclosed, and how much of it, would be very difficult, and the results would probably be so arbitrary as to bring the system into disrepute.

6.56 In any event, this suggestion is open to much the same objections as option 1. It cannot be assumed that previous convictions for similar offences will always have much probative value. According to the psychological research, the extent to which previous offences of a particular kind suggest guilt of a particular offence of the same kind will depend on the individual features of each situation and the character of the person concerned.[47] The criminal record in itself does not reveal enough about the previous misconduct for anyone to know how far, or in what

---

[44] Similarly, Judge Rivlin QC warned:
> I fear that if evidence of previous misconduct were admitted as a general rule it would quickly bring our system of criminal justice into disrepute. Take any of the high-profile appeals of recent years, and add into the equation that at the outset of the trial the jury were told of the defendant's convictions.

[45] Misuse of Drugs Act 1971, s 3.

[46] Eg taking a vehicle without consent (Theft Act 1968, s 12).

[47] See paras 6.11 – 6.21 of the consultation paper.

way, each conviction is relevant to the current charge. The reason that a defendant's convictions even of similar offences are usually excluded at present is that they would often be prejudicial, and that that fact usually outweighs their probative value. We see no reason to suppose that such convictions are less prejudicial than they have hitherto been thought to be, or that they have greater probative value. Indeed, the limited research so far carried out suggests otherwise.

OPTION 2: ADDUCE THE DEFENDANT'S RECORD OF SEX OFFENCES IN SEX CASES[48]

6.57 Only the Association of Chief Police Officers was attracted by the prospect of following the lead of the United States Federal Rules of Evidence by putting in the defendant's record for sexual assault where he or she is charged with such an offence.[49] Several respondents strongly opposed this option. More than one respondent made the point that if, as a general rule, previous misconduct is excluded because it is irrelevant, prejudicial or both, this is no less so in respect of sexual offences. Indeed it is likely to be *more* unfair to introduce sexual misconduct, because of the greater risk of prejudice.[50] It would not only be unnecessary to have a special rule for sexual misconduct: it would be wrong.

6.58 It was argued, however, that we had not fully appreciated the potential probative value of sexual misconduct. Professor McEwan wrote:

> The Commission concedes that past behaviour can be probative, but does not acknowledge that some propensities can be more significant than others. ... Where a personality is abnormal, it appears to be a better predictor of behaviour than situation. The problem is how to identify the abnormal personality.[51]

She argued that research has shown that serial and sadistic offenders are abnormal, and expressed concern about three recent cases where information about the defendant ought, she thought, to have been available to the jury.

6.59 One of the main reasons mentioned in the consultation paper[52] for treating sex offences differently from other offences is that the perpetrators are psychologically

---

[48] Paras 9.24 – 9.38.

[49] In 1994 Rules 413–415 were added to the Federal Rules of Evidence. Rule 413 refers to offences of sexual assault, 414 to sexual abuse of children, and 415 to civil cases arising out of such offences. In cases of sexual assault or of molestation of children a party is now entitled to introduce evidence that a defendant has previously committed such an offence if it is relevant to any matter, including, presumably, the defendant's disposition or tendency to commit the act charged.

We take note of a critique of the new Federal Rules, published since the consultation paper, which contains a detailed and persuasive set of arguments to the effect that the new Rules are not only wrong in principle but are likely to backfire in practice: Katharine K Baker, "Once a rapist? Motivational evidence and relevancy in rape law" (1997) 110 Harv LR 563.

[50] The Jury Study confirmed this view.

[51] Jenny McEwan, "Law Commission Dodges the Nettles in Consultation Paper No. 141" [1997] Crim LR 93, 95–96.

[52] See paras 9.25 – 9.27.

different from the rest of the population in a way that other offenders are not.[53] It is argued that sex offenders are motivated by compulsions not shared by "normal people". While burglars, for example, attempt to pursue the normal social goal of acquiring property, but by illegal means, the desires of sex offenders are themselves deviant. This argument entails a belief that sexual offences result from the character traits of the perpetrator to a greater extent than other offences.[54] If this is the case, the fact that the defendant has such character traits, demonstrated by evidence of previous convictions, would be highly probative.

6.60 In the consultation paper we said:

> There are undoubtedly some individuals who form a "small but important sub-group of offenders ... for whom clinical or 'special' psychogenic[55] explanations remain highly relevant".[56] A possible solution would thus be to allow evidence of a defendant's past conduct to be adduced only if a psychiatrist were able to give evidence that the defendant has a personality defect that "causes" him or her to commit sexual offences.[57]

We added that the increased danger of prejudice in cases involving sexual offences must not be forgotten.

6.61 If, in a particular case, evidence of some personality defect or disposition is especially relevant because it is abnormal, then (unless it is also especially prejudicial) it should be admissible. For the purposes of evaluating option 2, however, the question is whether evidence of previous sexual offences should be admissible *without the need to show such relevance*, merely because both the offence charged is also sexual. We are still of the view that the case for such a rule has not been made out. Indeed, since sexual misconduct tends to be more prejudicial than other misconduct, the arguments for a general exclusionary rule seem if anything to be *stronger* in this case. We reject this option.

OPTION 3: ALLOW EVIDENCE OF THE DEFENDANT'S PREVIOUS MISCONDUCT TO BE ADDUCED *ONLY* WHERE IT IS AN INGREDIENT OF THE OFFENCE CHARGED

6.62 At the opposite extreme to option 1 is option 3, under which previous misconduct would hardly ever be admissible. The only exception would be where the misconduct is actually an element of the offence alleged. The defendant's previous disqualification, for example, is an element of the offence of driving while

---

[53] It was said in Congress that rapes are committed by a "small class of depraved criminals": 137 *Congressional Record* S3241, 13 March 1991.

[54] Ie, while non-sexual crimes may be the product of certain situations, sex offences stem from an inherent character defect in the offender.

[55] Something is "psychogenic" if it has an emotional or psychological origin.

[56] R G Broadhurst and R A Maller, "The Recidivism of Sex Offenders in the Western Australian Prison Population" (1992) 32 British Journal of Criminology 54, 72 (footnote added).

[57] Para 9.36.

disqualified. Subject to that necessary exception, previous offences could not be adduced even if their probative value were overwhelming.

6.63 However sceptical one might be of the value of bad character evidence, there are clearly some cases in which it is so probative that it should be admitted. Understandably, this option received no support at all, and we reject it.

OPTION 4: A SINGLE INCLUSIONARY RULE WITH AN EXCEPTION FOR EVIDENCE WHOSE LIKELY PREJUDICIAL EFFECT OUTWEIGHS ITS PROBATIVE VALUE[58]

6.64 A few respondents favoured introducing the record at the beginning of a trial as a matter of course, as in option 1, but would also give the court a discretion to exclude previous convictions which were too prejudicial. This amounts to our option 4. While it meets some of our objections to option 1, it also sacrifices one of option 1's main attractions – namely its (supposed) simplicity. We think it would make for complexity and delay if a judicial discretion had to be exercised in every case where a defendant has a criminal record.

6.65 More fundamentally, it is axiomatic that only relevant evidence should be admitted. Not all evidence of bad character is relevant to the issue of guilt. The admission of irrelevant bad character evidence might not matter if it were not prejudicial; but often it is. It can lead to a person being convicted on inadequate evidence, or where the fact-finders are not in fact sure that the charge has been made out. Therefore, bad character evidence which is not relevant should in our view be excluded *as a matter of course*, not merely as a matter of discretion. We therefore favour a general rule *excluding* bad character evidence (subject to exceptions) rather than a general inclusionary rule subject to a discretion to exclude.

OPTION 5: AN EXCLUSIONARY RULE WITH A SINGLE EXCEPTION FOR EVIDENCE WHOSE PROBATIVE VALUE OUTWEIGHS ITS LIKELY PREJUDICIAL EFFECT[59]

6.66 In our view, this option is something of an over-simplification. First, it offers no scope for *excluding* evidence whose probative value *does* outweigh its likely prejudicial effect. This might be desirable where, for example, the probative value outweighs the prejudicial effect, but both are of negligible significance, and introducing the evidence would simply distract the fact-finders from the real issues. Second, option 5 amounts to the complete abandonment of any attempt to minimise reliance on judicial discretion, the unpredictability of which we have identified as a defect of the present law. Our preference is for an exclusionary rule subject to exceptions which are not wholly dependent on judicial discretion, but are, as far as possible, objectively defined. We therefore reject option 5.

---

[58] Paras 9.58 – 9.69.

[59] Paras 9.70 – 9.71.

CONCLUSION: THE GENERAL APPROACH WE RECOMMEND

6.67 Our preference, therefore, is still for a structure along lines similar to option 6 – namely, an exclusionary rule with a specified exception or exceptions. Moreover, we now believe that the problems discussed in the consultation paper are best resolved by means of a general approach which extends to evidence of the bad character of witnesses and other non-defendants, rather than defendants alone. In the next Part we give an overview of this scheme.

PART VII
OVERVIEW OF OUR RECOMMENDATIONS

7.1 The overall aim is that all the rules on admissibility of evidence of a person's bad character should be set out in one statute. This entails replacing the existing mélange of rules deriving from statute and common law with a single comprehensive set of rules.[1]

7.2 At the heart of our proposals are five fundamental considerations, namely:

(1) No person who is involved in a criminal trial should be subject to a gratuitous and irrelevant public attack on their character.

(2) To adduce evidence of a person's bad character in a public forum is, prima facie, such an invasion of their privacy and so prejudicial to them that it should not be adduced where any relevance it may have to the issues the fact-finders have to decide is of no real significance or is only marginal.

(3) The fact-finders in any criminal trial must have all relevant material placed before them so as to enable them to perform their function, consistent with doing justice to the parties whose accounts they have to judge.

(4) Wherever it is appropriate for aspects of a person's character to be adduced in evidence it should only be permitted to the extent that it is relevant for the fact-finders to be aware of it for the performance of their task.

(5) In the case of evidence of the bad character of a defendant, the probative value must be sufficient to outweigh the prejudicial effect of the evidence (except where the evidence is being adduced by one defendant about another).

7.3 There are three organising principles of the new structure for the rules on evidence of bad character.

INSIDE OR OUTSIDE THE CENTRAL SET OF FACTS

7.4 First, a distinction is drawn between (i) evidence about the events for which the accused is being prosecuted, the investigation and the prosecution for offences arising out of those events ("the central set of facts"), and (ii) any evidence of bad character which goes outside that central set of facts. This distinction is central to our scheme.

7.5 In a criminal trial it is inevitable that assertions are to be made about the defendant's "bad character" in the sense that his or her conduct on, and related to, the occasion in question is said by the prosecution to be criminal. Whenever the trial is contested, it is highly likely that the defendant in putting forward the

---

[1] Clause 20 of the draft Bill abolishes the existing common law on admissibility of bad character evidence, and repeals s 1(e) and (f)(i) – (iii) of the 1898 Act which govern the admissibility of bad character evidence in cross-examination of the defendant.

defence will need to make imputations about the conduct of others. They may be prosecution witnesses or they may not be witnesses at all. The imputations may be as to their conduct on, or related to, the occasion in question or in relation to the conduct of the investigation or prosecution. In our view, imputations of bad character in relation to the events which are the subject of the trial or their investigation or prosecution, whether made by the prosecution or the defendant, must be admitted into evidence without fear of automatic penalty. They go to the core of the case which the fact-finders have to determine.

7.6 It has been a defect in our law that the defendant, in putting a case which makes imputations against the character of another, has had to run the risk that his or her entire previous character will be adduced in evidence on the issue of his or her credibility. This has led to a distortion of the issues and the evidence as presented to fact-finders at trial, by tempting defendants either to avoid putting their full case or to refrain from giving evidence to support it. The efforts of the courts to ameliorate this defect, either by construing the 1898 Act accordingly,[2] or by exercising discretion, have served to draw attention to the problem but have, perforce, addressed it inconsistently and unpredictably. We propose to introduce fairness, consistency and predictability, by reforming the law so that the defence, no less than the prosecution, should be able to make allegations of bad character in respect of the events the subject of the trial, or related thereto, and their investigation or prosecution, without running the risk that evidence of the defendant's bad character on other occasions will be adduced solely on the issue of credibility.

7.7 By way of contrast, where any party to the trial wishes, without the consent of another party, to adduce evidence of another person's bad character which goes *outside* the central set of facts, they must obtain the leave of the court. In determining whether to give leave, the court must first apply a common basic rule upon which all else will be built, namely: that a person's bad character may only be introduced into evidence if, and to the extent that, it is of *substantial* probative or explanatory value in relation to the issues in the case. The single standard of substantial probative or explanatory value is the one which should be applied whether it is the prosecution, or the defendant, or a co-defendant, who wishes to introduce the evidence and whether it is a defendant's character or that of a witness or another person who is involved in the events in issue which it is sought to put before the fact-finders.[3] We refer to it as "the enhanced relevance test".

"Substantial" probative value

7.8 Concern was expressed about the vagueness of the word "substantial", which we used in our proposal in the consultation paper, and the possible difficulties for courts in determining what counts as "substantial" in any individual case.

---

[2] Judicial effort in construction has largely been focused on what constitutes an "imputation" that will lose the defendant his or her shield. The current approach to the relevant section of the 1898 Act is described at paras 2.64 – 2.67 above.

[3] Note that where the prosecution seeks to adduce evidence of the bad character of a defendant, the value of the evidence is not the only test. See para 7.23 below.

However, very few respondents were troubled by the words "substantial" and "significant". Our view is that the use of such open-textured words indicates that there are issues where the court does not have an untrammelled discretion, but must nevertheless exercise its own judgment. This is the kind of decision-making with which courts are familiar, and as one respondent wrote, "Our law has managed for some time to cope with concepts such as significance and substantiality eg 'substantial cause of death', 'substantial risk that the course of justice will be seriously impeded'." Mr Justice Tim Smith, the Commissioner in Charge of the ALRC at the time of its review of the law of evidence, conducted some research amongst his fellow judges on the extent to which the addition of "substantial" as a qualifier was helpful to their decision-making. He concluded that greater consistency resulted. He commented, "True the expressions ['substantial' and 'significant'] are vague but that will not detract from their effectiveness."

7.9 The terms "substantial" and "significant" appear in the Australian Evidence Act 1995 (Cth) in the context of the rules on the admissibility of misconduct evidence. The Act sets a raised threshold for character evidence adduced to prove a person's *tendency* to act in a particular way or to have a particular state of mind,[4] or to disprove innocent coincidence,[5] or on the issue of the credibility[6] of a person as a witness. The raised threshold applies whether the evidence concerns the character of the defendant or another. Where the issue is "tendency" or coincidence the evidence must have "significant probative value"[7] to be even prima facie admissible. Evidence going to the credibility of any witness must be of "substantial probative value".[8] Additional protections apply where the person concerned is on trial.[9]

7.10 The statute does not spell out the ways in which such evidence on the issues of tendency or coincidence may have "significant" probative value, but it is clear from the evolution of the section that the ALRC had in mind that the past conduct and that to which it was said to be relevant must be "substantially and relevantly similar".[10] This was the implication they drew from the psychological studies.[11] They concluded, "To maximise the probative value and minimise the disadvantages of such evidence, the emphasis of the law should be on receiving

---

[4] Section 97. The Evidence Act 1995 (New South Wales) is drafted in the same terms.

[5] Section 98.

[6] Sections 102 and 103.

[7] Sections 97 and 98.

[8] Section 103.

[9] Sections 101(2) and 104(2), (4) and (6).

[10] This is the phrase used in the ALRC Interim Report No 26 (vol I) at para 809, and in cl 87 of the Bill appended to the final Report.

[11] These are the studies referred to at para 6.11 above and discussed more fully in the consultation paper, at paras 6.10 – 6.21.

evidence of past conduct of the relevant person occurring in similar circumstances."[12]

7.11 Where the issue is credibility only, the Evidence Act 1995 (Cth) does require the court to have regard to specific matters in judging whether the evidence has substantial probative value. They are (a) whether the evidence tends to prove that the witness knowingly or recklessly made a false representation when under an obligation to tell the truth; and (b) the period that has elapsed since the acts or events to which the evidence relates.[13]

7.12 In relation to section 103 of the Evidence Act 1995 (Cth) and the definition of "substantial probative value", it has been observed that

> evidence adduced in cross-examination must ... have substantial probative value in the sense that it could rationally affect the assessment of the credit of the witness. ... The addition of the word "substantial" nevertheless imposes a limitation upon the common law, when almost anything was allowed upon the issue of credit unless it clearly had no material weight whatsoever upon that issue. That limitation is an important one. Counsel must, however, be given some freedom in cross-examination – whether it relates to a fact in issue or to credit. They are not obliged to come directly to the point; they are entitled to start a little distance from the point and to work up to it.[14]

It is suggested[15] that where evidence would have a real, persuasive, bearing on the reliability of a witness, or the reliability of particular testimony of the witness, the test should be regarded as being satisfied,[16] at least where the testimony of the witness could reasonably be regarded as important to the outcome of the proceedings.[17]

7.13 The New Zealand Law Commission has recommended a restriction on evidence going to a person's truthfulness: evidence is only admissible if it is "substantially helpful" in assessing that person's truthfulness. The Commission says in its commentary:

> The Commission's desire is to propose a test of significant or heightened relevance so as to prohibit truthfulness evidence that is of limited value.[18] The substantial helpfulness test is aimed at admitting only evidence that will offer real assistance to the fact-finder. ...

---

[12] ALRC Interim Report 26 (vol I), para 794 (footnote omitted).

[13] Section 103(2).

[14] *RPS*, unreported, NSW CCA, 13 August 1997, *per* Hunt CJ.

[15] Watson, Blackmore, Hosking, *Criminal Law (NSW)* vol I, para 6.10860.

[16] *Fowler*, unreported, NSW Sup Ct, 15 May 1997.

[17] *McGoldrick*, unreported, NSW CCA, 28 April 1998.

[18] The concept of "heightened" relevance can also be found in s 13 of the Evidence Act 1908. As such it is not an unfamiliar concept (footnote in original).

Some commentators did not support introducing the substantial helpfulness test, arguing that such a test would cause unnecessary uncertainty. The Commission considered other tests (such as "necessity" or "direct relevance") but concluded, with the support of other commentators, that those alternatives would not provide any greater certainty.[19]

7.14 Little guidance is available in the case law on either side of the Atlantic on the meaning of "substantial relevance". There is little authority in this jurisdiction on the meaning of "substantial relevance" that is pertinent to bad character evidence. The closest is the advice given to judges to help them guide juries in the context of mental responsibility.[20] Juries are told to interpret the word "substantial" in the context of mental impairment in a broad common sense way, or to take it as meaning more than trivial but less than total.[21] In the United States, in the civil law, "substantial evidence" has been interpreted to mean such evidence that a reasonable mind might accept as adequate to support a conclusion, or evidence which possesses something of substance and relevant consequence.

7.15 The concept of "substantial effect" is utilised in the employment law area of disability discrimination. A "substantial effect" is one that is significant or greater than *de minimis*, in other words, more than minor or trivial, but it does not have to be large or considerable.[22] Factors for assessing what is substantial are set out in "Guidance" which is issued by the Secretary of State under section 3 of the Disability Discrimination Act 1995. The guidance gives illustrations and examples but is not a checklist.[23]

7.16 Professor McEwan wrote,

> There must be doubts as to the likely efficacy of [a provision limiting imputations to those which *substantially* undermine a witness's credibility] in the light of the disastrous failure of section 2 of the Sexual Offences (Amendment) Act 1976.[24] We clearly lack a common conception of relevance.[25]

There is some truth in this. We believe, however, that a requirement that all bad character evidence has to be of substantial probative value in order to be admissible can be made more effective in practice by spelling out the factors which a court should take into account when deciding whether evidence meets the raised standard.

---

[19] NZLC, *Evidence: Reform of the Law* (1999) Report 55(1), paras 157–158.

[20] *Egan* [1992] 4 All ER 470.

[21] *Lloyd* [1967] 1 QB 175.

[22] See A Samuels, "Disability Defined" [2000] 144 SJ 424.

[23] *Vicary v British Telecommunications Plc* [1999] IRLR 680, EAT.

[24] Z Adler, *Rape on Trial* (1987); S Lees, *Carnal Knowledge: Rape on Trial* (1995).

[25] Jenny McEwan, "Law Commission Dodges the Nettles in Consultation Paper No. 141" [1997] Crim LR 93, 102.

7.17 Thus we think that the concern that "substantial" is too vague is overstated. We think there is merit in the flexibility of the term. We said in the consultation paper that "we do not think it appropriate to prescribe in a statute which kinds of conviction are and are not probative",[26] and most of those who responded on the point agreed. In our view, the gist of "substantial" in this context is "more than minor or trivial" and that is the sense in which we use it.

Taking factors into account

7.18 The court, when deciding on admissibility of such character evidence, should be assisted in making its decision on the extent of its probative value by being required to have regard to all relevant matters, including such of a number of factors set out in the statute as are relevant. These factors include: (i) the kind of events or other things the evidence is about; (ii) how many of these there are; (iii) when they are alleged to have happened or (in the case of a state of affairs) to have existed; (iv) where the evidence is evidence of misconduct, and it is suggested that the evidence has probative value by reason of similarity between that misconduct and the alleged misconduct, the nature and extent of the similarities and the dissimilarities between each of the alleged instances of misconduct; (v) where the evidence is evidence of a person's misconduct, and it is suggested that that person is also responsible for the misconduct alleged, and the identity of the person responsible for the misconduct alleged is disputed, the extent to which the evidence shows or tends to show that the same person was responsible each time.

7.19 When deciding on admissibility of bad character evidence the court should be assisted in making its decision, both in relation to the assessment of probative value and of the risk of prejudice, by being required to have regard to all relevant matters, including such of a number of factors set out in the statute as are relevant. **We recommend that the legislation should set out the factors to which a court is to have regard when assessing the probative value of bad character evidence or where the interests of justice lie.**[27]

THE PURPOSE OF THE EVIDENCE

7.20 The second organising principle is the purpose of the evidence. The rules on the admissibility of evidence of a defendant's bad character which goes outside the central set of facts are to be organised according to the purpose for which it is admitted, namely whether it is explanatory, incriminatory, relates to credibility, or is corrective. We consider each of these purposes in detail in Parts X–XIII respectively.

WHO IS ADDUCING THE EVIDENCE?

7.21 The third organising principle concerns which party is seeking to adduce the evidence: the prosecution, or the defendant, or a co-defendant.

---

[26] Para 6.63.

[27] See cl 5(2), 9(7) and 10(8) of the draft Bill.

7.22 If it is the defendant who is seeking to adduce evidence of another person's bad character which goes outside the central set of facts, the only test which applies is the enhanced relevance test: it must be of substantial probative value to a matter in issue, *and/or* of substantial explanatory value for understanding the case as a whole. This is the case even where the other person is themselves a defendant in the proceedings.

7.23 By contrast, where the prosecution is seeking to adduce evidence of a defendant's bad character which goes outside the central set of facts, there is an "interests of justice" test in addition to the enhanced relevance test. The major component of the interests of justice test is a comparison of the probative force of the bad character evidence and the potentially prejudicial effect of the evidence. "Prejudice" is defined at clause 17(2). It has two aspects for our purposes: "reasoning prejudice", namely where there is a risk that the fact-finders would be so impressed by the fact of the previous misconduct that they would attach undue weight to it; and "moral prejudice", namely where the nature of the misconduct so poisons the mind against the defendant that the fact-finders would be prepared to convict without being satisfied that the defendant was in fact guilty. The important feature to note is that the burden is on the prosecution to establish that the interests of justice require the bad character evidence to be admitted notwithstanding its prejudicial effect.

PART VIII
BAD CHARACTER AND THE LEAVE REQUIREMENT

8.1 In this Part we consider the kinds of evidence that should fall within our proposed exclusionary rule, and should thus be prima facie inadmissible. In the consultation paper we proposed that the rule should extend to all evidence which the court thinks would be prejudicial, and to no other evidence. We are now persuaded that this approach was too broad brush, and that the rule needs to be more focused and easier to apply. We have concluded that there are three issues which need to be separately considered, namely:

(1) How should evidence of bad character be defined, for the purpose of a rule that such evidence is prima facie inadmissible (that is, admissible, if at all, only with leave)? Our provisional proposal was that such a rule should apply to any evidence about a person which, in the opinion of the court, the fact-finders might in fact find prejudicial. We have concluded, however, that such a rule would exclude too much. Under our recommendations, evidence would count as evidence of a person's bad character *only* if it reveals conduct (or a disposition towards conduct) *of which reasonable people might disapprove*. The possibility of wholly unreasonable prejudice is for this purpose disregarded.[1]

(2) Should evidence be exempt from the exclusionary rule if, though within the definition of bad character evidence, it relates directly to the offence charged? Our conclusion is that it should. For this purpose we have decided to make use of the concept of a *central set of facts* in defining the scope of the rule of prima facie exclusion. Evidence of bad character which falls within the central set of facts should be admissible without the need to obtain leave. Only bad character evidence which falls *outside* those facts should be prima facie inadmissible.

(3) Are there circumstances in which, though not directly related to the offence charged, bad character evidence should nevertheless be exempt from the requirement of leave which is the hallmark of the exclusionary rule? Our conclusion is that evidence which all parties agree should be admitted, and evidence of a *defendant's* bad character adduced by that defendant, need not be subject to the requirement of leave.

8.2 We recommend that the rule of prima facie inadmissibility should be structured as follows:

(1) Evidence of a person's bad character is admissible only with leave of the court, unless

(a) it falls within the central set of facts, or

---

[1] That possibility must, however, be taken into account in determining whether evidence which *is* evidence of bad character is admissible under an *exception* to the exclusionary rule.

(b) all parties agree it should be admitted, or

(c) the evidence is of a defendant's bad character and is adduced by that defendant.

(2) Leave may only be granted, where required, if the evidence falls within one of a number of categories which are the subject of detailed provisions.

8.3 The recommendations made in this Part are given effect by clauses 1 and 2 of the draft Bill.

DEFINING EVIDENCE OF BAD CHARACTER

The options considered in the consultation paper

8.4 In the consultation paper we discussed three different ways of drawing up a rule excluding bad character evidence.[2] The first, option A, was as follows.

> The most obvious approach is to confine the rule to evidence of certain kinds of *fact*. It might be provided, for example, that the rule should extend to any evidence that (or from which the fact-finders are likely to infer that) the defendant has committed a criminal offence, or done anything else that is likely to reflect adversely on the defendant in the minds of the fact-finders, other than the commission of the offence charged.[3]

8.5 This approach seemed attractively straightforward but we were concerned that distinguishing between conduct alleged to constitute the offence charged and *other* conduct was not a simple matter. In particular, there were difficulties inherent in the law on "background" evidence and so it would be hard to say what was "background" and what part of the offence itself.[4] We therefore provisionally rejected this option.

8.6 Whereas option A focused on the kinds of facts in question, option B focused on the kinds of inferences the fact-finders are invited to draw, or, put another way, the purpose of the evidence. We stated that it

> would involve asking what kinds of *inference* the fact-finders would be invited to draw from the evidence if it were admitted. In most cases of the kind with which we are concerned, the fact-finders are asked to infer that the defendant is likely to have committed the offence charged *either*
>
> > (1) because the evidence shows that the defendant has a propensity to commit offences of the kind with which he or she is charged, *or*

---

[2] Paras 9.74 – 9.92.

[3] Para 9.75.

[4] The law on background evidence was set out at paras 2.70 – 2.84 of the consultation paper, and is described more briefly at para 10.1 of this report. We had in mind particularly *Ellis* (1826) 6 B & C 145, 108 ER 406; *Rearden* (1864) 4 F & F 76, 176 ER 473; *Bond* [1906] 2 KB 389.

(2) because the evidence reveals a combination of circumstances that is highly unlikely to be attributable to coincidence alone.

The exclusionary rule might be formulated so as to extend to any evidence which is adduced as the basis for an inference of either of these kinds.[5]

8.7 Our principal criticism of option B was that, while it was capable of including the kinds of cases where a conviction is wrongly reached by a logical inference from bad character evidence (reasoning prejudice), it inevitably omitted the kinds of cases where a conviction was reached *irrationally* on the basis of such evidence (moral prejudice). Our view is that both kinds of prejudice need to be guarded against.

8.8 We therefore provisionally proposed option C, namely:

(1) that [subject to the exceptions proposed] evidence should be inadmissible if, in the opinion of the court, its admission would be prejudicial; and

(2) that, for the purpose of this rule, the admission of evidence should be regarded as prejudicial if there is a risk that

(a) the fact-finders might treat the evidence as being more probative of guilt than it really is, or

(b) it might lead them to convict the defendant without being satisfied that he or she is guilty as charged.[6]

This option focused on the actual risk of prejudice to the defendant – in other words, the prejudicial qualities of the evidence, irrespective of the use to which it might *rationally* be put. It had the advantages, in our view, first that no evidence which bore a risk of prejudice would be outside the rule, because the rule itself required the court to consider that risk, and secondly that it avoided the problem identified with option A.

Objections to our provisional proposal

8.9 Various respondents raised the issues of the impossibility of second-guessing the jury and the danger of usurping the role of the jury which seemed to be thrown up by option C. The underlying concern is the difficulty of assessing exactly how fact-finders will use a particular piece of evidence. Some respondents were concerned that an exclusionary rule drawn in this way, although purporting to cover all prejudicial evidence, would in fact become impotent as regards certain pieces of evidence.

---

[5] Para 9.77.

[6] Para 9.92.

Evidence of criminal offences

8.10 Paul Roberts, Reader in Criminal Justice at Nottingham University, wrote:

> However, the Commission seems unaware of potential drawbacks in its own preferred scheme. For one thing, if the existing statute and common law on a defendant's previous misconduct were abrogated without specific statutory replacement, the courts would be at liberty to decide that the new statutory scheme was narrower in scope than the old common law. The judges might, for example, decide to adopt a practice of routinely allowing defendants' credibility to be impeached by evidence of their previous convictions of dishonesty offences, the *specific* prohibition on questions tending to show convictions currently contained in proviso (f) having been replaced by the new, non-specific statutory wording. On one view of the meaning of credibility, the prosecution might even be permitted to adduce such evidence in chief, regardless of whether the defendant testifies or not. No doubt this argument is tendentious, or even disreputable, but that fact alone is not proof against its success. And if this type of argument were to find favour with the courts, the Commission's carefully worded exceptions to its general exclusionary rule would be *pro tanto* pre-empted, outflanked like an adjectival Maginot Line.[7]

8.11 We find this objection persuasive. We agree that, where the evidence in question shows or tends to show that a person has committed a criminal offence, it should not be possible for a court to by-pass the exclusionary rule by deciding that that evidence is not prejudicial. Moreover, to be strictly accurate, evidence of a conviction is not itself a form of bad character: it is merely what the court accepts as prima facie conclusive evidence that the person convicted had *committed* the offence of which he or she was convicted. It is the act of committing the offence that amounts to bad character. We do not think it is necessary to exempt minor criminal conduct (such as parking offences) from the exclusionary rule altogether, on the basis that it is unlikely to be prejudicial: that can be taken into account in deciding whether one of the exceptions to the rule applies. In our view, evidence that a person has committed a criminal offence should automatically count as evidence of that person's bad character. This is one respect in which our recommendation departs from our provisional proposal.

Evidence of bad character not amounting to an offence

8.12 Clearly, however, "bad character" cannot be defined *solely* in terms of committing an offence. Evidence of conduct can be highly prejudicial even if that conduct is not a crime. The conclusion reached in the preceding paragraph is therefore not a complete solution to the problems inherent in making the exclusionary rule hinge solely on the court's assessment of the evidence's likely prejudicial effect. The problem would still arise in the case of evidence that a person has acted in a way which, though arguably discreditable and therefore prejudicial, would not amount

---

[7] P Roberts, "All the Usual Suspects: A Critical Appraisal of Law Commission Consultation Paper No 141" [1997] Crim LR 75, 84–5.

to any criminal offence. It would similarly arise in the case of attitudes or beliefs, as distinct from conduct, or personal qualities (such as sexual orientation).

8.13 The focus of this report has changed somewhat from the consultation paper. We are concerned to seek to achieve a single consistent approach to the admissibility of evidence of bad character in respect both of defendants and non-defendants. Thus the concept is to be applied to a wider range of persons and, in particular, includes those of whom the fact-finders are not required to make a decision to which criminal sanctions attach. Given the wider range of persons for whose protection our recommendations seek to provide, it would not be satisfactory, in our view, for the question whether evidence is even prima facie inadmissible to be determined on the basis of the court's guess whether the fact-finders would be prejudiced by it. In particular, for reasons connected with ensuring that the defendant has the maximum freedom to conduct his or her case, we do not recommend that prejudicial impact should be a factor when determining whether a non-defendant's bad character should be adduced in evidence. The only condition we require to be satisfied is that the evidence is of substantial probative value on a matter of substantial importance in the context of the case as a whole. It would undercut this approach to require the court to assess the likely prejudicial effect of the evidence at the prior stage of deciding whether the evidence in question is evidence of bad character at all, and therefore requires leave to be adduced. Even in the case of a *defendant's* character, we think the perceived prejudicial impact of the evidence is best considered in relation to whether leave should be *granted*, not at the stage of determining whether leave is *necessary*.

8.14 It would be particularly unsatisfactory if the question whether leave is required in the *magistrates'* court were to depend whether the magistrates think the evidence would prejudice *them*. One respondent wrote:

> Magistrates might be tempted to turn the test on its head, quickly and instinctively reaching the conclusion (perhaps based on perceptions of experience) that a piece of evidence is likely to be more probative than prejudicial. This might lead to decisions that the evidence is not prejudicial and so does not come within the scope of the exclusionary rule at all. If there was a tendency for this to happen, full arguments might not be heard and the desired structured regime for full consideration of admissibility of the evidence might be truncated.

8.15 Another respondent thought, "The magistrate, having estimated the true probative value of the evidence, is then to consider whether there is a risk that *he* might treat the evidence as being of more probative value than it really is! Of course he wouldn't." Unsurprisingly, some magistrates who responded had rather more confidence in the ability of magistrates to keep their various functions distinct.

8.16 In view of this difficulty we have concluded that the concept of bad character evidence, and thus the scope of the exclusionary rule, should not (as we proposed in the consultation paper) be defined in terms of the effect that the evidence, if admitted, would in fact be likely to have on the particular fact-finders. Rather, it should, as far as possible, be defined according to objective criteria. It seems to us that the most appropriate criterion for this purpose is whether a *reasonable person* might disapprove of what the evidence reveals about the person to whom it relates. If the definition of bad character were to include that which only the wholly unreasonably intolerant or irrational might find morally dubious, the court would become embroiled in a guessing game as to the particular moral views of the fact-finders in the particular case. That would be wrong in principle and utterly impracticable. If an advocate thinks that the magistrates or jury will display unreasonable prejudices there are other avenues, concerning time, venue, discharge of jurors, or even staying of the proceedings, by which the defendant can be protected from that prejudice.

8.17 Sometimes, of course, even the question of whether a *reasonable* person would disapprove of particular conduct will be a matter of opinion. Some kinds of conduct are thought discreditable by some people, but are not criminal and are thought by many to be morally inoffensive. In these cases we think a court should be capable of deciding, in a judicial manner, whether disapproval is *within the range* of responses open to a reasonable person. An affirmative answer would not amount to judicial disapproval of the conduct in question, because the court might recognise that some reasonable people would disapprove of it while others would not.

DISPOSITION

8.18 We have considered whether evidence that a person has a *disposition* to commit offences or otherwise to act in a way of which reasonable people might disapprove should be within the concept of "bad character". Although our terms of reference refer to "previous misconduct", we do not think it would be sensible to draw a distinction between evidence of conduct and evidence of a disposition which has not (or cannot be shown to have) manifested itself in conduct. For example, a rule incorporating such a distinction would fail to require leave for evidence that a man had admitted to a sexual interest in children, whilst denying ever having acted on that interest; yet such an inclination would clearly be a highly prejudicial fact about his character, and we think that whilst it may be right to adduce it as evidence it should be justified before leave is given for it to be adduced. The same would apply to evidence of manifestations of attitudes or views which might be highly eccentric or obnoxious and capable of giving rise to high levels of prejudice and which similarly should be subject to justification before they may be adduced with leave.

Our recommendation

8.19 **We recommend that evidence of a person's bad character should be defined as evidence which shows or tends to show that that person**

    (1) has committed an offence, or

    (2) has behaved, or is disposed to behave, in a way of which a reasonable person might disapprove.

BAD CHARACTER EVIDENCE NOT SUBJECT TO THE EXCLUSIONARY RULE

The central set of facts

8.20 An unattractive feature of the proposal made in the consultation paper is that it would have required the exclusionary rule to be applied even to evidence of the alleged offence itself which on any view is evidence of "bad character". It would be ludicrous if the prosecution had to seek leave to adduce such evidence. We had tried to meet this point in our option A by distinguishing between the offence itself and "other" misconduct, but rejected that option on the ground that the distinction was too hard to draw.[8] Having now rejected option C, however, we have to renew the attempt.

8.21 The response of our consultant on the consultation paper, Peter Mirfield of Jesus College at the University of Oxford, was very helpful on this point. He wrote:

> I am not really clear about the line between option A and option C. I can pose a question which describes my doubt. In para 9.76, it is said that to define the rule in terms of discreditable nature of the facts which the evidence tends to establish leads to problems with so-called "background evidence". Clearly, the prosecution must be able to adduce evidence of the crime charged. ... *But*, the problem is not so much in drawing a line between evidence of commission of the crime charged and evidence of other crimes or bad conduct, but one of drawing a line between evidence without which it is impossible to provide a coherent account of the commission of the crime charged and other evidence. ... Let me put it this way. Does the Commission wish (genuine) *res gestae* evidence to be caught by the exclusionary rule or not?

8.22 The answer to Peter Mirfield's question was "no". As we note above, one aspect of the difficulty of distinguishing between the offence itself, and "other" misconduct, was the law as it stood on "background" evidence. In the consultation paper[9] we had identified four "indicators" which had, in some cases, taken evidence outside the normal exclusionary rule. They were:

(i) the evidence may be close in time, place or circumstances to the facts or circumstances of the offence charged;

(ii) the evidence may be necessary to complete the account of the circumstances of the offence charged, and thus make it comprehensible to the jury;

(iii) the accused may have had a relationship with the victim of the offence charged, and the previous misconduct evidence may relate to this victim rather than the victims of other offences;

(iv) the evidence may assist in establishing the motive behind the offence charged.

---

[8] See para 8.5 above.

[9] At para 2.81. The footnotes are omitted. For the authorities supporting this para, see para 10.1 below.

8.23 We discuss categories (ii)–(iv) and our solution in Part X below, but note here that only category (i) seems to describe evidence which ought properly to avoid an exclusionary rule altogether (as distinct from possibly qualifying for admission under an exception to that rule). Having concluded that bad character should be defined in terms of objective facts rather than the risk of prejudice, we must now formulate the exclusionary rule in such a way that it does *not* exclude evidence which goes directly to the facts of the alleged offence, or evidence of misconduct in the course of that offence or close to that offence in time, place or circumstances.

8.24 We took account of our tenet that fact-finders are, prima facie, entitled to have placed before them all the relevant evidence which is available, and of the general weaknesses and risks entailed in extraneous evidence of bad character, and formed the view that the distinction between central and extraneous evidence should be one of the organising principles of our recommendations.

8.25 We were encouraged to note that, in the context of restrictions on evidence going to a defendant's credibility, section 104 of the Australian Evidence Act 1995 (Cth) referred to

    (a) the events in relation to which the defendant is being prosecuted; or

    (b) the investigation of the offence for which the defendant is being prosecuted

and that this formulation did not appear to have generated major problems of interpretation.

8.26 It seemed to us that this offered a way forward, and that evidence of the events charged, and of the investigation of that offence, should be admissible without being subject to any exclusionary rule, no matter which party seeks to adduce it. This would include any incidental misconduct, such as the criminal damage caused by a burglar who broke items in the course of the burglary. It would extend too to the surrounding facts (such as the appropriation, the day before, of a car which was to be used in the burglary) and to an allegation that a witness is lying about the alleged facts of the offence.

8.27 The reference to the *investigation* of the offence charged would mean that a defendant would not need leave to adduce evidence that, for example, an alleged cell confession was never made, or that a confession was extracted under threat or the offer of a reward, or that an officer had destroyed evidence inconsistent with the defendant's guilt. It would extend only to misconduct committed in the course of the investigation or prosecution, and not to evidence of misconduct on other occasions which was uncovered in the investigation. For example, it would not permit an officer, when innocently asked "And what did you do then?" to reply, "I rounded up all those with known records of offences of this type, including the defendant."

8.28 We also think that the exclusionary rule should not apply to evidence about things done in the course of the proceedings, if relevant, even if they cannot be said to be part of the investigation – for example, evidence that a defendant has absconded in the course of the proceedings, or has sought to dissuade a witness from testifying. Such evidence might of course be excluded on the grounds that it has no relevance or under section 78(1) of PACE on the ground that it is too prejudicial, but we do not think it should be prima facie inadmissible on the basis that it is evidence of bad character. Similarly, it would be anomalous if the defence had to ask leave to adduce evidence that, after the trial had started, an officer in the case had tried to discourage a defence witness from testifying: this kind of allegation is on a par with an allegation that evidence was fabricated in the course of the investigation.

Evidence which all parties agree should be admitted

8.29 Clearly no purpose would be served by requiring leave to adduce bad character evidence if all the parties consent to the evidence being admitted. In these circumstances, therefore, our proposed exclusionary rule would not apply.

Evidence of a defendant's bad character, adduced by that defendant

8.30 In the consultation paper we proposed that the defendant should not have to obtain leave to adduce evidence of his or her own bad character.[10] We still take this view. As one respondent wrote,

> The defence should ... always have the right to adduce evidence of a defendant's previous convictions if it felt that it would be helpful to do so. The most obvious example is where the defendant had an alibi because he was in prison at the relevant time.

Our recommendations

8.31 **We recommend that evidence of a person's bad character should be automatically admissible if**

   (1) **it has to do with the offence charged, or is evidence of misconduct in connection with the investigation or prosecution of that offence; or**

   (2) **all parties agree to its admission; or**

   (3) **it is evidence of the defendant's bad character which the defendant seeks to adduce.**

8.32 **We recommend that**

   (1) **all other evidence of bad character should be admissible only with the leave of the court, and**

   (2) **leave should be granted only if the evidence falls within one of the exceptions we recommend below.**

---

[10] Provisional proposal 21, and para 10.114 of the consultation paper.

8.33 The definition of bad character is key, and appears at the head of the Bill, in clause 1. Clause 2 then describes the circumstances in which leave is not required for evidence of bad character to be admissible. The aim here is to "ring-fence" evidence of the offence itself, and it is important that this subclause delineates the boundary around the central set of facts as accurately as possible. The purpose of the examples given in the explanatory notes is to give as clear an indication as we can where the boundaries lie.[11] The section would, of course, be interpreted in the light of the other clauses in the Bill, and that fact in itself would indicate that it, and in particular subsection (1)(a), is not an open door through which any evidence, however loose its connection with the charges, might pass.

8.34 The structure of the Bill is put into diagrammatic form on the next page.

---

[11] We note that a court may have recourse, for the purposes of clarification, to explanatory notes attached to a statute, as stated by Lord Hope in *A* [2001] UKHL 25, para [82].

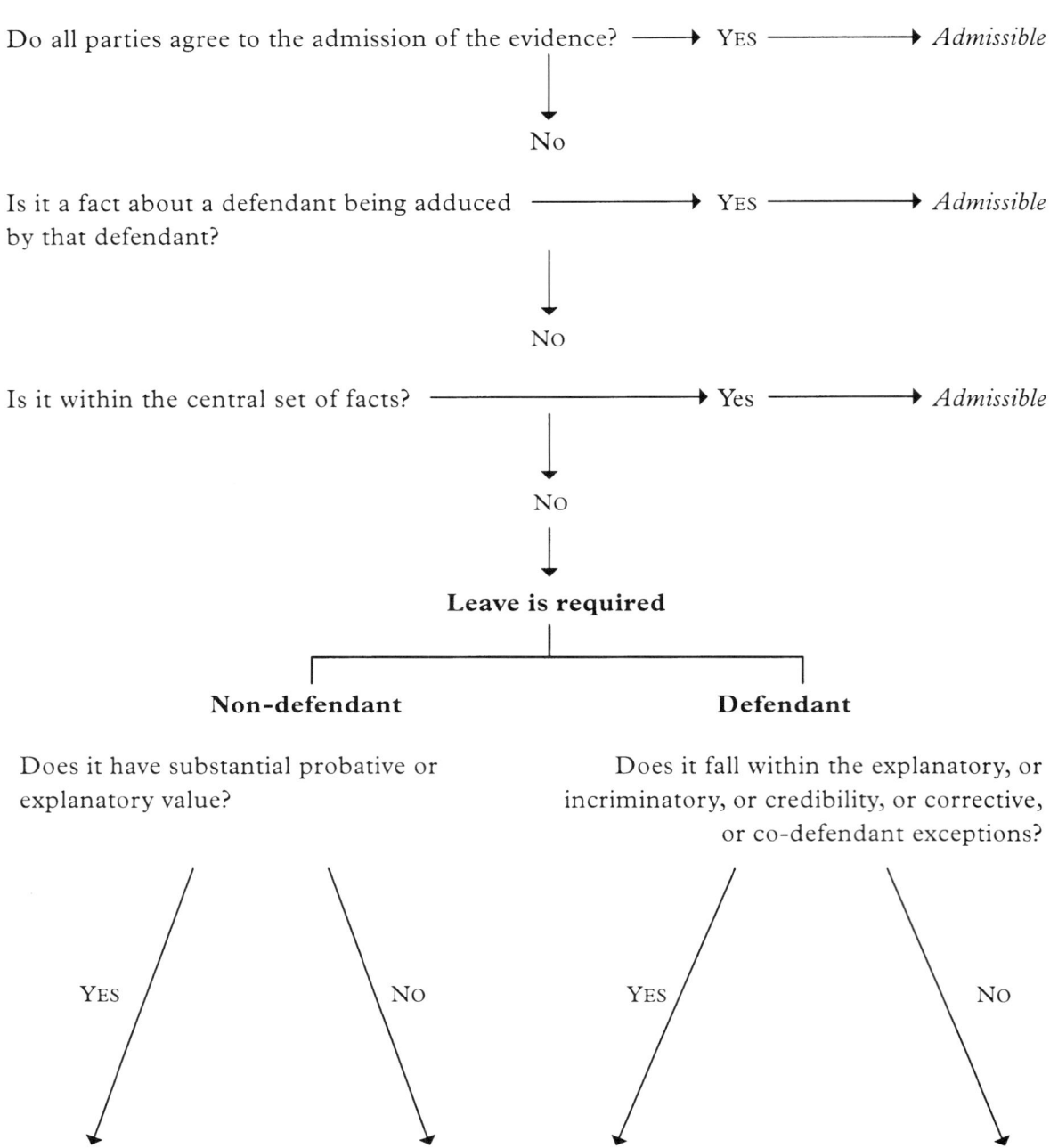

Structure of the draft Bill

PART IX
EXCEPTIONS APPLICABLE TO NON-DEFENDANTS

9.1 As regards defendants, the principle that evidence of other misconduct should be prima facie inadmissible is already embedded in English law.[1] There are two bases for this principle. The first is that such evidence is irrelevant; the second is that it is prejudicial. This principle does not extend to witnesses, but there are sound arguments for saying that it should.

9.2 In the consultation paper we raised the possibility of restricting cross-examination of witnesses to that which would be substantially relevant to the witness's credibility. We now take the view that a requirement of enhanced relevance for *all* evidence of the bad character of non-defendants, not just that going to credibility, is an important element in the package of measures we now recommend to secure a trial which is fair to the defendant, but which also safeguards witnesses and others from gratuitous attack.

THE CURRENT POSITION

9.3 It is trite law that only "relevant" evidence is admissible. That is the only evidential restriction on bad character evidence that may be adduced about a person who is not a defendant.[2] Where a person testifies, questions put in cross-examination which go to the witness's credibility "must relate to his likely standing after cross-examination with the tribunal which is trying him or listening to his evidence".[3]

9.4 Where a person's credibility is the issue, he or she may be asked questions about his or her criminal record, associations or way of life which might discredit his or her testimony in the eyes of the fact-finders.[4] Questions can be put to a witness about any improper conduct to test his or her credit. The general rule is that where a witness is cross-examined as to credit, evidence is not admissible to contradict his or her answers.[5] There are a number of exceptions to this general rule. Evidence is admissible to contradict a witness's answer under cross-examination on credit to prove bias;[6] previous convictions;[7] reputation for

---

[1] Viscount Sankey LC described it as "one of the most deeply rooted and jealously guarded principles of our criminal law" in *Maxwell v DPP* [1935] AC 309, 317.

[2] With the exception of complainants in "sexual offences": see para 2.69 above.

[3] *Sweet-Escott* (1971) 55 Cr App R 316, 320, *per* Lawton J.

[4] See *Archbold* para 8–138.

[5] *Harris v Tippett* (1811) 2 Camp 637.

[6] *Thomas v David* (1836) 7 C & P 350.

[7] Criminal Procedure Act 1865, s 6.

untruthfulness;[8] or medical reasons for unreliability of evidence.[9] The list of exceptions is not closed.

Judicial control

9.5 The court has the power to control cross-examination. Cross-examination is not confined to issues raised in evidence in chief, but if the cross-examiner strays outside the issues in the case (including the credit of the witness), then the court should disallow questions which are irrelevant or vexatious, or which are designed to prolong the case unnecessarily.[10] It is erroneous for a court to take the view that cross-examination cannot be stopped because there is some tenuous legal reason for it.[11] Where the defendant is unrepresented, the court still has the power to control cross-examination conducted by the defendant.[12]

9.6 The court does, moreover, have a discretion to excuse an answer to a question when that answer would not, in the court's opinion, affect the credibility of the witness.[13] One could argue that, given the dictum of Lawton J in *Sweet-Escott*,[14] the court has a *duty*, not just a discretion, to excuse an answer in these circumstances.

9.7 Questioning by an advocate is also subject to the professional Code of Conduct.[15]

THE OPTION PUT FORWARD IN THE CONSULTATION PAPER

9.8 In the consultation paper[16] we thought that the time had come "to question how far it is appropriate to allow a party free rein in attacking witnesses' characters, on the basis that the focus of cross-examination should be the *probative* credibility[17] of the witness ... The onus should be on the party seeking to introduce the incriminating evidence to show how it is directly relevant, or of significant weight." We referred to the Australian Evidence Act 1995 (Commonwealth), sections 102–103, which provide that evidence going only to credibility must have "substantial probative value", and to section 2 of the Sexual Offences

---

[8] *Brown and Hedley* (1867) LR 1 CCR 70.

[9] Expert medical evidence is admissible to show that a witness suffers from some disease, defect or abnormality of mind which affects the reliability of his or her evidence: *Toohey v Metropolitan Police Commissioner* [1965] AC 595.

[10] *Kalia* (1974) 60 Cr App R 200; *Maynard* (1979) 69 Cr App R 309.

[11] *Flynn* [1972] Crim LR 428.

[12] *Brown (Milton)* [1998] Cr App R 364.

[13] *Hobbs v Tinling* [1929] 2 KB 1, 51, *per* Sankey LJ.

[14] See para 9.3 above.

[15] The Code of Conduct of the Bar of England & Wales, para 708(g), reads: "[Counsel] must not make statements or ask questions which are merely scandalous or intended or calculated only to vilify, insult or annoy either a witness or some other person". This Code does not, however, bind the courts: *McFadden* (1976) 62 Cr App R 187. The Law Society's Code for Advocacy replicates these provisions at para 7.1(e) and (f).

[16] At para 12.92.

[17] This is Zuckerman's term. What he calls "probative credibility" we called "specific credibility". See A Zuckerman, *The Principles of Criminal Evidence* (1989) p 248.

(Amendment) Act 1976.[18] We considered the possibility of a rule that "evidence may be called, and questions asked, as to an aspect of a witness's character only where it would be unfair to the defendant for them *not* to be asked – in other words, where the evidence (or the question) might reasonably lead the fact-finders to take a different view of the witness's evidence". Provisional proposal 35(D) set out for consultees' consideration the following option:

> allowing imputations to be made against a witness only where, if true, they would *substantially* undermine the witness's credibility.[19]

9.9 We stated that we saw some merit in this option, but did not feel able to put it forward as a proposal because, by going beyond admissibility of a *defendant's* bad character, it appeared that it might raise issues going beyond the subject-matter of the consultation paper.[20] We therefore simply invited views.

The views of respondents

9.10 Four respondents were in favour of this proposal and thought that it did not fall outside the scope of this paper. Three respondents argued against it. Among the four in favour, the justices of Uxbridge Magistrates' Court said there was some practical support for this option. They felt that, although it could present practical difficulties, it would make for a "clearer" trial and allow magistrates to concentrate more on the facts of the case.

9.11 Professor Jackson addressed the point in detail in his response. He thought that judges should take

> a much firmer stance against ... allowing witnesses' characters being attacked. In this regard I would adopt option D in para 35. I consider the Commission is wrong to consider that the question of cross-examination lies outside the scope of a paper on the previous misconduct of defendants. If a tougher line were to be taken by judges to limit the scope of cross-examination as to credit, then many of the tit-for-tat problems which the 1898 Act have given rise to could be avoided. The suggestion in para 12.91 that this would amount to requiring a higher standard of legal relevance for character evidence than for other evidence is questionable in the light of the low probative value that character evidence generally has in relation to both

---

[18] Since repealed: see para 2.69 above. Section 2(1) of the Sexual Offences (Amendment) Act 1976 provided that "no evidence and no question in cross-examination shall be adduced or asked at the trial, by or on behalf of any defendant at the trial, about any sexual experience of a complainant with a person other than that defendant" unless the court gives leave. Section 2(2) specified that leave should be given "if and only if" the judge was satisfied "that it would be unfair to that defendant to refuse to allow the evidence to be adduced or the question to be asked."

[19] Para 12.118 and provisional proposal 35(D) in Part XVI.

[20] In fact, the terms of reference ask the Commission to "consider the law of England and Wales relating to ... evidence of previous misconduct in criminal proceedings; and to make appropriate recommendations, including, if they appear to be necessary in consequence of changes proposed to the law of evidence, changes to the trial process." There is no explicit restriction to previous misconduct *of the defendant*.

credibility and facts in issue. In any event, the suggestion that bad character imputations should only be made where they would substantially undermine the witness's credibility is not far removed from the existing common law boundaries on cross-examination. According to Sankey LJ in *Hobbs v Tinling* [1929] KB 1, 50-51, such questions are only proper if they are of such a nature that the truth of the imputation conveyed would seriously affect the opinion of the court on the credibility of the witness. The problem would seem to be that trial judges are reluctant to circumscribe cross-examination to this extent. More stringent limits on cross-examination as to credit would not merely protect defendants but would also go a long way to protect the dignity of victims who are so commonly castigated during cross-examination.

Professor McEwan shared this view: "We should be instead be looking closely at ways to control unacceptable cross-examination."[21]

9.12 Those who argued against provisional proposal 35(D) were concerned that the test of "substantiality" was too vague and would provoke legal argument, and that it would involve the court in the difficult task of determining when a witness's credibility is substantially undermined. We discuss the test of substantiality and conclude that it is not too vague to be useful at paragraphs 7.8 – 7.17 above.

9.13 It is, however, clear that if a test of enhanced relevance were to apply only to evidence which is relevant via credibility, as we suggested, then this would add unwelcome complications to the law. There would be a high risk that advocates and courts would become embroiled in analyses of the ways in which evidence is said to be relevant.[22] In what follows, therefore, we have in mind a rule which extends to *all* bad character evidence which is outside the central set of facts,[23] not just to evidence going to credibility.

---

[21] Jenny McEwan, "Law Commission Dodges the Nettles in Consultation Paper No. 141" [1997] Crim LR 93, 102.

[22] Eg, if it is part of the defence case that a witness for the prosecution is the culprit, the advocate may initially argue that evidence of the witness's character is relevant to his or her credibility, so attracting the test of enhanced relevance. However, the advocate could argue that the witness's character is directly relevant to a fact in issue, in which case the enhanced relevance requirement would not bite.

The difference an analysis can make is illustrated also by *Edwards* [1991] 1 WLR 207. It was argued that the confession obtained from the defendant was fabricated, and in order to support this contention the defence sought to adduce evidence of how the police officers had fabricated confessions in other cases. On one analysis it is the *defendant's* credibility which is in fact at stake, namely the credibility of his evidence that he never made the confession, and in that event a test of enhanced relevance limited to attacks on a witness's credibility would not be applicable.

But if the officers are cross-examined on the existence of the confession, which they presumably were, then the evidence of what happened in the other cases reflects on *their* credibility, and so the test *would* be satisfied.

[23] The concept of the "central set of facts" is explained at paras 8.26 – 8.28 and 8.31 above.

THE DANGERS OF BAD CHARACTER EVIDENCE

Its irrelevance

9.14 We have considered in Part VI above what evidence there is to show how and to what extent past conduct might be relevant at trial (to propensity and to credibility) in relation to *defendants*. The conclusions we draw have the same force in relation to *non*-defendants. We concluded that in relation to propensity, past behaviour can be probative on the question whether the defendant is likely to have acted in the way alleged, but the probative value of a single previous instance can be easily over-estimated, and this would seem to be as true for non-defendants as for defendants. In relation to credibility, we concluded that previous misconduct *may* be relevant to a witness's *general* credibility; but, since little significance can in any event be attached to that credibility or the lack of it, the witness's previous misconduct is generally of little value in determining the issues in the case. A person's specific credibility – that is, the extent to which, in the circumstances of the individual case, the witness appears to have a *reason* to lie – is of far more importance in a case, as Professor Eggleston, an Australian judge, wrote:

> For my own part, I would ... limit severely the scope of cross-examination as to credit. As most witnesses will lie if the motive is strong enough, and many will lie merely to save lengthy explanations about matters that they think have nothing to do with the case, I do not regard the demonstration that a witness has lied about some irrelevant matter as affording much help in deciding whether he is telling the truth about the facts in issue.[24]

9.15 The New Zealand Law Commission took the view that bad character evidence is generally unhelpful on matters of truthfulness, and that restrictions are needed in respect of truthfulness, evidence showing a propensity in the defendant, and evidence about the sexual experience of a complainant. The restriction on evidence going to a person's truthfulness reads:

> A party may offer evidence in a civil or criminal proceedings about a person's truthfulness only if the evidence is substantially helpful in assessing that person's truthfulness.[25]

The Commission has also recommended special rules for propensity evidence about defendants and about sexual experience of complainants.[26]

---

[24] R Eggleston, *Evidence, Proof and Probability* (2nd ed 1983) p 77.

[25] Clause 39(1). Additional rules apply if the person whose truthfulness is in issue is a defendant in criminal proceedings.

[26] Propensity evidence which the prosecution seeks to adduce about a defendant must be about acts or omissions that are prima facie those of the defendant, relate to an issue in dispute, and have a "probative value ... which clearly outweighs the risk that the evidence may have an unfairly prejudicial effect on the defendant" (cl 45). Clause 46 contains the restrictions on evidence of a complainant's sexual experience.

Its prejudicial effect

9.16 It does not necessarily follow that just because evidence has little probative value it should be inadmissible. As the ALRC said, "If one accepts the view that [evidence of character] is of little value in a trial setting, that does not necessarily justify its exclusion".[27] However, the case for excluding evidence of bad character of non-defendants rests not just on its general irrelevance, but also on its potential for distorting the verdict by the prejudice which such evidence may introduce in respect of a witness whose evidence may be crucial. That this is so is demonstrable by the panoply of special rules and statutory provisions on limiting cross-examination about the previous sexual experience of complainants in sex cases where it is not merely the question of irrelevance which is to the fore but also the invitation to prejudice which underpins its attractiveness as a tool for the defence. In this respect we can see little reason, in principle, to treat witnesses any less favourably than defendants in considering the level of probative value which should be achieved before evidence should be admissible.

9.17 We note the words of Lord Steyn in *A*, where he accepted that past sexual behaviour has been adduced to the unfair disadvantage of the complainant:

> Nevertheless, it has to be acknowledged that in the criminal courts of our country, as in others, outmoded beliefs about women and sexual matters lingered on. In recent Canadian jurisprudence they have been described as the discredited twin myths, viz "that unchaste women were more likely to consent to intercourse and in any event, were less worthy of belief": *R v Seaboyer* (1991) 83 DLR (4th) 193, 258, 278C *per* McLachlin J. Such generalised, stereotyped and unfounded prejudices ought to have no place in our legal system. But even in the very recent past such defensive strategies were habitually employed. It resulted in an absurdly low conviction rate in rape cases. It also inflicted unacceptable humiliation on complainants in rape cases.[28]

9.18 Two questions arise: (1) does evidence of the bad character of non-defendants also have potential for distorting the verdict? and (2) are there considerations *other* than irrelevance and distortion of verdict which militate against admitting such evidence?[29] The ALRC sought to justify a raised threshold on the grounds that the existing law has "underestimated" the capacity of character evidence "to distort the fact-finding process".[30] These distortions arise because there is "a real danger that evidence from which a character inference can be drawn will be given disproportionate weight ...", and, particularly in the case of complainants in

---

[27] ALRC Interim Report No 26 (vol I), para 799.

[28] [2001] UKHL 25, para [27]. See also A Zuckerman, *The Principles of Criminal Evidence* (1989) pp 271–275.

[29] We address the second of these questions at paragraph 9.19 below.

[30] ALRC Interim Report No 26 (vol I), para 799. In its Final Report, the ALRC proposed a general exclusionary rule prohibiting the use of evidence of character, reputation or conduct, or tendencies to prove a tendency (cl 86), with an exception for evidence of conduct, and a general rule for evidence of credibility, limiting it to evidence of substantial probative value (cl 96(2)).

sexual cases, the fact-finders will be inclined to make a general moral assessment of the complainant.[31]

9.19 The Australian and New Zealand views are confirmed by research in this jurisdiction. The research concentrates on rape trials, where the problem seems to be especially acute. It has been found that, in some cases, advocates ask questions which are clearly irrelevant, or even questions which breach their own professional code.[32] Professor Temkin has written of research into the views and experience of barristers who prosecute and defend in rape trials. She found that defence counsel tend to avoid hectoring and harassing witnesses, partly because it can be counter-productive. She found also that both prosecuting and defence counsel took seriously the limitations on sexual history evidence which were then in force, and thought judges took them seriously too. Nevertheless, the applications of defence counsel to cross-examine on the basis of the complainant's sexual history were frequently made and rarely turned down. Discrediting the complainant was a "central strategy in the defence armoury" – as confirmed by recent Home Office research[33] – and one that was likely to succeed, despite the court's power to control cross-examination and specific legislative provisions designed to give the court control over the fairness of attacks on the witness's credibility. As Lord Steyn recently concluded, the regime provided for by section 2 of the Sexual Offences (Amendment) Act 1976 had not been effective in protecting complainants:

> Section 2(2) provides that the judge shall only give leave "if and only if he is satisfied that it would be unfair to that defendant to refuse to allow the evidence to be adduced or the question to be asked." The statute did not achieve its object of preventing the illegitimate use of prior sexual experience in rape trials. In retrospect one can now see that the structure of this legislation was flawed. In respect of sexual experience between a complainant and other men, which can only in the rarest cases have any relevance, it created too broad an inclusionary discretion. Moreover, it left wholly unregulated questioning or evidence about previous sexual experience between the complainant and the defendant even if remote in time and context. There was a serious mischief to be corrected.[34]

---

[31] *Ibid*, para 807 ff.

[32] See, eg, S Lees, *Carnal Knowledge: Rape on Trial* (1995) pp 136–142, 192–3, and 249. See also Paul Rook, *The English Crown Court* for examples of cross-examination at Wood Green Crown Court, and Helena Kennedy QC, *Eve Was Framed* (1992) ch 5. We note that only one respondent expressly doubted that this problem exists.

[33] Professor Temkin writes: "In the Home Office study, barristers considered that 'the defence has little choice but to seek to undermine the credibility of the complainant'", referring to *A Question of Evidence? Investigating and Prosecuting Rape in the 1990s* (1999) Home Office Study 196, p 36: J Temkin, "Prosecuting and Defending Rape: Perspectives From the Bar" Jo Law and Society 27(2) (2000) 219-48, 234. She also cites a report from the Scottish Office which found the same approach: G Chambers and A Millar, *Prosecuting Sexual Assault* (1986) Scottish Office Central Research Unit.

[34] *A* [2001] UKHL 25, para [28].

9.20 We would add a further concern: even if the fact-finders did base their verdict on the evidence unaffected by the relative moral standing of the parties, the witness might suffer humiliation and distress in the process. The feelings of the witness are a matter of public interest – witnesses who undergo humiliating or distressing cross-examination will report this experience to others, and witnesses will be deterred from testifying.[35]

> *W is a middle-aged woman, who is raped by an acquaintance. D says she consented. The police explain to her that, when she gives evidence, which she must for the prosecution to succeed, she might be asked about a 20-year old shoplifting conviction. Neither her husband nor her children nor her friends know about this conviction. The fear that it would be mentioned in public is enough to dissuade her from giving evidence.*

9.21 We do *not* argue that the sensibilities of witnesses should be protected at the expense of the defendant's rights, but, where the questions which the defence would like to ask do not substantially advance the defence case, then we do say that such questions should not be allowed.[36]

9.22 We therefore agree with the conclusion of the ALRC: evidence which distorts the fact-finding process and promotes an inaccurate verdict should be subject to restriction, whether the distortion favours the defendant or disadvantages the defendant.

9.23 While it may be right for a complainant in a sexual case to be protected from questioning about previous sexual experience which is irrelevant or insufficiently relevant, it does not follow that any other kind of character attack on a witness is justifiable. (Indeed, unequal treatment of prosecution and defence witnesses could itself lead to unfairness.)[37] Our conclusions relate, therefore, to all non-defendants, not just complainants, and across all kinds of cases.

---

[35] Consider the case of *Eccleston* [2001] EWCA Crim 1626, where the witness was not a complainant. Her evidence supported that of the complainant in one important respect. It was not put to her that she was lying. The defence appealed on the basis that the conviction was not safe because the witness's convictions for loitering as a prostitute, use of a controlled drug, and theft were not adduced. The Court of Appeal held that they made no difference because they were of only marginal relevance, but might she not have been deterred from giving evidence if she had thought they would be brought out in open court?

[36] See the guiding principle at para 5.20 above.

[37] As described in debate by Dale Campbell-Savours (MP for Workington):

> Another important question is whether the witnesses were treated equally. Why was J [the complainant] given anonymity, whereas the character of the only other eye-witness [a witness for the defence] was torn to shreds before the jury?

Hansard (HC) 5 March 1998, col 1277. The complainant was protected from certain kinds of questions by s 2 of the Sexual Offences (Amendment) Act 1976, but this protection did not extend to the eye-witness. The verdict depended on whether the jury believed the complainant or the eye-witness.

The effect of a statutory test of enhanced relevance

9.24 Putting the requirement that bad character evidence achieve a certain standard of relevance into statutory form, and raising that required standard, would require advocates and courts to consider whether questions put will elicit evidence which indeed has that enhanced level of relevance. For example, presently judges and magistrates may be reluctant to intervene to prevent irrelevant questioning because they are not confident that an appellate court would agree that the question was wholly irrelevant. Given the existence of a statutory structure by which leave was required, the advocate would need to show that the evidence had some relevance and that it is of more than minimal significance. If a line of questioning is not relevant at all, the advocate will not be able to argue either that it is directly probative or that it casts light on the person's truthfulness, let alone that it does so to an enhanced degree.

9.25 In making the application for leave, an advocate would have to point to the features of the evidence which support the argument that the evidence is substantially relevant – for example, how recent was any alleged misconduct, and how similar to any misconduct alleged in relation to the facts of the offence charged (which may include the giving of false evidence as to those facts).

9.26 Applying the rigour of requiring the advocate to satisfy the court of the enhanced level of relevance would mean that evidence going to the "specific credibility" of a witness (that is, evidence which suggests that the witness has an incentive to lie *on this occasion*) would be more likely to have the required level of relevance than evidence which merely suggests that the witness *might* lie if he or she *did* have an incentive to do so.

9.27 A leave requirement would also have the effect, first, that the court would turn its mind to the question of the relevance of the evidence; and second, that where the court decides to admit it, the process of reasoning by which the evidence is deemed to be substantially probative would be made explicit.[38]

Would a test of enhanced relevance prevent the defendant from having a fair trial?

9.28 A test of enhanced relevance would represent a restriction on the evidence that a defendant may adduce. We have considered very carefully the argument that a defendant should not be fettered in the presentation of his or her defence, and especially whether there would be any danger of a wrongful conviction resulting from a court's refusal to permit bad character evidence which would be permitted under the current law.

9.29 The question whether the defendant receives a fair trial also has significance in the light of Article 6 of the European Convention on Human Rights. The Strasbourg Court leaves evidential rules to the domestic courts and looks at the totality of the evidence against someone when deciding whether there has been a fair trial.[39]

---

[38] See our recommendation that a court should give its reasons, at para 17.15 below.

[39] See para 3.4 above.

Moreover, following the incorporation of the Convention into English law, where evidence is inadmissible on the ordinary rules of construction, the English courts will consider whether the trial is thereby rendered unfair, with explicit reference to Article 6 and the rights implicit in it. The approach a court is recommended to adopt is described in general terms at paragraphs 3.21 – 3.36 above.

9.30 Given this context, would a rule preventing a defendant from putting certain questions to a prosecution witness render the trial unfair, and thus infringe Article 6? We do not think so, for the following reasons. We note two general points first: that rules of evidence are a domestic matter, and the important question is not whether a rule in the abstract is fair, but whether the defendant has had a fair trial, and second, that there is no explicit right in the Convention to adduce whatever evidence the defence wishes to adduce.[40] The right to present one's defence is a constituent part of the right to a fair trial.

9.31 The recent authority of *A*[41] is instructive in this regard. That case concerned the application of sections 41–43 of the Youth Justice and Criminal Evidence Act 1999, which, subject to certain exceptions, provide that a defendant charged with a sexual offence may not cross-examine a complainant about his or her sexual behaviour on other occasions in support of a defence of consent. It was argued that these provisions infringed the defendant's right to a fair trial under Article 6. The House of Lords agreed that a literal reading might result in the exclusion of evidence necessary to a fair trial, particularly where the evidence was of a previous sexual relationship between the complainant and the defendant himself. With the help of section 3 of the HRA 1998,[42] however, their Lordships construed the legislation so as not to exclude any evidence which is so relevant to the issues that its exclusion would endanger the fairness of the trial under Article 6.[43]

9.32 The importance of this decision for present purposes lies not so much in the fact that the House was prepared to give the legislation a flexible interpretation in order to avoid finding it incompatible with Article 6: we strive to produce draft legislation that is Convention-compatible even if it is read in accordance with ordinary principles of statutory interpretation and without resort to section 3 of the HRA.[44] Rather, the crucial point is their Lordships' recognition that the exclusion of relevant defence evidence does not *in itself* render the trial unfair.[45] It depends *how* relevant the excluded evidence is to the crucial issues in the case.

---

[40] See, eg, *Breen* [2001] EWCA Crim 1213 in which it was made quite clear that D was not entitled to adduce evidence of a defence not recognised in English law.

[41] [2001] UKHL 25.

[42] See paras 3.29– 3.35 above.

[43] [2001] UKHL 25, para [46], *per* Lord Steyn.

[44] Any Bill that is presented to Parliament has to be certified by a Minister as compatible with the Convention rights: HRA 1998, s 19. It does not have to be compatible without recourse to s 3 for the purpose of certification.

[45] [2001] UKHL 25, para [34], *per* Lord Steyn.

> *D is charged with theft. W, who was D's employee at the time of the alleged offence, is a witness who will give incriminating evidence which a jury could hardly accept without convicting D. The bad character evidence in question is the fact (not disputed by the prosecution) that, in her previous job, four years before the time of D's alleged offence, W was dishonest in her expenses claims. D says that the witness is incompetent and therefore mistaken. It is hard to conceive that the evidence would be admissible under our enhanced test.*

> *Alternatively, D is charged with theft, and wishes to ask W about an allegation that she was dishonest in her previous job. In this example, D's case is that W is lying, not incompetent. The fact that in the relatively recent past she has been guilty of dishonesty at the work place might well surmount the test of enhanced relevance.*

> *A third variation: D is charged with theft and wishes to ask W about an allegation of dishonesty 10 years previously, or in a non-work context. The court might well take the view that it did not pass the enhanced relevance test.*

9.33 Presently, the evidence of W's past might well be put in or allowed in under all three scenarios or, at the least, under the latter two on the basis that as there is a general dispute about the reliability of her evidence any evidence which might reflect on her reliability as a witness could be admitted, especially if the defendant does not himself have any previous convictions. Under an enhanced relevance test, the court would force the advocate to consider and articulate why it is that the evidence should be admitted as satisfying that test. The outcome might be that a witness was saved a public humiliation for a cause which could not sensibly have been thought to advance the defendant's case. At the very least the defence will have been forced to sharpen up the focus of its attack.

9.34 It follows, from the decision in *A*, that a requirement of enhanced relevance for bad character evidence would risk infringing Article 6 *only* if the required level of relevance were set so high that evidence sufficiently probative to be necessary for a fair trial might nevertheless fail to satisfy it. This result could be avoided by formulating the requirement in such a way that it will *inevitably* be satisfied whenever the exclusion of the evidence might render the trial unfair. We therefore do not accept that the introduction of a test of enhanced relevance would necessarily risk infringing Article 6. That risk can be eliminated if the test is properly formulated and applied.

OUR CONCLUSION

9.35 We think it right to have a rule of law that, where evidence of the bad character of a non-defendant is barely or only minimally relevant, it should be excluded. We have reached this conclusion because

(1) of the special power of bad character evidence to distort the fact-finding process;

(2) of the need to encourage witnesses to give evidence, by making it known that witnesses will not have their past exposed publicly where it is at best of only minimal relevance to the questions in issue, such as whether they are telling the truth; and

(3) it will give courts a clear supportive framework to control gratuitous and offensive cross-examination which has little or no purpose other than to intimidate or embarrass the witness or muddy the waters.

FORMULATING THE TEST OF ENHANCED RELEVANCE

9.36 We argued above that the risk of rendering the trial unfair by excluding relevant defence evidence can be avoided by ensuring that evidence would not be excluded if that would be its effect. We will need to do this if the rule we recommend is not to infringe Article 6. One way to do it would be by expressly formulating the test in terms of whether the defendant could have a fair trial if the evidence were excluded. This would ensure that the trial was not rendered unfair; but it would go further than we think necessary. Our object in raising the standard of relevance is not to exclude as much bad character evidence as Article 6 will allow. Rather, it is to exclude only bad character evidence which is of *trivial* relevance – the kind of evidence which cannot be said to be entirely irrelevant, but which adds very little. We are not seeking to raise the standard as high as that currently applicable to "similar fact evidence".[46] Nor do we suggest that evidence of bad character should be excluded merely because it *could* be excluded without depriving the defendant of a fair trial.

9.37 We therefore conclude that the criterion should be formulated, not in terms of whether the defendant can have a fair trial, but expressly in terms of the degree of relevance that the evidence has to the issues in the case. This means, however, that we must express the required degree of relevance in such a way that evidence will inevitably satisfy that requirement if its exclusion would render the trial unfair. We now consider how this can be done.

The importance of the matter in issue

9.38 The value of evidence is made up of its relevance to a matter in issue *and* the importance of that matter in issue in the context of the case as a whole. Even bad character evidence which is highly probative on a particular issue may not have sufficient probative value to justify its admission if that issue is itself of trivial importance. For example, a fact may have substantial relevance to the credibility of a person whose credibility is in issue, and thus to the matter in issue on which she gives evidence, although that matter is not of substantial importance in the context of the case as a whole. If the matter on which she gives evidence is of only marginal relevance to the central issues in the case, then no amount of relevance

---

[46] See para 2.5 above.

to her credibility can ever amount to *substantial* importance in the context of the case as a whole.

9.39 We conclude that, in order to meet the purposes for which it is designed, the test of enhanced relevance should be whether the evidence has substantial probative value in relation to a matter in issue which is itself of substantial importance in the context of the case as a whole. Our use of the word "substantial" in this context is parallel to its use as described in Part VII above.

Ensuring a fair trial

9.40 We now return to the question whether such a test would risk infringing Article 6, by excluding evidence which needs to be admitted if the defendant is to have a fair trial. This depends whether a court might conceivably decide that certain bad character evidence which a defendant seeks to adduce is not of substantial probative value (or is of substantial probative value only in relation to a matter in issue which is not itself of substantial importance to the case) *although* the defendant cannot have a fair trial if the evidence is excluded. We think this would be a self-evidently contradictory position for a court to adopt. If it is unfair to the defendant to exclude the evidence, this can only be because the evidence does have substantial probative value in relation to the crucial issues in the case. Indeed, a court might reasonably approach the question of whether particular evidence has substantial probative value by first asking itself whether the defendant could have a fair trial if the evidence were excluded. A negative answer to this question would inevitably mean that the evidence did have sufficient relevance to be admitted.

OUR RECOMMENDATIONS

Exceptions: non-defendants: substantial probative value

9.41 **We recommend that leave may be given to adduce evidence of the bad character of a person other than a defendant if it has substantial probative value in relation to a matter in issue in the proceedings which is of substantial importance in the context of the case as a whole.**[47]

Exceptions: non-defendants: substantial explanatory value

9.42 As we explain in relation to bad character evidence to be adduced against defendants,[48] some character evidence is not strictly speaking *probative*, in that it does not of itself *prove* any fact, but it is nevertheless significant in making other evidence comprehensible. Some evidence about people other than defendants may serve this kind of purpose in a trial, and **we therefore recommend that leave may be given to adduce evidence of the bad character of a person other than a defendant if it has substantial explanatory value.**[49]

---

[47] This recommendation is given effect by cl 5 of the draft Bill.

[48] See Part X below.

[49] This recommendation is given effect by cl 4 of the draft Bill.

9.43 Thus, for example, in a case of intra-familial abuse, it was not only abusive behaviour by the defendant on occasions other than that charged which was valuable in explaining the case as a whole to the jury, but also abusive behaviour by other members of the family.

The consequences for the defendant

9.44 Where the defendant does obtain leave to adduce evidence of another's bad character under either of these recommendations, this may make it possible for the prosecution to apply for the defendant's own bad character to be admitted. It is possible that evidence of the defendant's own bad character will attain a probative value it did not have before the bad character evidence of the other person was adduced, and so the prosecution might make an application under the rules that we recommend in Parts X, XI, and XII respectively.

The relationship with section 41 Youth Justice and Criminal Evidence Act 1999

9.45 At the time of writing, section 41 of the Youth Justice and Criminal Evidence Act 1999 lays down rules for the admissibility of sexual history evidence of complainants in sexual cases, as described above. Our recommendations would involve no changes to those provisions. Where those provisions apply, our proposed test of substantial probative value would have to be satisfied as well; but it is almost certain that evidence of sexual experience which is ruled admissible under section 41 will have substantial probative value, with the result that it would be ruled admissible under our recommendations too. Our recommendations, however, cover a far wider range of cases and people than does section 41, as they are not restricted to complainants, nor to sexual cases, nor even to witnesses.

> *D is charged with rape. He wants to ask the complainant about her convictions for possession of unlawful drugs. It is not "sexual behaviour" so section 41 does not apply. He will, however, have to obtain leave under clause 4 or 5 of our draft Bill.*

> *D is charged with indecent assault. He says the complainant consented. He wants to question the complainant about his sexual experiences with a mutual friend. He will have to obtain leave under section 41(3) of the 1999 Act. If, and only if, evidence of those sexual experiences count as "bad character" then he will have to obtain leave under clause 4 or 5 of our draft Bill as well.*

PART X
THE EXPLANATORY EXCEPTION

THE DEFECTS OF THE CURRENT LAW

Res gestae and background evidence

10.1 The present law is that evidence which falls within the "res gestae" or is "background" evidence may be admitted as evidence. It does not therefore have to be examined to determine whether it can be described as "similar fact" evidence. In the consultation paper we identified four "indicators" which may enable evidence to avoid the normal exclusionary rule on the basis that it is background evidence.[1] They are as follows:

(1) the evidence may be close in time, place or circumstances to the facts or circumstances of the offence charged;[2]

(2) the evidence may be necessary to complete the account of the circumstances of the offence charged, and thus make it comprehensible to the jury;[3]

(3) the accused may have had a relationship with the victim of the offence charged, and the previous misconduct evidence may relate to this victim rather than the victims of other offences;

(4) the evidence may assist in establishing the motive behind the offence charged.[4]

10.2 Background evidence is admitted because it is "so closely entwined and involved with the evidence directly relating to the facts in issue that it would amount to distortion to attempt to edit it out".[5] However, highly prejudicial evidence can be

---

[1] Para 2.81. The case law is discussed in some detail at paras 2.70 – 2.84 in the consultation paper.

[2] See *Archbold*, para 13-35: "the evidence must have clear probative value and the more remote from the date of the offence the incident sought to be proved is, the clearer the probative value must be." See also *Berry* (1986) 83 Cr App R 7, 10, *per* Watkins LJ, referred to at para 2.75 of the consultation paper, and *Sidhu* (1994) 98 Cr App R 59.

[3] This is taken from the Court of Appeal's judgment (*per* Purchas LJ) in the unreported case of *Pettman*, 2 May 1985, CA No 5048/C/82: "where it is necessary to place before the jury evidence of part of a continual background of history relevant to the offence charged in the indictment and without the totality of which the account placed before the jury would be incomplete or incomprehensible, then the fact that the whole account involves including evidence establishing the commission of an offence with which the accused is not charged is not of itself a ground for excluding the evidence." This passage is also referred to in *Fulcher* [1995] 2 Cr App R 251, 258D–E, *per* Kennedy LJ, and in *Stevens* [1995] Crim LR 649.

[4] See *Ball* [1911] AC 47, 68.

[5] *Cross and Tapper*, p 343.

admitted as "background" without any adequate assessment of its prejudicial effect.[6] To quote McHugh J:

> Great care needs to be taken ... in determining whether evidence, disclosing other criminal conduct, is evidence concerning the res gestae or is merely circumstantial evidence. By applying labels such as "one transaction", "connected series of events", "system", "history", "completeness" and "part of one chain of relevant circumstances", evidence which is in truth purely circumstantial improperly avoids the tests of admissibility which the modern cases expound.[7]

OUR ANALYSIS

10.3 We have concluded that there are two different reasons for admitting such evidence. Some evidence (res gestae) is so inextricably linked to the facts about the offence charged, by reason of its close connection with them in time and space, that it should be automatically admissible; on the other hand, some evidence, though not forming part of the alleged facts, is nonetheless linked to those central facts by virtue of its force in making them comprehensible. That evidence *should*, in our judgment, have to pass a test of admissibility.[8]

Evidence which is part of the narrative of the offence

10.4 While it could be argued that all prejudicial character evidence should be prima facie inadmissible, in the words of McHugh J, some evidence "is so fundamental to the proceedings that its admissibility as a matter of law cannot depend upon a condition that its probative force transcends its prejudicial effect".[9] It would, for example, be very strange if evidence of an assault committed in the course of a rape, but not separately charged, were to be treated as prima facie inadmissible; or if, on a charge of murder by firing a bullet through a window, the prosecution had to seek leave to adduce evidence that the defendant had not only killed the deceased but also broken the window; or if, on a charge of burning down a hostel

---

[6] Eg, *Fulcher* [1995] 2 Cr App R 251 in which the Court of Appeal held it was right that, where the defendant was charged with the murder of his infant son, evidence of the defendant's previous violence towards the victim was admissible as background as evidence of motive. Its prejudicial effect was not taken into account. The Court of Appeal commented at p 258, "Of course, a court always has power to exclude evidence which it finds to be more prejudicial than probative," but no application was made for it to be excluded on that basis, and the court thought any such application would have been unlikely to succeed.

[7] *Harriman v The Queen* (1989) 167 CLR 590, 633–634.

[8] The ALRC wrote that

> surrounding detail puts a narrated transaction in context, assisting evaluation of the truth of the narration and thus is "indirectly" relevant to the issues. Information which aids in the understanding of other relevant evidence is also relevant.

ALRC Report, vol 2, para 59. We think that the evidence described in the first sentence, and the evidence described in the second, should be handled differently.

[9] *Harriman v The Queen* (1989) 167 CLR 590, 633.

for ex-prisoners, leave were required to prove that the defendant was a resident of that hostel.[10]

10.5 The fact that a rapist committed an assault in the course of the rape *may* of course be relevant to a fact in issue: for example, it may suggest an absence of consent. But, even if that fact has no real bearing on any issue in the case – because the issue is not whether the complainant was raped but whether it was the defendant who did it – it would in our view be unrealistic to suggest that the prosecution may not prove that fact without first satisfying the court that the interests of justice require that it be allowed to do so. The assault is relevant not for any light it throws on the defendant's character, and thus on the likelihood that he committed the rape, but because it is part and parcel of what is alleged.[11] Therefore we believe that it should be admissible without more, and not required to fall within an *exception* to the exclusionary rule.

10.6 Under our recommendations, this is achieved by the rule that bad character evidence does not require leave if it has to do with the alleged facts of the offence charged. Evidence which forms part of the narrative of the offence (approximating to res gestae, or indicator (1) in paragraph 10.1 above) will inevitably satisfy this requirement, and therefore does not require leave to be adduced.[12]

Explanatory evidence

10.7 The *probative* value of a fact is its value in proving the truth or falsity of a fact in issue. Often, however, the value of the kind of fact which provides essential background is not that a specific fact in issue can be inferred from it, but simply that if the fact-finders did not hear of it they would find it harder to understand the nature of what is alleged. Strictly speaking, it has *explanatory* value, not probative value. Under the present law such evidence is admitted as "background" evidence without any assessment of its potentially prejudicial effect. The obvious examples of "explanatory evidence" arise in the contexts of complex financial fraud and abuse of one person by another over a long period.

---

[10] Cf *Neale* (1977) 65 Cr App R 304. In our Hearsay Report we referred to the difficulties created for witnesses giving oral evidence when they are stopped, in the middle of a natural account of an event, for fear that they are about to break a rule of evidence. See Law Com 245, paras 12.13 – 12.14 and paras 7.74 – 7.75 of the Hearsay Consultation Paper No 138 (1995). If this kind of evidence was prima facie inadmissible, more of those interruptions would occur.

[11] As Professor Murphy wrote in his response, "it is inevitable that some evidence involving an aspect of the accused's character should be introduced, but *the evidence is admitted, not because it involves character, but despite the fact that it does so*".

[12] Clause 2(1) of the draft Bill. See paras 8.31 and 8.32 above.

> *X sets up a company, as sole shareholder and executive director. Its ostensible purpose is to make investments on behalf of clients. X asks D to be a non-executive director. X tells D that the company will seek to "minimise" corporation tax payments, and D will occasionally be asked to sign off on misleading accounting documents to that end. Over a number of months, both X and D sign off on false accounting documents. Then X disappears overnight. The company's client account has been cleaned out. D is charged with false accounting and conspiracy to defraud the company's clients. D pleads guilty to the false accounting charges, and the convictions are recorded. However, D pleads not guilty to conspiracy, claiming to have been unaware of X's fraud on the clients. At D's conspiracy trial, the prosecution will need to refer to D's previous convictions and the wrong-doing that lay behind them, because the false accounting documents were used to effect the fraud on the clients.*

> *D is charged with repeated sexual abuse of his sister. In order to explain why she did not turn to her parents to be protected from her brother, the prosecution has to explain the history of abuse within the family, which shows the defendant as a victim of abuse himself as well as a perpetrator.*

10.8 Where the evidence falls outside the central facts, however, and therefore under our scheme requires leave to be admitted, we do not think it should be exempted from the principles applicable to such evidence merely because it satisfies one or more of indicators (2)–(4) in paragraph 10.1 above. Those principles dictate that leave should not be given unless the evidence has *substantial* explanatory value. The court must be satisfied that, without the evidence, the court or jury would find it impossible or difficult properly to understand other evidence in the case *and* that its value for understanding the case as a whole is substantial.[13] This test applies whether the evidence relates to a defendant or anyone else.[14]

10.9 Where the evidence is of a *defendant's* bad character, however, we recommend an additional test to be satisfied, namely that the interests of justice require it to be adduced *notwithstanding any prejudicial potential* it might have.

10.10 The test for evidence of this kind, where it applies to a defendant, has the same structure as for incriminatory evidence. The only difference from that test is that the value of the evidence is not, strictly speaking, "probative", in that it does not directly *prove* anything; it explains other evidence. It is therefore not the *probative* value of the evidence that must be weighed against the risk of prejudice, but its value *for understanding the case as a whole*.

---

[13] Clause 4 (a) and (b), cl 7 (1), (2) and (3).

[14] For its application to non-defendants, see Part IX above.

10.11 The difference between our policy and the current law is that, under the current law, if evidence of the defendant's other misconduct comes into the category of "background" evidence, it is admitted without any assessment of its prejudicial effect, whereas under our recommendation, the risk of prejudice does have to be taken into account. In our view, this requirement will secure a fair, rational and consistent approach to the inclusion of such evidence.

10.12 **We recommend that leave may be given to adduce evidence of the bad character of a defendant if it has substantial explanatory value and the interests of justice require it to be admissible, even taking account of its potentially prejudicial effect.**[15]

---

[15] This recommendation is given effect by cl 7 of the draft Bill.

PART XI
THE INCRIMINATORY EXCEPTION

INTRODUCTION

11.1 In Part VIII we explained our recommendation that leave should be required for evidence of bad character which falls outside the central set of facts. This Part describes the second of the exceptions for evidence of the bad character of a defendant. This exception is for evidence of substantial probative value which goes to a matter in issue. It will enable the prosecution, in certain circumstances, to adduce evidence of the defendant's bad character as part of the prosecution's case.

11.2 In Part X of the consultation paper we took the view that the present law, based on the concept of similar fact, is unsatisfactory, and set out six options for consideration. We start by explaining what the responses were to those options, and how they have informed our recommendation. At the end of this Part, we address three special cases where evidence of the defendant's bad character might form part of the prosecution case.

THE OPTIONS FOR REFORM AND THE RESPONSE ON CONSULTATION

11.3 The first option considered was for no change. We rejected that option in the light of the problems we thought exist in the current law.[1] A substantial number of respondents addressed this, but only a small minority thought the law should be left as it is. Most of those thought that the difficulties are not attributable to the law itself but are inherent in the nature of the problem.

Option 2: adducing bad character evidence to prove mens rea[2]

11.4 This option would allow evidence of an accused's previous convictions to be adduced where the conduct is admitted but there is an issue whether it was performed with any criminal knowledge or intent. For example, where a person with convictions for burglary is charged with having entered a building as a trespasser with intent to steal[3] and his defence is that he entered the building only to sleep,[4] evidence of previous convictions for burglary would be admitted, even without particular similarities between the past conduct and the charge.

11.5 We pointed out in the consultation paper that, in practice, this option would not in fact lead to the automatic admission of previous convictions for the same offence. The bare fact of the conviction would have little probative value but its prejudicial effect could easily be more than trivial, and so the defence would, no doubt, apply for the evidence to be excluded by the judge or magistrates, pursuant

---

[1] Paras 10.20 – 10.22 of the consultation paper.
[2] Paras 10.23 – 10.36 of the consultation paper.
[3] Contrary to the Theft Act 1968, s 9(1)(a).
[4] See *Cokar* [1960] 2 QB 207, n 47 in Part IV above.

to the common law rule[5] or section 78(1) of PACE. The net result would be that probative value would have to outweigh prejudicial effect.

11.6 We identified the disadvantages of this option: a significant danger of wrongful convictions; past miscarriages of justice would be compounded; defendants would be unlikely to admit the conduct if the consequence was the admission of similar previous convictions; and difficult in practice to determine in a particular case whether the conduct is admitted or denied.

11.7 Only four respondents specifically addressed this option and, of those, only one gave it any support. That respondent was concerned that evidence of bad character which tends to disprove an innocent explanation should be admissible. We reject this option. Our recommended exception would make evidence which tends to disprove an explanation given by the defendant admissible where its value in so doing outweighs the prejudice attaching to it, but without the attendant disadvantages of this option.

Option 3: adducing bad character evidence to show disposition[6]

11.8 In the consultation paper we considered a reform proposed by the CLRC,[7] which would allow evidence of "a disposition to commit the kind of offence with which [the defendant] is charged … if the disposition which the conduct tends to show is, in the circumstances of the case, of particular relevance to a matter in issue …".[8]

11.9 We did not favour this option because: it would allow evidence of disposition to be given without that evidence being "highly relevant"; and it proposed (in clause 3(2)(c)) that disposition evidence be admitted where it "tends to confirm the correctness of an identification of the accused". We noted that identification evidence is recognised as giving cause for especial concern,[9] and we were troubled by the prospect of it being supported by prejudicial evidence.

11.10 Only two respondents mentioned this option, and neither of them thought it was preferable to other options. We do not pursue this option any further.

---

[5] *Sang* [1980] AC 402.

[6] Paras 10.37 – 10.46 of the consultation paper.

[7] Although it was presented by the Committee as making no change to the then existing law, it would in fact have extended the circumstances in which previous misconduct was admissible. See para 10.38 of the consultation paper.

[8] Clause 3(2) of the Bill accompanying the CLRC Evidence Report.

[9] Hence the guidelines for trials involving disputed identification laid down in *Turnbull* [1977] QB 224.

Option 4: the Australian common law test, namely whether there is any reasonable explanation for the similar fact evidence other than that the defendant is guilty[10]

11.11 The fourth option which we canvassed was the Australian common law test, as stated in *Pfennig*:[11] the evidence is inadmissible unless there is no rational view of the evidence that is consistent with the innocence of the accused. The majority in *Pfennig* said that

> for propensity or similar fact evidence to be admissible the objective improbability of its having some innocent explanation [must be] such that there is no reasonable[12] view of it other than as supporting an inference that the accused is guilty of the offence charged.[13]

This test is simple, and it minimises the risk of wrongful convictions: as Roderick Munday put it, "Practically speaking to admit similar fact evidence at all is to determine that, barring a miracle, the defendant will be convicted".[14]

11.12 We identified three disadvantages of this option. We thought the test stricter than necessary, and likely to lead to the exclusion of evidence which was probative and of little prejudicial effect. We noted that, because it requires the judge to assess the strength of the evidence, it would require the judge to apply the same test to the evidence as the jury would have to apply, if it were admitted. Thirdly, we feared that adoption of this test would lead to an increase in the need for voir dires.

11.13 Only five respondents referred specifically to the Australian common law test. Three of them preferred it. We take the point made by one respondent who said that the Australian common law test is "clear, understandable, and appears likely to ensure that justice is done to the defendant", but, given the breadth of evidence to which this test is to apply, we do not think it is the right one. The test in *Pfennig* is not necessarily appropriate for bad character evidence of a different kind from that in issue in *Pfennig*: bad character evidence is not always either so probative, nor so prejudicial. We are still of the view expressed in the consultation paper: we think wrongful acquittals would result from setting the test so high, and we do not favour the consequences for the judge's role and the trial process which would follow from it. We note also that this option has no particular advantage in the

---

[10] Paras 10.47 – 10.59 of the consultation paper.

[11] (1995) 127 ALR 99. This authority has been superseded in those jurisdictions where the Evidence Act 1995 (Cth) and the Evidence Act 1995 (New South Wales) apply.

[12] The majority regarded "reasonable" and "rational" as synonymous in this context: *ibid*, at p 114.

[13] *Pfennig* (1995) 127 ALR 99, 113, *per* Mason CJ, Deane and Dawson JJ, summarising the effect of *Hoch* (1988) 165 CLR 292, 294. *Pfennig* has since been applied in, eg, *Robertson* (1997) 91 A Crim R 388: the defendant was charged with administering a stupefying drug or thing and indecently assaulting the complainant. Accounts from others who claimed he had drugged their drinks and possibly acted indecently towards them were permitted as evidence against R on the basis that, once concoction was excluded, there was no rational explanation other than that they supported an inference of guilt.

[14] R Munday, "Similar Fact Evidence and the Risk of Contaminated Testimony" [1995] CLJ 522, 524.

magistrates' courts where the justices decide on the admissibility of evidence and on the question of guilt. We therefore believe that this option should be rejected.

Option 5: the scheme of the Australian Evidence Act 1995 (Cth)[15]

11.14 The Evidence Act 1995 (Cth) provides that all relevant evidence is admissible unless excluded by the Act, but has two exclusionary rules that are relevant for present purposes: one is confined to "tendency" and "coincidence" evidence, and the other extends to any evidence adduced by the prosecution.

11.15 Under the "tendency" and "coincidence" rules, evidence may not be adduced to show

(i) that a person has a tendency to act in a particular way, or

(ii) that a person did a particular act (or had a particular state of mind) because two or more events have occurred which are unlikely to have occurred by coincidence,

unless the evidence has *significant probative value*.[16] In addition, tendency evidence and coincidence evidence adduced *by the prosecution about a defendant* may not be used against the defendant unless its probative value *substantially outweighs any prejudicial effect* that it may have on the defendant.[17]

11.16 Finally, *any* evidence adduced by the prosecution (not just tendency and coincidence evidence) must have probative value which outweighs the danger of prejudice.[18]

11.17 The effect is that prejudicial evidence adduced by the prosecution is admissible only if the following conditions are met:

(i) the evidence's probative value must outweigh the danger of prejudice;[19] *and*

(ii) *if* the evidence is tendency or coincidence evidence, its probative value must in addition

- *substantially* outweigh the danger of prejudice,[20] *and*

- be *significant*.[21]

11.18 Four of the five respondents who commented on this option were in support of the Australian statutory scheme. We address the points they made in the following paragraphs.

---

[15] Paras 10.60 – 10.72 of the consultation paper.

[16] Evidence Act 1995 (Cth), ss 97(1)(b), 98(1)(b).

[17] *Ibid*, s 101(2).

[18] *Ibid*, s 137.

[19] *Ibid*.

[20] *Ibid*, s 101(2).

[21] *Ibid*, ss 97(1)(b), 98(1)(b).

11.19 In the consultation paper we set out three drawbacks to the Australian statutory scheme.[22] First, we were unsure what it might mean for the probative value of evidence to outweigh the risk of prejudice *substantially*, or for evidence to have *significant* probative value as opposed to *some* probative value. Secondly, we thought the effect of the rules was that tendency and coincidence evidence would sometimes be inadmissible even if its probative value outweighed its prejudicial effect. Thirdly, we thought the Australian statutory scheme unnecessarily complicated.

Option 6

11.20 The preferred option in the consultation paper[23] was to allow bad character evidence to be adduced if

(i) it is relevant to a specific fact in issue; and

(ii) on the assumption that the evidence is true, the *degree* to which it is relevant to that fact (in other words, its probative value) outweighs the risk that, if admitted, it might

(A) result in prejudice;

(B) mislead, confuse or distract the fact-finders; or

(C) cause undue waste of time.

11.21 Of those making specific comments on this proposal, 27 respondents were in favour and ten were against it. The responses from consultees on this option and on option 5 informed our views on the following issues.

OUR CONCLUSIONS

A test of enhanced relevance

11.22 The Australian statutory scheme requires the bad character evidence itself to have "significant" probative value, whereas our preferred option did not set a standard of enhanced relevance for the probative value of the evidence. As will have been seen from our recommendation for a test of enhanced relevance for all evidence of bad character which goes outside the central set of facts,[24] we now accept that there is a meaningful difference between evidence having some probative value and having substantial probative value. We think evidence which the prosecution wishes to adduce as part of its case against the defendant should meet this test of enhanced relevance.

The relationship between probative value and prejudicial effect

11.23 The Australian statutory scheme requires the evidence in question substantially to outweigh the danger of prejudice. Our preferred option merely required the

---

[22] See paras 10.64 – 10.70.

[23] Provisional proposal 16, set out at paras 10.73 – 10.85.

[24] See para 7.7 above and the discussion of "substantial" at paras 7.8 – 7.17 above.

probative value to outweigh the risk that, if admitted, it might (inter alia) result in prejudice.

11.24 We were concerned that the result of the Australian statutory scheme "must be that tendency and coincidence evidence adduced by the prosecution is sometimes inadmissible *even if its probative value outweighs the risk of prejudice. ...* [I]f the evidence's probative value outweighs the risk of prejudice, we see no reason why it should be excluded merely because it does not *substantially* outweigh that risk."[25]

11.25 Mr Justice Tim Smith, Commissioner in Charge of the ALRC Report and a respondent to the consultation paper, expressed grave concern that the preferred option failed to give sufficient weight to the risk of wrongful convictions. He thought that the test proposed was not sufficiently strict:

> In paragraph 10.84 the paper refers to what I see as the major difficulty with the proposal and that is its potential to increase the risk of wrongful conviction. It is said that this is always a risk with this kind of evidence but the view of the Commission is that this option would reduce it "as far as is reasonably practicable". I would prefer to phrase the issue slightly differently – whether the option would reduce the risk of wrongful conviction to an acceptable level. ..., something would be need to be added to the discretion to ensure that evidence would only be admitted in cases where it is clear that the probative value will outweigh its likely prejudicial effect.
>
> Ultimately, the problem is that the rule, however it is formulated, will let into evidence before the tribunal of fact evidence which carries with it a risk of wrongful conviction because of its prejudicial effect. ... If a balancing test is to be used, however, one which incorporates the requirement that the probative value of the evidence substantially outweigh any probative effect would seem to me to be the minimum requirement if the concern to minimise wrongful conviction is to be adequately addressed.

11.26 The point made by Mr Justice Tim Smith is that the judge may underestimate the prejudicial effect of the evidence and, if he or she does so, then the risk of wrongful conviction is greatly increased. If, on the other hand, the evidence is only admissible if there is a significant margin between its probative value and its prejudicial effect then a minor under-estimation will not result in the admission of evidence which is in fact more prejudicial than probative.

11.27 The counter-argument is that, if there has to be a significant margin, it is possible for evidence which is more probative than prejudicial to be excluded. In the consultation paper we gave an example of a case where the higher standard would lead to the exclusion of evidence which we thought should not be excluded:

> the fact-finders might already know (perhaps because the fact has been admitted as "background" evidence, or because the defendant is notorious) that the defendant has a long history of serious crime. The

---

[25] Para 10.65 (emphasis in original). The omitted section of the para addressed (and rejected) the possible requirement that the evidence have "significant" probative value.

additional prejudice likely to result from the revelation of one more minor offence is very small, and would be outweighed by a comparatively small degree of probative value. In such a case we think that the evidence ought to be admissible, even if the probative value of the evidence is not "significant". Similarly, if the evidence's probative value outweighs the risk of prejudice, we see no reason why it should be excluded merely because it does not *substantially* outweigh that risk.[26]

11.28 Because we are now proposing a test of enhanced relevance for all bad character evidence,[27] this example is not so convincing: if the prejudice attaching to the evidence is indeed slight, then given that the character evidence must be of substantial probative value, it is likely that the probative value *would* substantially outweigh the prejudice.

11.29 The question is what degree of risk of wrongful conviction is acceptable. We acknowledge that there is some force the point made by Professor McEwan[28] that people do not agree on when one fact tends to prove or disprove another, let alone about the degree to which one fact tends to prove or disprove another. Although there might be consensus about the cases at each end of the scale, so that most courts, if not all, would allow bad character evidence in one situation and would disallow it in another, there is a body of cases in the middle of the spectrum where it is likely that courts will differ on whether the probative value of the evidence in question outweighs the prejudice attaching to it. If the test is that the probative value must substantially outweigh the prejudice, then a court will exclude evidence which it might have let in after hesitation.

11.30 Our view is that such an approach runs the risk of focusing on a question which, though it might be useful to ask, is not the real issue to be addressed. The purpose of a trial is to do justice. We believe that there is no better way to express the test than in terms of this central purpose. Thus the test is best expressed in qualitative rather than quantitative terms, that is, what the interests of justice require. This test will apply in circumstances in which the prosecution is seeking to adduce evidence about the defendant. Just as the burden of proof falls on the prosecution in criminal proceedings, so this test should place the onus on the prosecution to show that the interests of justice require that the evidence be admitted.

The importance of the matter in issue

11.31 As we say in relation to non-defendants, the value of evidence is made up of its relevance to a matter in issue and the importance of that matter in issue in the context of the case as a whole. The court must therefore have regard to the significance of the issue on which the evidence in question is said to be probative in the context of the case as a whole.[29]

---

[26] Para 10.65 (emphasis in original).

[27] See para 7.7 above.

[28] See para 7.16 above.

[29] See cl 8(2)(b) and 8(3)(b)(iii) of the draft Bill.

The defendant's propensity to be untruthful

11.32 In the majority of contested cases, whether the defendant is telling the truth or whether the defence is true is itself an issue in the case. It is possible that evidence of bad character could have some value in indicating whether the defendant is generally untruthful. We take the view, however, that the defendant's general propensity to be untruthful is not a matter which it would be fair to allow the prosecution to assert as part of its case against the defendant. Where the defendant simply denies the truth of some or all of the prosecution's evidence in relation to the offence charged, and makes no attempt to attack anyone *else's* credibility, we think it virtually inconceivable that evidence of the defendant's general untruthfulness could ever have sufficient probative value to outweigh the risk of prejudice. Rather than relying on courts to find that such evidence in fact fails to meet the requirements of the incriminatory exception in any case where it is tendered, we have decided that such evidence should not even be *eligible* for admission under this exception.

11.33 We believe that evidence of a defendant's propensity to be untruthful should be admissible in certain limited circumstances, but only if certain further conditions are satisfied *in addition* to those required by the incriminatory exception. For simplicity we treat these further conditions as representing a separate "credibility" exception, which we explain in Part XII below. Thus, where the evidence has probative value *only* in showing that the defendant has a propensity to be untruthful, leave may not be given unless the requirements of the credibility exception are satisfied.

The credibility of a defence

11.34 Sometimes the prosecution will seek to argue that the defendant's explanation is so similar to one advanced by the defendant on a previous occasion that it is unlikely to be true. For example, in *Reid*[30] the defendant, charged with robbing a mini-cab driver at knife-point, claimed that he had entered the cab only after the robbery had taken place – which was almost identical to a defence which he had earlier raised, unsuccessfully, to a similar charge of robbery. The similarity of the defence would, in that case, still have been probative even if it had previously been successful.

11.35 In that case the similar defences were unusual, and their similarity was therefore probative in itself, but if a defence is a common one, then repetition of it is not very significant. There is usually a limited range of defences available to most criminal charges, and it has therefore been argued that a court should not place too much weight on the fact that the accused has used a similar general defence (such as self-defence) in the past.[31]

11.36 In the consultation paper, we expressed the provisional view that where a defendant has previously put forward substantially the same, unusual defence, that

---

[30] [1989] Crim LR 719.

[31] R Munday, "The Paradox of Cross-Examination to Credit – Simply Too Close for Comfort" [1994] CLJ 303, 315-316.

fact may be relevant to his or her credibility.[32] This view was largely supported on consultation.[33] Evidence of other misconduct might have substantial probative value on the credibility of the defence that is being advanced, as held by Gage J:

> Similarities of defences which have been rejected by juries on previous occasions, for example false alibis or the defence that the incriminating substance has been planted and whether or not the accused pleaded guilty or was disbelieved having given evidence on oath, may be a legitimate matter for questions. These matters do not show a disposition to commit the offence in question; but they are clearly relevant to credibility.[34]

11.37 There is, however, a distinction between the credibility of the *defendant* and that of the *defence*. Where the defendant is putting forward a defence which would be persuasive if she had not run it before, the fact that she has run it before goes to whether her defence in these proceedings is truthful, not to whether she is generally disposed to be untruthful. The point can be illustrated by supposing that Reid had been acquitted of the first robbery. On that hypothesis, his previous reliance on a defence which had on that occasion been successful would not in itself suggest that he had a propensity to lie; and in this respect it would make no difference that he was now relying on the same defence again. What the similarity between the two defences *would* suggest, however, is that on the second occasion the defence was unlikely to be true. Under our recommendations, therefore, the fact that Reid had run the same defence before would be eligible for admission under the incriminatory exception, if it satisfied the requirements of that exception. The only evidence that is ineligible for admission under the incriminatory exception, and admissible instead under the credibility exception, is evidence going to the defendant's *propensity* to be untruthful – *not* evidence which goes directly to the central issue of whether the defendant's version of events is in fact true or false.

The additional value of the evidence

11.38 Evidence might have substantial probative value in relation to a central issue in a case if taken on its own, but its value might be considerably reduced if there has already been, or it is clear that there will be, other, less prejudicial, evidence to prove the fact. We therefore think that the court should also have regard to what the evidence in question adds to the other evidence in the case.[35]

11.39 We can see no reason for any artificial limit to be included prescribing that evidence of bad character going to a matter in issue must be adduced as part of the prosecution's case in chief. It may be that issues arise later in the case, possibly

---

[32] Para 6.73.

[33] Sixteen respondents addressed this provisional view. Thirteen agreed, (although two added caveats), and one substantially endorsed it. One respondent thought that we had understated the case, but one would state the proposition more narrowly, and would agree "only were the description 'unusual' to be narrowly interpreted so that it meant, in effect, 'peculiar'."

[34] In a judgment prepared by Stuart-Smith LJ, in *McLeod* [1994] 1 WLR 1500, 1512H–1513A.

[35] See cl 8(3)(b)(i) and (ii) of the draft Bill.

as a result of evidence elicited or adduced by the defendant, which alter the probative value of evidence of the defendant's bad character. The essence of the test should be the relationship between the probative value of the bad character evidence and the risk of prejudice.

Statutory guidance

11.40 We have said at paragraph 5.3 above that the test to be applied by the court should be capable of being applied predictably and consistently but be sufficiently flexible to cater for the infinite variety of factual situations which will occur. We believe this is best achieved by a test which leaves a court some room for individual judgment, while guiding that judgment on the matters to be borne in mind.

Provisional proposals on statutory guidelines

11.41 As part of our preferred option in the consultation paper we proposed that the court be required to take certain factors into accounts, and we proposed that they should include

    (i)   in the case of the evidence's probative value,

        (A)   the extent (if any) to which the evidence tends to suggest that the defendant has a *propensity* to act in the manner alleged;

        (B)   any *similarities* between the facts revealed by the evidence and those now alleged;

        (C)   the extent to which any such similarities may reasonably be attributed to coincidence; and

        (D)   any *dis*similarities between the facts revealed by the evidence and those now alleged; and

    (ii)   in the case of the evidence's likely prejudicial effect,

        (A)   the risk of the fact-finders attaching undue significance to the evidence in question in determining whether the defendant is guilty as charged; and

        (B)   the risk of their convicting the defendant on the basis of his or her conduct on some other occasion or occasions, rather than because they are satisfied that he or she is guilty as charged.[36]

11.42 One of our main criticisms of the test in *DPP v P* was, and still is, that it does not give sufficient guidance to courts on how to apply the test that it prescribes. We therefore proposed an approach based on structured guidelines. Three respondents supported it on the basis that it will promote greater consistency as between different judges and will ensure that all the various factors are taken into account. Three others were apprehensive about the proposal because of the perceived risk that adopting a "structured discretion" would generate a large number of appeals based on the precise meaning of the words used. Three

---

[36] Paras 10.79 and 10.80 and provisional proposal 17 of the consultation paper.

respondents did not favour the guideline approach and argued that it is essential that, in the context of similar fact evidence, maximum flexibility is retained. For example, Ian Kennedy J said that

> the variety of points which call for consideration in similar fact cases ... is so wide that no structure could hope to highlight all of them, and the longer the list the more easy it is to argue that Parliament can not have given much weight to the unlisted point.

11.43 The argument *for* the guidelines is one of accessibility: that it is desirable for all parties and the court to know what features of evidence are pertinent to the question of admissibility. The danger is said to be that if it is spelt out exactly what the court ought to have been taking account of, then the defence have ammunition to appeal if the court failed to mention relevant factors. Of course, if the defence are right and the court not only failed to mention them but failed to take them into account, there can be no objection to the defence appealing against the ruling. The real fear is of encouraging unmeritorious appeals. One might argue that this should be met by training magistrates and judges to give reasons for their decisions.

11.44 Guidelines are not a panacea: reaching the decision about whether it is fair to admit potentially prejudicial evidence is an intrinsically difficult task, and will always require the careful exercise of judgment. But we do not accept that guidelines would be useless or, worse, a positive nuisance to those performing this balancing exercise. We note that the NZLC has recommended the following draft clause:

> *Propensity evidence offered by prosecution about defendants*
>
> 45(3) When assessing the probative value of propensity evidence, the judge may consider, among other matters, the following:
>
> (a) the frequency with which the acts or omissions which are the subject of the evidence have occurred;
>
> (b) the connection in time between the acts or omissions which are the subject of the evidence and the acts or omissions which constitute the offence for which the defendant is being tried;
>
> (c) the extent of the similarity between the acts or omissions which are the subject of the evidence and the acts or omissions which constitute the offence for which the defendant is being tried;
>
> (d) the number of persons making allegations against the defendant that are the same as or similar to that which is the subject of the offence for which the defendant is being tried and whether those allegations may be the result of collusion or suggestibility;
>
> (e) the extent to which the acts or omissions which are the subject of the evidence and the acts or omissions which

constitute the offence for which the defendant is being tried are unusual.[37]

11.45 We are still of the view that structured guidelines on how to apply the test are conducive to comprehensible and consistent application of the requisite test, and we recommend that the legislation set out factors for the court to take into account.[38]

THE RECOMMENDATION: EVIDENCE OF SUBSTANTIAL PROBATIVE VALUE

11.46 **We recommend that leave may be given to the prosecution to adduce evidence of the bad character of a defendant if**

 (1) the evidence has substantial probative value in relation to a matter in issue (other than whether the defendant has a propensity to be untruthful) which is itself of substantial importance in the context of the case as a whole, and

 (2) the interests of justice require it to be admissible, even taking account of its potentially prejudicial effect.[39]

11.47 We now address three special cases where evidence of bad character may be relevant to the case against the defendant.

THE THEFT ACT 1968, SECTION 27(3)

11.48 Section 27(3) of the Theft Act 1968 permits the prosecution to adduce in chief evidence of criminal disposition, in the form of evidence of prior possession of stolen goods (section 27(3)(a)) or previous convictions (section 27(3)(b)) in order to prove that the defendant knew or believed the goods to be stolen.[40]

The defects of the current law and the proposals in the consultation paper

11.49 We have set out the problems in this subsection at paragraphs 4.17 – 4.23 above.

11.50 In the consultation paper, we considered the possibility of proposing that evidence of previous convictions should be admissible in handling cases where the accused admits the conduct alleged, but denies criminal knowledge. This option was proposed by the CLRC in its Evidence Report,[41] and was adopted by the Royal Commission.[42] It has one striking advantage over the existing provision in that it enables the prosecution to rely only on previous *convictions*, whereas paragraph (a) permits evidence of the mere fact that the defendant has had stolen goods in his or her possession, albeit without knowledge or belief that they were stolen.

---

[37] NZLC, *Evidence: Reform of the Law* (1999) Report 55.

[38] See para 7.19 above.

[39] This recommendation is given effect by cl 8 of the draft Bill.

[40] The case law on this provision is described at paras 2.27 – 2.30 above.

[41] Para 92.

[42] Report of the Royal Commission, ch 8 para 31, and Recommendation 192.

11.51 However, we suspected that if this proposal were implemented, its effect could be easily avoided by disputing some other ingredient of the offence. For example, if it were disputed that the goods in question were stolen, it would not be possible to invoke the proposed rule as there would be an outstanding issue in the case other than knowledge. We had little doubt that this would seriously undermine the usefulness of this option, and we rejected it in the consultation paper.[43]

11.52 We provisionally proposed that section 27(3) be repealed, and that handling cases be dealt with under the same rules as other cases.[44] There are many other instances where the mental element of an offence may be difficult to prove, and previous misconduct might be of assistance – though this may be less of a problem now that inferences can be drawn from a defendant's failure to give evidence[45] – and we see no reason to single out one such offence for special treatment. Evidence of previous misconduct is not necessarily more probative, or less prejudicial, in the case of handling than in any other case. We did not think that any special rule for handling cases was needed or justified.

The response on consultation

11.53 Thirty-three respondents addressed this proposal explicitly. Of those, 27 respondents were in favour of the provisional conclusion and three were against. Two respondents favoured the second option, and one thought the provision should remain as it is on the basis that it "does little, if any, harm and sometimes may do some good". One of the three who were against the proposal conceded that if our other proposals were to be implemented, section 27(3) would become otiose. One respondent thought the provision should be amended, so that such evidence could only be used in rebuttal.

11.54 Our view, that the provision is unnecessary under the current law, and would continue to be so following our recommendations for incriminatory evidence, was fortified by the views of respondents. The most common argument given in support of our proposal was that the section is very rarely used. The Criminal Bar Association commented that "if the prosecution does not have a sufficient case without resorting to this provision, then the general thinking is that the prosecution ought to fail".

11.55 As no strong arguments have been put forward which cause us to change our view from that in the consultation paper, **we recommend that section 27(3) of the Theft Act 1968 should be repealed.**[46]

THE OFFICIAL SECRETS ACT 1911, SECTION 1(2)

11.56 Section 1(2) of the Official Secrets Act 1911 allows the accused's purpose (an element of the offence) to be proved by reference to his or her "known character

---

[43] Provisional proposal 43(2). Paras 14.11 – 14.12.

[44] Provisional proposal 44. Para 14.13.

[45] Criminal Justice and Public Order Act 1994, s 35. See para 4.40 above.

[46] See cl 20(3)(b) of the draft Bill.

as proved".[47] In the consultation paper we invited views as to whether this provision should be repealed or amended.[48] Eighteen respondents expressed a view on this proposal, eight thinking it should be repealed, and eight thinking it should not be changed.[49]

11.57 The main argument in favour of repeal was that the provision is unfair to the accused. Some respondents suggested that evidence introduced under this provision should be required to meet a specific standard of probative value before it is admitted. Those who opposed change pointed to the unusual nature of the offence and the circumstances in which it arises, argued that "the difficulty of proving this offence requires this special provision", or referred to the fact that the Attorney General's consent is required as an important safeguard against its abuse.

11.58 We have taken account of the views of experienced respondents that this is an offence with unique difficulties for the prosecution, given that the subject matter may inhibit the calling of certain types of evidence. The character of the accused is not an element of the offence charged. It is merely one route by which one element, namely purpose, may be proved.

11.59 It is not for us, dealing as we are with matters of evidence, to address the substantive question whether, as a matter of policy, the purpose of a person charged under the Official Secrets Act should be capable of being proved by reference solely to character. It is, however, within our remit to consider how, and by reference to what mechanisms and tests, such evidence may be admitted given that the explicit terms of the section require the person's character to be "proved". There is nothing in section 1(2) which is inimical to the application of the principles we have identified as appropriate to determining when evidence of bad character may be admitted.

11.60 The statutory provisions in the draft Bill (which set limits on how certain matters of character may be proved) will apply where the prosecution seeks to prove a person's known character under section 1(2). An application to admit such evidence would be made under clause 8 and the evidence would only be admitted if it were of substantial probative value, and the interests of justice required it to be admissible, taking account of the risk of prejudice.

11.61 **We recommend that the admissibility of evidence of the defendant's bad character pursuant to section 1(2) of the Official Secrets Act 1911 should be determined by the above rules.**

---

[47] See para 2.31 above.

[48] Provisional proposal 42, para 14.3.

[49] One advised amendment, rather than repeal, and one collective response was divided on the matter.

THE EFFECT OF AN EARLIER ACQUITTAL

11.62 The law as it stood at the time of the consultation paper had the effect that, no matter how probative evidence of previous alleged offences might be in relation to a new prosecution, if the defendant had previously been acquitted of them, no evidence could be adduced of them.[50] We did not explore this issue in the consultation paper, but simply proposed no change. We did, however, explore this issue in depth in our double jeopardy consultation paper, and proposed that the law should be changed.[51] This is no longer held to be the law in consequence of a decision of the House of Lords last year in a case where evidence of previous acquittals was admitted under the "similar fact" rubric.[52] The result of that decision is to effect the change which we had thought was required: there is now no special rule of inadmissibility for evidence of previous offences of which the defendant has been acquitted.[53] This effect, which would apply to all the exceptions we recommend but would be particularly applicable to the incriminatory exception, is preserved by the terms of the draft Bill appended to this Report. The defence would still be able to apply to have the evidence excluded under section 78(1) of PACE.

---

[50] The rule in *Sambasivam v Public Prosecutor, Federation of Malaya* [1950] AC 458.

[51] See Double Jeopardy (1999) Consultation Paper No 156, Part VIII and provisional proposal 24.

[52] *Z* [2000] 2 AC 483.

[53] We therefore did not make any recommendation for abolition of the *Sambasivam* rule in Double Jeopardy and Prosecution Appeals (2001) Law Com No 267 paras 2.22 – 2.28.

PART XII
THE CREDIBILITY EXCEPTION

INTRODUCTION

12.1 In Part XI we explained when leave may be given under the incriminatory exception for evidence of the defendant's bad character which is of substantial probative value in relation to a matter in issue. We noted that evidence which is relevant to a matter in issue only by virtue of its relevance to the defendant's credibility may *not* be admitted under that exception. This Part explains when evidence going to the defendant's credibility might become admissible.

12.2 We have recommended that evidence going only to the defendant's credibility should not be admissible merely because the court thinks that its probative value outweighs the risk of prejudice. We nevertheless believe that in certain limited circumstances the interests of justice may require the admission of such evidence. In many cases, the fact-finders are presented with competing accounts and their task is to decide who to believe. In some cases the defendant will seek to support his or her case by obtaining leave to adduce evidence outside the central facts which shows that another person has a general propensity to be untruthful. If there is evidence available about the defendant which shows that he or she also has a propensity to be untruthful, our view is that, in those circumstances it would be misleading if the fact-finders were not provided with that information as well. It may, therefore, be fair for evidence of the defendant's propensity to be untruthful to be admitted.[1] We now explain when evidence should be admissible on the issue of the defendant's credibility. At the end of this Part (paragraphs 12.22 – 12.24) we explain what kinds of attacks by the defendant will *not* trigger this exception.

THE RECOMMENDATION

The defendant will have obtained leave to attack the other's character

12.3 If the defendant wishes to attack another person's character by adducing evidence, or by eliciting evidence in cross-examination, of another's bad character falling outside the central set of facts then leave must be obtained by the defendant pursuant to clause 5. Leave will only be given if that evidence is of substantial probative value.[2] We anticipate that this kind of attack, in turn potentially triggering a cross-application by the prosecution to adduce evidence of the defendant's character, ought to occur less frequently than it does now. To mount such an attack, the defendant's advocate would have to show that the person's history of truthfulness or character generally was *substantially* relevant to the

---

[1] As recommended by Sir John Nutting QC in his response, "Once a ruling has been obtained the witness can be cross-examined as to his credit. If that is done the defendant loses the shield and will be vulnerable to cross-examination on the same basis."

[2] See Part IX above.

likelihood that he or she was lying in the case in hand, and therefore to a fact in issue.

12.4 A defendant need not testify personally in order to make an attack on the general credibility of another person. An attack is also made if evidence is given of an attack made by the defendant out of court, on an occasion when he or she has been cautioned. An example would be where the defendant, when interviewed by the police, says of the principal prosecution witness, "You can't believe a word he says, given his record" and that part of the interview is evidence in the case.

12.5 One of the advantages of our recommendations requiring leave for the introduction by the defendant of evidence of a person's bad character outside the central set of facts[3] is that they ensure the court is clear about the *purpose* of the defendant's proposed attack on the other person. Thus any application by the prosecution for leave to adduce the defendant's character on the basis of credibility may be judged by reference to the purpose, nature, extent and effectiveness of the defendant's attack. In that case only evidence of the defendant's character which relates to it will be admitted. Further, in the Crown Court, requiring the defendant to obtain leave gives the judge the opportunity before matters have gone too far to form a preliminary view whether permitting the attack might in turn trigger a successful application by the prosecution to adduce evidence of the defendant's character. The judge can then give an appropriate warning to the defence of the risk of pursuing the application in good time for them to consider it out of hearing of the jury so that if, on reflection, they think better of pursuing the application they may withdraw in good order and without embarrassment before the jury.

12.6 Where, therefore, the defendant makes an attack on a person's character on matters which fall outside the central set of facts and the effect of that attack is to suggest or support a suggestion that the person has a propensity to be untruthful, then the question arises whether evidence which shows a similar propensity in the defendant should itself be admissible.

The comparison

12.7 If the defendant's own credibility is in issue and there is evidence available which tends to show he or she also has a propensity to be untruthful, it could be misleading if that information were kept from the fact-finders. One of the guiding principles we have set out is that fact-finders should not be unnecessarily misled.[4]

The test of enhanced relevance

12.8 In accordance with our principle that evidence of bad character which goes outside the central set of facts must have enhanced relevance, so in these circumstances, the evidence which, it is said, shows the defendant has a general propensity to be untruthful must have substantial probative value on that issue.

---

[3] See paras 8.26 and 8.31 above.

[4] See para 5.9 above.

The interests of justice test

12.9 Wherever evidence of a defendant's bad character is tendered by the prosecution our scheme requires the court to take account of the risk of prejudice in deciding whether to admit it. Therefore, even where the bad character evidence in question has substantial value, and without it the fact-finders would have an inaccurate impression of the defendant's credibility as compared with the non-defendant's credibility, the overriding requirement is that the interests of justice require the admission of the evidence, having taken account of the risk of prejudice.

12.10 In making that judgment, the court must have regard to certain specific factors designed to limit the introduction of evidence on a tit-for-tat basis to those cases where it is truly required. The first is the extent to which the evidence sought to be adduced has probative value on the issue of the defendant's propensity to be untruthful. The second is the need to avoid an inaccurate impression of relative truthfulness in the context of the case as a whole. The third is whether the defendant's propensity to be untruthful may be shown by other evidence in the case.

12.11 The court is not, in this connection, concerned with bad character in any respect other than the relevance of the history of the defendant to his propensity to tell the truth. As Sir John Nutting QC put it:

> If the motive for putting to the witness his previous convictions is limited to an attack on his credit, permission should be sought from the Judge in advance so that a proper analysis can be made of what aspects of the witness's record relate to his credit. The most obvious examples are lies on oath in previous trials and convictions for dishonesty.

12.12 This should avoid the kind of unfairness that arose in S^5 where past convictions which had no obvious relevance to credibility were admitted.

12.13 **We recommend that leave may be given to the prosecution to adduce evidence of the bad character of a defendant which is relevant only to whether the defendant has a propensity to be untruthful if**

   (1) **the evidence has substantial probative value in showing that the defendant has such a propensity,**

   (2) **the defendant has suggested that another person has such a propensity,**

   (3) **the evidence adduced in support of that suggestion does not have to do with the offence charged, and is not evidence of misconduct in connection with the investigation or prosecution of that offence,**

   (4) **without the evidence of the defendant's bad character the fact-finders would get a misleading impression of the defendant's**

---

[5] See para 4.50 above.

> **propensity to be untruthful in comparison with that of the other person, and**
>
> **(5) the interests of justice require the evidence to be admissible, even taking account of its potentially prejudicial effect.**

12.14 This recommendation is reflected in clause 9. Leave may only be sought under this clause by the prosecution (subsection (8)).[6] If a co-defendant wishes to attack an accused's general credibility that would have to be done, if at all, under clause 11, as described in Part XIV.

> *D is charged with conspiracy to defraud. His advocate obtains leave to cross-examine one of the prosecution witnesses on her multiple convictions for theft, on the basis that they show she is generally untruthful. D can then expect his own conviction for perjury to be adduced by the prosecution under the credibility exception.*

12.15 As with the incriminatory exception, we believe it is desirable for the courts to be given guidance in applying this exception.[7] They will be particularly apposite on the issue whether the interests of justice require the evidence to be admissible. The draft Bill makes detailed provision in subsection (7) of clause 9.

12.16 The court should thus take into account the nature and number of the events to which the defendant's attack relates, and of those to which the evidence which the prosecution wishes to adduce in response relates.

12.17 Certain of the factors are tailor-made for this exception. Paragraph (c) requires the court to consider how important the defendant's propensity to be untruthful and the other person's propensity to be untruthful are, in the context of the case as a whole.

12.18 Paragraph (d) requires the court particularly to have regard to the question whether, although the defence advocate might have asked a witness questions which were clearly intended to elicit answers which would have been damaging to the witness's general credibility, those answers were in fact given. For example, the defendant might be given leave to put to the witness that she had been summarily dismissed from a job for misconduct involving the spreading of malicious and untrue rumours but which had not resulted in criminal proceedings. The witness might not agree but might assert that she had resigned to take up better paid employment. In that event, paragraph (d) requires the court to take into account the fact that the questions have not revealed any evidence of a tendency in the witness to be untruthful. The court might conclude that in view of her denials, the attack on her turned out to have little of substance in it. Alternatively, it might

---

[6] A simple false claim of good character by a defendant about his or her own propensity to tell the truth on oath might prompt the prosecution to seek leave to admit evidence showing that the defendant does have a general tendency to lie, but this will be under cl 10. See Part XIII below on corrective evidence.

[7] See para 7.19 above.

conclude that, even though the advocate did not obtain the answers he wanted, the witness's denials were so unconvincing that the fact-finders would still be likely to get an inaccurate impression of the defendant's propensity to be untruthful as compared with the witness's propensity to tell lies.

12.19 Paragraph (e) requires the court to assess how inaccurate the impression the fact-finders would have of the defendant's propensity to be untruthful in comparison with the other person's. Where a conviction is spent, paragraph (f) directs the court to take that fact into account.

12.20 Paragraph (g) requires the court to consider the overall impact of allowing the prosecution to ask such questions on the course of the trial: that is whether admitting the evidence would run the risk of confusing or misleading the fact-finders or would unduly prolong the proceedings.

12.21 In the Crown Court the judge may advise the jury on how they are to approach evidence admitted under this exception. Clearly, the *purpose* of any such evidence is to shed light on the defendant's propensity to tell the truth, and a judge would probably remind the jury of that. It may be that, in cases where the evidence also shows that the defendant has previously done the same kind of thing it will also be appropriate for the judge to explain why it is not being put forward for that purpose and to remind the jury they should not place undue weight on it. We think this approach is more realistic than the direction required by the current law, which is to the effect that the past behaviour is irrelevant to the question of whether the defendant committed the offence and directing the jury to ignore it for that purpose.

ATTACKS WHICH DO NOT RELATE TO THE PERSON'S PROPENSITY TO TELL THE TRUTH

12.22 An advocate may try to demonstrate that a person whose evidence is admitted is lying in the instant case in various ways and for different purposes. He or she may be cross-examined on, or the defendant may adduce evidence bearing on

(1) the possibility that the person is biased because there is a history of animosity between that person and the defendant;

(2) the possibility that that person is the real culprit; or

(3) by attacking the person's reputation for truthfulness, which may amount to a full attack on the person's character.[8]

12.23 Evidence of the person's bad character on occasions other than covered by the central set of facts may bear on any of these matters or for purposes other than propensity to tell the truth. The exception described in this Part covers only the third. If the defendant adduces evidence of another's bad character for some other reason, that might render the defendant's own character admissible under the incriminatory exception (clause 8) but it would not do so under the credibility exception.

---

[8] See A Zuckerman, *The Principles of Criminal Evidence* (1989) pp 247–248.

12.24 For example, if the advocate wishes to persuade the fact-finders that the witness is the real culprit, he or she may refer to previous convictions of the witness which indicate that he or she is disposed to commit, or has a history of committing, the kind of offence with which the defendant is charged. In such a case, if the defendant has a similar history, that may, by reason of the defence pursued attain increased probative value so as to become potentially admissible under the incriminatory exception. We thought the point was well put by Sir John Nutting QC:

> I add this thought. The test of what the motive is in putting the record to the witness should not be the only test. If there is a sensible possibility that the Jury will regard the introduction of the witness record as indicative of propensity, the defendant should lose the shield in a similar fashion whatever the motive for introducing the evidence.

PART XIII
THE CORRECTIVE EXCEPTION

13.1 The essence of the exception recommended in this Part is to allow evidence of a defendant's bad character to be adduced for its *corrective* value. The fact-finders should not be left with a misleading impression of the defendant's character.[1] This exception covers similar ground to that of the "good character" exception under the present law.[2]

13.2 In the consultation paper we made the following criticisms of the existing good character exception. First, behind the present law lies the doctrine that character is indivisible, which is not always a useful guide to whether evidence of bad character should be admitted. We discuss this concept in detail at paragraphs 13.22 – 13.28 below. Second, good character is treated as bearing both on a person's propensities and on truthfulness, whereas, inconsistently, evidence of bad character which is admitted to contradict a claim of good character goes only to credibility. Third, it is presently unclear what kinds of assertions will trigger the loss of the shield.[3] Fourth, a person might falsely claim good character through his or her dress or conduct, but non-verbal assertions fall outside the present exception. Fifth and finally, an anomaly may arise under the present law where the defendant seeks to suggest a favourable contrast with other possible culprits. If those others are prosecution witnesses in the defendant's trial, such a suggestion will amount to an "imputation" and the defendant will lose the shield.[4] If they are not witnesses against the defendant, the suggestion may be made without the loss of the shield. The rationale is supposedly that the defendant is challenging the witnesses' credibility and therefore the defendant's own bad character should be admissible. The reality is that the imputation is about a propensity to commit the offence, not directly about the witnesses' credibility at all. Under our recommendations, if a defendant made this kind of imputation, it might render his or her bad character admissible under the incriminatory exception, as we explain at paragraphs 13.51– 13.52 below.

---

[1] Stephen Seabrooke argued persuasively that the correction of a false impression is the true purpose of section 1(f)(ii): "Closing the Credibility Gap: A New Approach to section 1(f)(ii) of the Criminal Evidence Act 1898" [1987] Crim LR 231.

[2] The first limb of s 1(f)(ii) of the 1898 Act. It is described briefly at paras 2.53 – 2.61 above.

[3] Eg, it is not clear from the case law whether the section encompasses the mere repetition in court of words claiming a good character uttered upon arrest: *Solomon* (1909) 2 Cr App R 80. Nor is it clear whether a defendant asserts good character by claiming (truthfully) to be, eg, a solicitor or church warden. It has been held that evidence of good character has been given where the defendant had claimed to have been earning an honest living for a considerable time (*Powell* [1985] 1 WLR 1364), or to have performed kind or honest deeds on a previous occasion (*Samuel* (1956) 40 Cr App R 8).

[4] Under the second limb of s 1(f)(ii). See para 2.64 above.

WHEN A DEFENDANT IS RESPONSIBLE FOR THE MISLEADING IMPRESSION

13.3 In order to lose the protection of the presumption preventing prejudicial character evidence being adduced, the defendant must be responsible, directly or indirectly, for the misleading impression. This was our position in the consultation paper, as expressed in provisional proposal 28:

> the shield should be lost if the assertion of the defendant's good character is made
>
> (a) by the defendant in the course of his or her evidence in chief, or in re-examination;
>
> (b) by a witness for the defendant in the course of his or her evidence in chief, or in re-examination, unless it is made in response to a question which does not appear to the court to have been intended to elicit the assertion;
>
> (c) by the defendant or a witness for the defendant in cross-examination, unless it is a reasonable response to the question asked;
>
> (d) by a prosecution witness, a co-defendant or a witness for a co-defendant in cross-examination by or on behalf of the defendant, if it is made in response to a question which appears to the court to have been intended to elicit the assertion; or
>
> (e) in a hearsay statement adduced by or on behalf of the defendant.[5]

13.4 Twenty-four respondents addressed provisional proposal 28, or a paragraph thereof. Fifteen expressly agreed with the proposal, and three did so impliedly. Five had some reservations about the proposal or had additional comments to make.

13.5 None of the respondents would exclude any of the circumstances outlined in proposal 28. Only one respondent would extend the circumstances to include the situation where the defendant calls witnesses of fact who are of good character:

> It is not uncommon for a defendant of bad character to call as defence witnesses a string of people of impeccable character to convey the impression that, by association, he is one of them. The shield should also be forfeit in these circumstances.

13.6 We do not agree that a defendant whose factual witnesses are of good character should be taken to be making an assertion of his or her own good character by their mere presence. We doubt very much that fact-finders will be misled, especially if they hear of the witnesses' impeccable characters but nothing about the defendant's character.

---

[5] Para 11.39 of the consultation paper.

13.7 We remain of the view that it must be the defendant who, directly or indirectly, causes the misleading assertion to be put before the court. A defendant will be responsible within our recommendation if the assertion is made

- (1) by the defendant in the proceedings in the course of giving evidence, or through his or her representative;

- (2) in an assertion made out of court by the defendant after caution, and evidence of the assertion is before the court;

- (3) by a defence witness;

- (4) by any witness in cross-examination by the defendant, unless the question was not intended to produce the answer given; or

- (5) by anyone out of court, and the defendant adduces evidence of it.

13.8 Whether the defendant is responsible for an assertion is not the end of the matter; corrective evidence will only be admissible if the interests of justice so require. This enables the court to take all the circumstances in which the assertion was made into account. See paragraphs 13.29 – 13.36 below.

The non-testifying defendant

13.9 In some of the circumstances set out in paragraph 13.7 above the defendant may not have testified at all. This can arise under the present law, where a defence witness makes a false claim of good character on the defendant's behalf. In that situation, the prosecution can cross-examine the witness so as to show that the assertion is false or misleading and, if the witness does not admit it the prosecution can call evidence in rebuttal.[6]

13.10 In the consultation paper we discussed whether the prosecution ought to be permitted to correct a misleading impression created by the defendant *other than in cross-examination or in rebuttal*.[7] Such a situation might arise where the claim to good character is made in a hearsay statement, adduced by or on behalf of the defendant (as we proposed in the consultation paper) or where it is made by the defendant in an interview with the police which is put in by the defence or the prosecution (as we now recommend).

13.11 A false assertion of good character made by a defendant in the police interview will fall within the clause if it is admitted as part of the defence case or as part of the prosecution case. If it is the prosecution who are seeking to put the interview in for other evidential purposes, which is more usually the case, the false assertion may be edited out and the defence may request this. If the defence do not agree to its deletion, it seems fair that the court should have the option of allowing evidence which corrects the assertion. The prosecution might want to include a false assertion of good character made by the defendant in interview where, for example, it was impossible to edit it out without losing some other statement

---

[6] *Redd* [1923] 1 KB 104; see also *Waldman* (1934) 24 Cr App R 204.

[7] We sought respondents' views in proposal 31 (see para 11.48) and they were broadly supportive.

which they were entitled to put in. In those circumstances it would be surprising if the interests of justice required corrective bad character evidence to be admitted.

13.12 Where the prosecution knows, in advance of the presentation of the defence case, that a false assertion of good character will be made, there is no reason, in our view, why the prosecution should not be able to apply for leave to adduce the corrective evidence in chief.[8]

Implied and non-verbal assertions

13.13 In the consultation paper, we were concerned to address the *fact* that the fact-finders would be misled, not *how* they might be misled. We proposed that

> the statute should make it clear that an implied assertion of good character will result in the loss of the shield in circumstances where an express assertion would do so.[9]

13.14 Only three of the 30 respondents who addressed this view disagreed. Five of those who agreed had some reservations. One respondent stated that evidence of good character should only be admissible if highly relevant, and an implied assertion of good character cannot meet this standard of relevance. The question of admitting bad character to rebut an implied assertion would not therefore arise. We do not agree that an implied assertion can never be sufficiently relevant. We do think, however, that only bad character which is *substantially* relevant should be admissible to contradict an explicit or implied assertion. The other concerns expressed are relevant to assertions implied by non-verbal means as well as verbally, and we consider them when we address non-verbal assertions of good character in paragraphs 13.18 – 13.21 below.

13.15 We suspect that there may be cases in which it will be difficult to determine whether an assertion of good character has been made, but we do not think these difficulties are insuperable. (We note, for example, that the Magistrates' Association thought it perfectly feasible for magistrates to determine that an assertion had been made, whether implied or express.)

13.16 In the consultation paper we also proposed that where

(1) in the opinion of the court, a defendant's conduct in the proceedings is intended to give the impression that he or she possesses a specific attribute, and

(2) had the defendant expressly claimed to possess that attribute, he or she would have been regarded as implicitly asserting that he or she is of good character,

---

[8] There is, of course, a notice requirement. See para 17.3 below.

[9] Provisional proposal 26 and para 11.27 of the consultation paper. We noted that the CLRC proposed to apply the rule to the introduction of evidence "with a view to establishing directly or by implication that the accused is generally or in a particular respect a person of good disposition or reputation" (para 136 and cl 7(1)(a) of their draft Bill) and that the same approach has been adopted in the Evidence Act 1995 (Cth), s 110(2).

the defendant should be regarded as so asserting, and should therefore lose the shield.[10]

13.17 Thirty-seven respondents addressed this issue. Twenty-seven agreed with the provisional proposal, although some had slight reservations, and nine disagreed.

13.18 Respondents' concerns fell into two categories. They feared that a defendant might be taken to have made an assertion when none was intended. As one person wrote, "The need for the implication to be clearly established should be emphasised". Alternatively, they thought these two proposals unworkable, or even if workable, not worth the trouble they would entail.

13.19 An assertion about a person's character may be inferred from, for example, what he or she wears, such as where the defendant appears in court in clothing which implies that he or she holds a position of trust that would not normally be held by a person with a criminal record. It is therefore arguable that non-verbal assertions ought to be within the ambit of the section and that it is defective because it does not include such assertions. Thus if a defendant is to lose the shield if he tells the court he is a vicar he should nonetheless be liable to do so where he makes the same assertion in non-verbal form, such as by appearing in court a dog-collar.[11]

13.20 We are still of the view that it should make no difference whether the assertion is made explicitly, or implicitly, or non-verbally: if the policy is that the defendant is to lose the shield if he claims a good character he does not have, then he should do so if he implies the same fact. Whilst it may be rare that a defendant will convey a false impression by his or her conduct (including dress) during the proceedings, nonetheless, in a case where a court thinks it *is* just to treat a defendant as if he or she had made such an assertion, then the law should cater for that.

13.21 The paramount test for leave is whether the interests of justice *require* the corrective evidence to be admissible. The more doubt there is about whether an assertion was made at all, or whether it was intended, the less likely it becomes that the interests of justice will require it to be corrected.

THE CORRECTIVE EVIDENCE MUST HAVE SUBSTANTIAL VALUE

Divisibility of character

13.22 An assertion about a person's character may be about his or her character as a whole, or about a particular trait or traits. At common law, there is authority for the view that character is indivisible: an assertion about a particular aspect of a person's character can be rebutted by evidence about some other aspect.[12] One of

---

[10] Provisional proposal 27. See para 11.31.

[11] In the recent case of *Robinson* [2001] Crim LR 478, [2001] EWCA Crim 214, the trial judge held that the defendant was making an implied assertion of good character by waving a Bible around when giving evidence. As any defendant may take an oath on a holy book before giving evidence, it does not seem sensible to treat a defendant who brandishes that book around as making any further assertion about his or her character. This was the view of the Court of Appeal, with which we respectfully agree.

the main complaints about the first limb of section 1(f)(ii) was that the rule that character is indivisible can lead to injustice. Thus if a defendant is charged with an offence of assault, and claims always to have been honest, there is nothing in the subsection to prevent previous convictions for offences of violence being admitted. The defendant would have to rely on the court's discretion to keep those offences out. We were critical of this rule in the consultation paper, and provisionally proposed

> that the defendant should be open to cross-examination only on *that part* of his or her character or truthfulness about which an assertion of good character has been made.[13]

13.23 Thirty-two respondents addressed this proposal. Fifteen agreed with it. Two agreed that an element of divisibility should be introduced, but disagreed with the form of the proposal.[14] Thirteen disagreed with it, either expressly or by implication.[15]

13.24 There were three main arguments deployed against the proposal.[16] First, that it is unnecessary because the common law test of relevance applies so that irrelevant evidence is not admitted. One example was given of a prosecution for stealing in which "it would be irrelevant and therefore *inadmissible* that 20 years earlier the defendant had pleaded to an indecent assault. This point is not just a matter of discretion but of admissibility". The respondent is quite right that such a conviction would be logically irrelevant in such a case; few, if any, would disagree. The difficulties arise because agreement is not so easily reached in more mainstream cases. For example, in the consultation paper we expressed the provisional view that "behaviour not involving dishonesty is unlikely to be relevant to credibility".[17] Ten respondents disagreed with this view: five because they thought we had *over*stated the relevance of such behaviour to credibility, and five because they thought we had *under*stated it. By doing away with the common law rule that character is indivisible we intend to encourage advocates and courts to focus on the true relevance of the evidence which it is proposed to adduce.

13.25 The second criticism focused on the difficulty in practice of determining what is relevant. Five respondents said that our proposal 29 would not be practicable. The following response is typical:

---

[12] *Winfield* (1939) 27 Cr App R 139. See para 2.59 above.

[13] Provisional proposal 29 (emphasis in original). See paras 11.40 – 11.42.

[14] Respondents commented that bad character evidence to refute an assertion of good character should be limited to evidence going to credibility, and the fault with the current law was that it permitted bad character evidence going beyond credibility.

[15] In relation to many of our proposals, some respondents merely made a general statement of agreement with our proposals, without addressing the issue specifically, or said that where they did not mention a proposal specifically, it could be assumed they agreed with it.

[16] Four respondents thought it should be left to judicial discretion to disallow evidence which is "patently inappropriate". If previous misconduct is so irrelevant it should, in our view, be inadmissible as a matter of law, not as a matter of discretion.

[17] Provisional proposal 2(3).

> It is, in my view, entirely artificial to dissect good character into sections. If that were what reforms of the law were to require in this area it seems to me they would lead to endless argument and be difficult to apply.

13.26 The third criticism is linked to the second: limiting what counts as relevant would give defendants an unfair advantage, by allowing them to paint a misleading picture. For example, one person wrote,

> This wording could, inadvertently, provide an unscrupulous defendant with an advantage. "I would never do anything indecent/improper to a little child"; he has previous convictions for indecent assault on an adult. There are various other possibilities. There is a good argument for saying that a person's character cannot be rigidly "compartmentalised".

13.27 We acknowledge that dividing character into rigid classifications could lead to injustice and that it is not desirable for a statutory provision to dictate what propensity is relevant to another. It does not, however, seem to us that it would be so hard to determine what bad character evidence is relevant in the light of an assertion of good character in an individual case. To a certain extent, the defendant's claim sets the parameters, as one respondent (who supported the proposal) wrote:

> What is relevant must depend on the assertion made by the accused. If the assertion is specific, e.g. "I have never been in trouble with the law", a specific rebuttal would be to adduce evidence of the accused"s previous convictions. If, on the other hand, the accused makes a broad assertion, e.g. "I am a person of unimpeachable moral character", then a much broader rebuttal becomes relevant, dealing with virtually anything discreditable known about the accused, and including his reputation.

13.28 What we seek is on the one hand to get away from the position that obtains under the current law whereby "character" is seen as a whole, and on the other hand to give the court enough flexibility to allow evidence of previous misconduct to be given to contradict an assertion, even though it reveals a propensity which is not identical to the propensity which the defendant claims not to have. Thus our recommendations abandon the rule that character is indivisible, but do not prescribe what counts as relevant.[18] They do, however, in common with all the other categories of potentially admissible bad character evidence for which leave is required, prescribe an enhanced degree of relevance: bad character evidence is to be admissible only if it is of substantial relevance to that part of the defendant's character about which the magistrates or jury are likely to be misled. Thus bad character evidence cannot be admissible under the exception if it goes further than is necessary to correct the misleading impression, and so the whole of a person's character is not admissible merely because he or she has falsely asserted good character.

---

[18] In the Bill, cl 20(1) repeals the common law rules governing the admissibility of evidence of bad character.

THE INTERESTS OF JUSTICE TEST

13.29 The value of the evidence is only one side of the question for the court. The ultimate test should be whether the interests of justice *require* the admission of the evidence. In reaching a decision on admissibility, the court should take into account the factors which militate against the admission of the evidence, particularly the risk of prejudice.

Factors to take into account

13.30 A court should consider the following, when applying the interests of justice test:

(1) how much value the evidence has in correcting the false or misleading impression;

(2) what other evidence on the matter is available; and

(3) how important it is in the context of the case as a whole to prevent the false or misleading impression.[19]

13.31 In assessing the value of the evidence, we envisage that the court will consider the correspondence between the aspect of character for which the prosecution is seeking leave and the aspect of character about which the fact-finders might be misled, as well as matters generally concerning the quality of the evidence.

13.32 In applying the interests of justice test, the court must consider whether the false impression can be or has been corrected in some less prejudicial way.

13.33 The requirement that it is in the interests of justice for the corrective evidence to be admitted should be read in the context of the whole case, and the importance to the case of the impression created. If a defendant creates a particular impression as to his or her character, and the prosecution have evidence which incontrovertibly shows that impression to be false, in one sense this evidence does have substantial value in correcting the misleading impression. But it may be that the impression created by the defendant is itself of very limited relevance to the issues in the case; and, if so, evidence which serves only to correct that impression cannot have much value *in the context of the case as a whole.*

13.34 In addition to these matters, where the court is considering whether the two conditions are met, it must have regard to a number of factors. Those which address the nature and extent of the misleading impression which has triggered the application for leave are:

- the nature and degree of falsity or extent to which the fact-finders would be misled by the material sought to be corrected;

- by whom and in what circumstances the assertion was made, including the extent to which the defendant is personally responsible for the assertion;

---

[19] These factors appear at cl 10(4)(b)(i), (ii) and (iii) respectively of the draft Bill.

- and the effect on the conduct of the trial in terms of the time that would be spent hearing the corrective evidence and its distorting effect.

13.35 A court might take into account the circumstances in which the assertion was made in the following way. For example, where the assertion is made by a witness, whether that witness was called by the prosecution, the defendant or a co-defendant, any connection between the witness and the defendant, what the witness said, how misleading it was, and the weight which might be accorded to it, as well as how spontaneous it appeared to be. Another example might be where a defence witness gives an unsolicited (and false) eulogy in response to a question in cross-examination. In such a case the defendant will be prima facie responsible, but the court may decide that it would not, in the circumstances, be fair to admit corrective evidence.

> *Unknown to the witness, the court has already heard about some of the defendant's convictions. The court is content simply to ignore what the witness has said.*

> *The witness is the defendant's mother. The court decides not to place too much weight on what she says and does not allow the prosecution to prove he does not have the good character she claims for him.*

> *D has convictions for theft. His employer, who does not know this, speaks about D's trustworthiness. In such a case, the convictions may well be sufficiently relevant for leave to be given.*

13.36 A court could also consider whether the defendant has been unfairly caught out by the prosecution or a co-defendant in the course of cross-examination. Although a defendant will be held prima facie responsible for an assertion of good character which he or she makes when being cross-examined, if the court thinks the defendant has been tricked or unfairly led (possibly through incompetent questioning) into making a claim which is misleading and which triggers the exception, it may nevertheless refuse to allow the assertion to be corrected.

Practice in the magistrates' courts

13.37 Where the issue arises before magistrates there is a particular problem in that it may be thought inappropriate for magistrates to hear the details of evidence of previous convictions which they then rule inadmissible. Although magistrates may be confident that, although they have heard about the defendant's discreditable past in the course of entertaining an application, they can ignore it, the research does suggest to the contrary. In any event, the defendant might not be so easily convinced. In order to reduce this possibility, we propose a new procedural step. We recommend that magistrates make a ruling, in advance of being given the details of the evidence sought to be adduced, whether the assertion it is sought to correct is unimportant in the context of the case as a whole for it to be corrected. If they so rule then no evidence can fall within the provision in relation to that assertion. Subsection 10(9) provides for this new procedural step.

USE OF THE EVIDENCE

13.38 The direction a court should give for evidence admitted under the first limb of section 1(f)(ii) is that the evidence goes only to the defendant's credibility. In the consultation paper we noted that this direction may be illogical, and it may be unrealistic.

13.39 Where the defendant claims good character, he or she expects to benefit not just by being thought of as more likely to be truthful, but also by being thought of as less likely to commit the offence, whatever it is.[20] The direction on good character explicitly instructs juries to see "good character" as reflecting on the defendant in both these ways.[21] It is therefore illogical for bad character evidence admitted to counteract an assertion of good character to be treated as relevant only to the defendant's credibility. We set out our views on the rationality and usefulness of the direction given under the first limb of section 1(f)(ii) in provisional proposals 23 and 24:

> We believe
>
> (1) that it is unrealistic to distinguish between the use of previous convictions to rebut false claims of good character, and their use in assessing how truthful the rest of the defendant's testimony is likely to be; and
>
> (2) that, in some cases, it may also be unrealistic to distinguish between using the evidence of bad character to assess the likelihood that the defendant is telling the truth, and the likelihood that he or she committed the offence.[22]

13.40 Thirteen respondents addressed proposal 23 without distinguishing between 23(1) and 23(2). Twelve of those agreed with the beliefs expressed. Only one addressed 23(1) specifically and he disagreed with it. Ten addressed 23(2). Of these, six clearly agreed with it and one clearly disagreed. Disagreement with paragraph 23(2) can be inferred from a further four responses.

13.41 Provisional proposal 24 concerned the effectiveness of judicial directions:

> Our provisional view is that, since evidence of previous misconduct adduced to refute a false assertion of good character may in truth relate not only to credibility but also to propensity, judicial warnings that it relates only to credibility are of little, if any, use.[23]

---

[20] See para 11.11 of the consultation paper.

[21] *Vye* [1993] 1 WLR 471.

[22] Provisional proposal 23 and para 11.12 of the consultation paper.

[23] See paras 11.13 – 11.14.

13.42 Thirty-two respondents addressed this proposal, or made comments clearly applicable to it. Seventeen agreed with it, and twelve disagreed.

13.43 While it may be possible for a jury to comply with the standard direction in some cases, where for example the previous misconduct is not obviously similar to the offence charged, in those cases where the conduct is similar to that charged, following such a direction becomes very difficult. Some respondents warned of the admission of bad character evidence by the "back-door":

> What is important is that an assertion of good character should not become an automatically-opening back-door for the admission and improper use of otherwise inadmissible similar fact evidence or character evidence. On the other hand there will be cases in which the evidence is so strongly relevant that a judge should not direct the jury to use it simply on the issue of credibility.

13.44 We made the following proposal in the consultation paper:

> We provisionally propose that where the assertion of good character, and the evidence adduced to rebut that assertion, are directly relevant to the accused's propensities, the fact-finders should not be directed to treat the evidence as bearing solely on the accused's credibility.[24]

13.45 Thirty respondents addressed this issue, or made comments which are clearly applicable. A further three made comments which had indirect relevance to the issue. Twenty agreed with the provisional proposal, either expressly or impliedly. Seven disagreed with the provisional proposal.

13.46 We understand the concern that an exception could be used to admit evidence which is not admissible in chief against a defendant because it is too prejudicial, but which is then treated as going directly to the question of guilt. Our view is that the risk that the evidence might be thought to bear directly on the charge (because, for example, it is of similar behaviour to that charged) must be taken into account when deciding whether leave should be given, but if leave is given, it serves no purpose to tell a jury it is irrelevant to the question of guilt.

13.47 What a judge should do, in our view, is remind the jury of the purpose for which the evidence has been admitted, and, if appropriate, continue in the vein advised by Swinton Thomas LJ in his response: the jury must nevertheless be given a "clear direction that evidence in relation to previous convictions or misconduct does not prove guilt on the charge they are trying, but they must be cautious in their approach to that evidence, and must not place undue weight on it".[25]

THE RECOMMENDATIONS

13.48 **We recommend that leave may be given to the prosecution to adduce evidence of the bad character of a defendant if**

---

[24] Provisional proposal 30. See para 11.44.

[25] See paras 17.19 – 17.20 below.

> (1) **the defendant is responsible for an assertion (express or implied) which creates a false or misleading impression about the defendant,**
>
> (2) **the evidence has substantial probative value in correcting that impression, and**
>
> (3) **the interests of justice require it to be admissible, even taking account of its potentially prejudicial effect.**[26]

13.49 The circumstances in which we think a defendant should be prima facie "responsible" for an assertion are set out at paragraph 13.7 above.

13.50 **We recommend that, where the prosecution seeks to rely on this exception in summary proceedings, it should first indicate to the court that the impression created is false or misleading and that the prosecution has evidence to controvert it; the bench should then rule on whether the impression is important enough to need controverting; only if the bench so rules may the prosecution detail the nature of its corrective evidence, and proceed with the full application to introduce it.**[27]

WHERE THE DEFENDANT SETS UP A FALSE OR MISLEADING COMPARISON

13.51 Finally, we describe what the result might be where a defendant adduces or elicits evidence of *another's* character, such that the fact-finders are likely to be given a misleading impression of the defendant's character (or an aspect of it) when compared with the impression they have been given of that of the other person. This might occur where the defendant gives evidence that other possible culprits have previous convictions for offences similar to that charged. Where those other people do not give evidence, the shield presently remains intact.[28] We noted this anomaly of the current law in the consultation paper.[29]

13.52 Our Bill precludes this anomalous result: the appropriate exception is the incriminatory exception. Suppose, for example, that the defendant is charged with theft. The defence is that A, one of the prosecution witnesses, committed the theft. (For argument's sake, assume that the defendant's criminal history is not at this point sufficiently relevant for it to be admissible under the incriminatory exception.) If the defence were allowed[30] to adduce or elicit evidence of A's *other* misconduct, on the basis that it has substantial probative value in showing that A has a propensity to commit this sort of theft, the fact-finders would be likely to infer that A has a *greater* propensity to do so than the defendant does. If the defendant's history reveals a similar propensity, but it were not admitted, the fact-

---

[26] This recommendation is given effect by cl 10 of the draft Bill.

[27] See para 13.37 above.

[28] If they give evidence for the prosecution, the shield will be lost under the second limb of s 1(f)(ii).

[29] Para 11.20.

[30] Ie, have obtained leave under cl 5(1).

finders would be left with a misleading impression of the *comparative* propensities of A and the defendant. Were the case to take such a turn, it could well be argued that the defendant's history has, in that event gained a greater probative value than before. In that case it *might* well then have enough probative value to be admissible under the incriminatory exception (clause 8) even though it would not fall within clause 10 as there would be no misleading impression of the defendant's character.

PART XIV
THE CO-DEFENDANT EXCEPTION

INTRODUCTION

14.1 Evidence of a co-defendant's bad character may presently be adduced by two different routes, under the common law provisions and under section 1(f)(iii) of the 1898 Act. Under the common law, if the evidence of the bad character of a co-defendant is relevant to the defendant's defence it may be adduced. The reason for this is that a defendant should not be inhibited in the presentation of his or her defence. The test of relevance is strictly applied but there is no discretion to exclude the evidence.[1] Under statute, section 1(f)(iii) of the 1898 Act allows evidence of a co-defendant's bad character to be adduced *in cross-examination* if the co-defendant has given evidence against the defendant. That evidence is only admitted as relevant on the issue of the defendant's credibility and not on the issue of his or her propensity to commit the offence charged. If the case falls within the subsection the co-defendant has a right to cross-examine the defendant on his or her character. There is no discretion in the court to decline to admit such evidence.

14.2 In this Part, for clarity we shall refer to the defendant who gives evidence against his co-defendant as D1 (male) and the co-defendant as D2 (female). Typically this rule comes into play where two defendants run "cut-throat" defences, that is, each in their evidence blames the other for the offence or where, falling short of the full "cut-throat" defence, evidence is given by D1 which supports the prosecution case against D2 or undermines D2's defence. In either of these circumstances D2 has the right to cross-examine D1 on his bad character for the purpose of suggesting that D1's evidence should not be relied on.[2] The court has a discretion to order separate trials of the defendants to prevent the prejudice that might otherwise result.

14.3 The central problems with the present law are: that the court has no discretion to refuse to admit bad character evidence which may be of little probative value but significant prejudicial effect; the difficulty that fact-finders, magistrates and juries alike, inevitably experience in separating the evaluation of a defendant's truthfulness from that of the defendant's propensity to commit crimes; section 1(f)(iii), which only takes effect in cross-examination, may inhibit defendants from giving evidence, for fear of exposing themselves to cross-examination on their character; finally, it can produce an unbalanced and misleading picture to the fact-finders by revealing the bad character evidence of one defendant but not the other.[3]

---

[1] See para 2.40 above.

[2] Although see n 201 in Part II above.

[3] See paras 4.70 – 4.78 above.

OUR PROVISIONAL PROPOSALS

14.4 In the consultation paper we made several provisional proposals for reform of the admissibility of the bad character evidence of a co-defendant.

Bad character evidence adduced by a co-defendant

14.5 To address the problem of lack of discretion to refuse bad character evidence on the ground of its prejudicial effect, we sought views on the question whether one defendant should always be entitled to call or elicit evidence of previous misconduct by a co-defendant if it had some relevance, or whether the question of admissibility should require the balancing of the evidence's probative value against its likely prejudicial effect.[4]

Cross-examination of a co-defendant

14.6 We discussed seven possible options for the reform of cross-examination of a co-defendant. Six of them, which we provisionally rejected, were: (i) replicating the existing law; (ii) introducing an unstructured judicial discretion to permit cross-examination under section 1(f)(iii); (iii) repealing section 1(f)(iii) so neither defendant would lose the shield; (iv) introducing a rule that both defendants lose the shield if one attacks the other; (v) a presumption that evidence of D1's character may be admitted if he attacks D2 but a discretion to exclude this evidence; and (vi) a presumption against the lost of shield coupled with a discretion to admit evidence of bad character.[5]

14.7 We provisionally proposed our seventh option[6] – that, where D1, in the course of his evidence, or through his witness or representative, undermines the defence of D2 charged in the same proceedings,

(i) if the challenge to D2's account concerns her conduct in the incident in question, or in the investigation of it, the shield should not be lost; but

(ii) if this is not the case, any party to the proceedings, that is D2 or the prosecution or any other defendant, should be entitled to apply to the court for leave to adduce evidence of D1's character.

14.8 We provisionally proposed that once D1 had lost his shield in this manner, evidence of his bad character should only be admitted with the leave of the court. If D2 applied for leave we proposed a presumption in favour of leave unless it would be contrary to the interests of justice. Conversely if another party to the case applied for leave, the presumption should be against granting it unless it was in the interests of justice to do so.

14.9 In deciding whether to grant leave, we proposed a court should have regard, amongst any other relevant considerations, to

(1) the degree to which D2's defence had been undermined;

---

[4] At para 10.118 of the consultation paper.

[5] These are detailed in the consultation paper at paras 13.18 – 13.40.

[6] See paras 13.41 – 13.47 of the consultation paper.

(2) how unavoidable it was for D1 to undermine D2's defence;

(3) the nature, number and age of the matters of bad character which it is sought to adduce; and

(4) the relative characters of all the accused as they would appear to the fact-finders if the evidence of bad character were allowed.

14.10 We also provisionally proposed that where leave was given for one co-defendant to adduce evidence of the other's bad character, the fact-finders should be permitted to use that character evidence on the issue of guilt as well as on the issue of credibility, and that, in the Crown Court, the jury should be guided by the judge in assessing its probative value, as well as being warned about its potential for prejudice.[7]

14.11 This option would result in D1 only losing his shield if the evidence adduced or statement made against D2 did not concern the central facts of the case. This would enable D1 to put forward his defence freely without fearing cross-examination as to character. Where, however, D1 chooses to put in issue D2's character by raising matters *outside the central facts*, D1 would potentially expose his own previous bad character. The court would retain a structured discretion whether to give leave to adduce evidence of D1's character.

Attacks on a co-defendant by a defendant who does not testify

14.12 Under this option it was not necessary for D1 to have given evidence about D2 in order to trigger the entitlement to adduce evidence about his character, nor was it necessary for D1 to give evidence in order for the evidence of his character to be placed before the fact-finders.

THE VIEWS OF RESPONDENTS

A question of balance

14.13 Forty-one respondents addressed this issue, on which we had simply invited views.[8] Opinions were divided. Five were clear that there should be some balancing of probative value and prejudicial effect, and a further five thought that there should be a balancing test in some circumstances. Sixteen thought there should be no balancing test and a further three held that same view subject to certain conditions. Four respondents saw severance as the only solution. The remainder either argued that the current law involves an element of balancing, or submitted ambiguous or split responses.

14.14 Not all the respondents who supported a balancing test gave reasons for their support. Two respondents recognised that there was a strong argument against fettering the defendant's right to adduce relevant evidence, but argued that the interests of justice nonetheless demanded that a balancing exercise be carried out. One practitioners' organisation conceded that the basic rule should be that an

---

[7] See paras 13.51 – 13.53 of the consultation paper.

[8] See para 14.5 above and paras 10.115 – 10.118 of the consultation paper.

accused can adduce all evidence relevant to his or her defence, but argued that this could lead to injustice: not only by the wrongful conviction of D1, but also by the wrongful acquittal of D2. Another view was that the same standard of admissibility ought to apply to a co-defendant as to the prosecution.

14.15 Of the sixteen respondents who thought there should be no balancing test, seven respondents specifically argued that it would be unfair to fetter the defendant's right to adduce relevant evidence. The response of Professor McEwan was typical:

> ... there are more factors to balance than that of prejudice against probative value. It must be unfair to deprive the co-defendant of evidence relevant to his defence, whatever the effect on the defendant might be. Hence it seems that the current rule is the right one, that if a co-defendant wants to adduce evidence of previous misconduct by the defendant, the only test for admissibility is one of relevance.[9]

14.16 Another respondent commented that the balancing of probative value and prejudicial effect was an inappropriate consideration in assessing the position between defendants. A further six thought that the discretion to exclude evidence should be exercised only where the evidence was irrelevant, as is prescribed by the current law, although they did not base this specifically on an argument about fairness to the defendant.

Cross-examination of a co-defendant

14.17 Of the options we rejected the only one to attract significant comment (42 respondents) was that of retaining the current law. The vast majority of these respondents advocated change. But there was no real consensus about exactly what the problems, or their solutions, were.

14.18 The main argument for reform was that the current law is unfair to D1 who gives evidence against D2. The response from a practitioners' organisation, for example, said:

> We believe that the unfettered right of a co-accused to cross-examine under this subsection can lead to wholly disproportionate damage being done to the case of the accused whose character has been adduced.

14.19 Three respondents were concerned that the lack of discretion resulted in irrelevant or barely relevant evidence of bad character being adduced by D2. These respondents held differing views on whether this was because the issue of relevance was rarely raised with the judge or because judges were too willing to allow D1 to undermine D2's defence in the first place, since such evidence itself was often insufficiently relevant.

14.20 Those respondents who disagreed that reform was desirable thought that the introduction of an element of discretion would inhibit D2 in the presentation of

---

[9] Jenny McEwan "Law Commission Dodges the Nettles in Consultation Paper No. 141" [1997] Crim LR 93, 97.

her defence, arguing that it was only fair that, in the capacity of a witness, D1 should be cross-examined as to his previous convictions. A prominent practitioner said

> In the practical world of the hard fights in contested criminal cases with, in so very many instances, much hard lying taking place, it is improvident to put a premium upon the invention of cunning false stories giving rise to immunity from credit being properly tested.

14.21 However, this argument can be turned on its head and applied to D1. If D1 automatically loses the shield by undermining D2's, his defence might be equally inhibited. This point was endorsed by one judicial respondent.[10]

Our proposal

14.22 Thirty-five respondents addressed the option we had provisionally proposed in the consultation paper.[11] Twelve respondents agreed with the proposal. A further seven respondents had some reservations, but generally agreed with our proposal. Three respondents disagreed but suggested a scheme which was similar to that proposed.[12] Eight respondents did not agree with our proposal.

14.23 Most of those who agreed with our preferred option did so without further substantial comment. One respondent who agreed with the entire scheme of proposals in the consultation paper thought it was logical that the same test should be applied to the undermining of the co-accused. One academic stressed that

> Defendants should not generally be allowed to undermine the defence of a co-accused except where the challenge concerns the co-accused's conduct in the incident or investigation in question, in which case the shield would not be lost under the proposal.

A few other respondents agreed but had reservations about the rigidity of the proposal.

14.24 There were two main reasons for not agreeing with our proposals: dislike of the immunity afforded defendants who confine their attacks to the co-defendant's behaviour in the incident in question or the investigation, and dissatisfaction with the operation of the discretion.

14.25 The responses in favour of our proposals tended also to support the reasoning behind it. Respondents agreed that when putting forward a defence D1 should be able to challenge evidence concerning the incident in question, but that attacks on D2's character outside that parameter should open up the issue of D1's own credibility.

---

[10] The point was also referred to in the consultation paper: see paras 13.16 and 13.45.

[11] Provisional proposal 38. See para 13.46 in the consultation paper.

[12] All three thought that there should not be an immunity for defendants who confined their attacks to the co-accused's behaviour in the incident in question.

WHO SHOULD BE ABLE TO APPLY?

14.26 We proposed that *any* party to the proceedings ought to be entitled to apply to the court for leave to adduce evidence of D1's character.[13]

14.27 Three respondents addressed this issue and they all argued that the prosecution ought not to be able to adduce evidence of D1's character in these circumstances. All three believed that that the prosecution should not be able to take advantage of an exception aimed at allowing one defendant to cast doubt on the credibility of the other. We find this argument convincing. If the evidence would not have been sufficiently relevant to be adduced by the prosecution were the defendants tried separately, they should not be able to adduce the evidence merely because the defendant has undermined the co-defendant's defence. The rationale of the exception is that, because D1 has undermined D2's defence, D2 has a right to adduce evidence relevant to D1's credibility. This should not allow another co-defendant, D3, or the prosecution to adduce evidence in D2's stead where D2 has not sought to do so.

ATTACKS ON D2 BY D1 WHERE D1 DOES NOT TESTIFY

14.28 In the consultation paper we proposed that an application might be made to adduce evidence of D1's bad character on the ground that he had undermined the defence of D2, even though he had not given evidence, provided the nature of his defence was such as to put his own credibility in issue.[14] We concluded provisionally that the attack has a similar impact on the fact-finders whether or not it comes directly from D1. Whilst there is some logic in the traditional view that if the relevance of such bad character is to D1's credibility then if D1 does not give evidence, there is nothing to which the bad character evidence can be relevant, it was, and remains, our view that this understanding of credibility is too limited. The reality is that a defendant's credibility might be put in issue by out-of-court statements by the defendant or by the nature of the defence.[15]

14.29 Twenty-four respondents addressed this proposal. Seventeen agreed with our view. A further three agreed to a large extent. Only two disagreed with the proposal.[16] Most respondents who agreed did so without further comment. The only reason given for agreement was consistency with the proposals regarding prosecution witnesses. The respondents who agreed apparently accepted that the credibility of a non-testifying defendant may be put in issue.

14.30 The responses give strong support for our view that, as far as D2 is concerned, the effect on her defence is the same whether the attack comes directly or indirectly from D1. We maintain our view that D1's credibility may be brought into issue even though he does not testify. Thus evidence should be admissible through

---

[13] Para 13.46 of the consultation paper.

[14] See paras 13.48 – 13.50 of the consultation paper.

[15] The case for maintaining the traditional view of when credibility is in issue is set out at para 4.62, and our response, at para 4.65 above.

[16] One of these seemed to disagree only to a certain extent.

cross-examination of D1 or otherwise where D1 undermines D2's defence, whether in the course of his evidence, or through his representative or witness.

RELEVANCE OF BAD CHARACTER TO GUILT AS WELL AS CREDIBILITY

14.31 In the consultation paper we considered the use to which previous misconduct adduced under section 1(f)(iii) could be put.[17] The traditional justification for loss of the shield under section 1(f)(iii) is that a co-defendant should be able to "discredit someone who has given evidence against him".[18] However, where a comparative assessment is being made of the truthfulness of two defendants, it is difficult to distinguish guilt and credibility. Both factors are in issue where the person against whom the imputations are being made is on trial. We therefore proposed the abolition of the common law rule that, where evidence of an accused's bad character is admitted under section 1(f)(iii), it is directly relevant only to the accused's credibility.[19]

14.32 Thirty-two respondents addressed this issue, the majority of whom were strongly in favour of the provisional proposal. Twenty-five respondents thought that evidence admitted under section 1(f)(iii) should not be relevant only to credibility. Only two respondents disagreed with the proposal.

14.33 Four thought that the distinction between evidence relevant to guilt and evidence relevant to credibility was illogical, since evidence of previous misconduct must always be relevant to guilt. Seven thought that evidence might be relevant to guilt depending on the circumstances. One judicial respondent gave an example of scenario he had come across as a judge where two defendants were jointly charged with robbery. There was little evidence against D1 and rather more against D2. D1 had several previous convictions for robberies of a similar nature. D1's defence necessarily involved the imputation that D2, who was of good character, committed the offence rather than him. D1's previous convictions were, in consequence, revealed. The jury duly convicted D1 and acquitted D2. The only reason our respondent could put forward for this outcome was "that in the majority of cases the practical effect of previous misconduct has little or nothing to do with credibility and everything to do with propensity".

14.34 One of the respondents who disagreed with our proposal said that "the manner in which the defendant conducts his case should not call into question anything other than his credibility or the credibility of the defence case". The Crown Prosecution Service said that the conclusions reached in the consultation paper did a "disservice to juries", whom it felt were entirely capable of distinguishing questions such as "Is D1 telling the truth when he says that D2 did it?" from the question "Is D1 guilty?"

14.35 We can quite see that there is a distinction between saying that evidence is relevant only for the purpose of assessing credibility and not propensity. We also

---

[17] See paras 13.51 – 13.53.

[18] *Murdoch v Taylor* [1965] AC 574, 585D, *per* Lord Morris of Borth-y-Gest.

[19] See para 14.2 above.

understand that in some cases, principally where the offence charged is of a similar kind to the bad character evidence to be revealed, it is asking a great deal of fact-finders to disregard that evidence completely on the question of guilt but to regard it solely on the question of credibility. This will be particularly so where the question of guilt and credibility may be intimately bound up. Indeed it may well be regarded by juries as bizarre to direct them to ignore certain evidence (which may plainly go to propensity) for purposes other than testing the credibility of D1. In our view, giving juries directions which they will find bizarre or incomprehensible, or which require them to engage in mental gymnastics, does no credit to the law. In our view the way forward is to seek to ensure that the evidence which is adduced is limited to that which is substantially relevant to the issues of importance between the defendants and not marginal to the issues in the trial. Where, as inevitably will sometimes be the case, evidence is admitted on the issue of truthfulness but is also likely to impinge on the question of propensity, the judge should address the problem in a straightforward manner by warning the jury of the dangers of inferring from past conduct that the defendant is guilty of the offence charged.[20]

OUR RECOMMENDATION

14.36 Our provisional proposal embodied a number of elements:

(1) that D1 should be able to adduce evidence about D2's bad character in respect of the central set of facts (as we then defined them) without triggering any right of D2 to adduce evidence of D1's bad character which went outside those facts;

(2) if D1's character became an issue because of an attack made on D2 then any party to the proceedings could attack his character;

(3) no one would have the right to adduce evidence of D1's character, but it would always be a matter of discretion;

(4) the discretion was to be structured so that there was a presumption in favour of admitting evidence if the application was by D2 but against admissibility if the application to admit was by any other party. In each case the presumption was to be displaced on an interests of justice basis;

(5) there were a series of factors to be considered in exercising the discretion involving consideration of the damage done to D2's case, how gratuitous the attack had been, the number and nature of D1's convictions sought to be adduced, and the impact of admitting the evidence.

14.37 We have retained a number of features of our provisional proposals but have recalibrated them in order to achieve a uniformity of approach in the overall scheme we propose. We regard such uniformity of approach as an important feature of our recommendations.

---

[20] See paras 17.18 – 17.19 below.

14.38   We have, however, abandoned certain elements of the provisional proposals as we have been persuaded by the responses to the consultation paper that they were erroneous as a matter of principle.

14.39   In particular we think it right that D2 should be entitled as of right to adduce evidence of D1's bad character if the requirements are satisfied. We accept that each defendant should be permitted to pursue his or her defence legitimately without regard to the impact on the other defendants. On the other hand, we accept that the only party who should, on this ground, be free to adduce evidence of the bad character of D1 should be D2. If D2 does not wish to do so then we do not now think that the prosecution, or other defendants, should be able to jump on that bandwagon and adduce such evidence where they have no independent entitlement to do so.

14.40   Our first recommendation is that each defendant should be free to make attacks on the character of co-defendants in respect of matters falling within the central set of facts, as we have defined them,[21] without seeking leave of the court and without thereby automatically entitling co-defendants to adduce evidence of bad character which goes outside the central set of facts.[22] In this respect their freedom to adduce evidence will be no different from their freedom to adduce evidence attacking prosecution witnesses or others.

14.41   In common with our other recommendations, if a defendant wishes to adduce evidence about another defendant which goes outside the central set of facts then the leave of the court must be obtained.

14.42   Consistent with our recommendations in respect of adducing evidence of the defendant's character by the prosecution, or of a non defendant's character by any party, such leave will only be given if the evidence is of substantial probative value to an issue between the defendants, which issue is itself of substantial importance in the context of the case as a whole.

14.43   This recommendation mirrors our other recommendations in respect of evidence sought to be adduced about bad character evidence outside the central set of facts. The enhanced relevance test is designed to prevent evidence of bad character extraneous to the events in question being admitted where it is of only minimal relevance to a central issue, or where the issue to which it is relevant is itself marginal to the case.[23]

14.44   In this way the court will require each defendant who wishes to attack the character of a co-defendant, by drawing attention to character evidence which is extraneous to the central set of facts, specifically to justify its introduction. In so doing we aim to avoid material of great potential prejudice to another defendant being placed before the fact-finders for no reason other than that it may be of

---

[21] See para 8.31 above.

[22] Though the co-defendant may be granted leave to adduce such evidence: see paras 14.44 – 14.46 below.

[23] See para 9.35 above.

some marginal relevance, or relevant to some marginal issue or, as at present, because a defendant has been unwise enough to step across a line in the evidence given against that co-defendant.

14.45 If, however, the material does satisfy the test of enhanced relevance, then, because the defendant has the right to have his or her case presented, there is a right to have it adduced. There is no exclusionary discretion, such as we propose in the case of the *prosecution* seeking to introduce evidence of the defendant's bad character, requiring the court to have regard to the prejudicial impact of the evidence.

14.46 Where, however, the issue between D1 and D2 is whether D1 has a propensity to be untruthful, leave may only be given if, in addition to the other requirements, the nature or the conduct of D1's defence is such as to undermine D2's defence.

14.47 In assessing the probative value of evidence for the purposes of these provisions we require the court to have regard to the same factors as where it is considering the admissibility of other bad character evidence which is outside the central set of facts.[24]

14.48 Where the evidence of D1's bad character, outside the central set of facts, is admitted at the behest of D2, on whatever basis, we recommend no specific limit to the use to which the fact-finders may put that evidence. We envisage that the judge in summing up will routinely place such evidence in context, explaining the issue in the case to which it is relevant. Where it is admitted only in respect of the question of D1's propensity to untruthfulness, we envisage that the judge will make that clear to the jury. In every case, but in particular in relation to evidence which is admitted only on the issue of propensity to be untruthful, we would expect the judge to warn the jury that they must be very careful in the use to which they put such evidence and that it can be very dangerous to assume that a person has done something on this occasion merely because in the past he may have done something similar. We believe that reminding the jury that they should take this common sense approach to such evidence is much more likely to be understood and complied with than requiring them, as a matter of technical legal rules, to perform bizarre mental gymnastics.

The operation of the exception

14.49 We can illustrate the effect of the new test by returning to the scenario described by one of our respondents.[25]

---

[24] See para 7.19 above and cl 5(2) of the Bill.

[25] As described at para 14.33.

> *D1 and D2 are jointly charged with robbery. D1's defence is that D2 did it on her own. In order to get D1's criminal record admitted under the co-defendant exception on the basis that D1 has undermined D2's case, D2 must show that his convictions show he is likely to lie on oath. What is in issue is D1's propensity to tell the truth not his propensity to rob.*

14.50 The evidence is less likely to be admitted in relation to credibility than under the current law. It would be clearer than it is under the current law that *only* evidence of D1's bad character which was relevant to his credibility would be admissible, and there would be no danger of bad character evidence of little probative value (but significant prejudicial effect) being admitted.

> *D2 might seek to have D1's convictions admitted on the basis that they are substantially relevant directly to the issue of who committed the robbery. If D1 has recent convictions for robbery, they are more likely to be admissible on this basis, whereas other kinds of dishonesty offence might not be sufficiently relevant.*

14.51 It may be that the evidence of D1's previous convictions is directly relevant to the central issue of who committed the robbery even though it could have a similar prejudicial effect to that described by the respondent. However, the evidence would have to be substantially probative to be adduced, rather than creep in under the guise of credibility.

Severance

14.52 We believe that the need for severance of defendants would arise less frequently under our recommendation simply because evidence of the bad character of one defendant will be admitted at the behest of a co-defendant less easily than under the present law.

14.53 **We recommend that leave may be given to a co-defendant to adduce evidence of the bad character of a defendant where it has substantial probative value in relation to a matter in issue between the co-defendant and the defendant where that issue is itself of substantial importance in the context of the case as a whole – except that, if it has probative value only in showing that the defendant has a propensity to be untruthful, leave may not be given unless, in addition, the defendant's case is such as to undermine that of the co-defendant.**[26]

---

[26] This recommendation is given effect by cl 11 of the draft Bill.

PART XV
THE QUALITY OF TENDERED EVIDENCE

INTRODUCTION

15.1 In this Part we consider what approach the court should take to the quality of the evidence which a party wishes to adduce. Should the court make some assumption about the veracity or reliability of the witnesses and the overall quality of the evidence, or investigate for itself? We conclude that in considering admissibility, the court should not make its own enquiry, but should take the evidence at face value (unless it is unrealistic to do so).

15.2 The problems posed by this issue arise most acutely where it is alleged that the quality of the evidence is affected by contamination or collusion. We therefore consider additionally what a court should do where bad character evidence has been admitted but turns out to be so affected. We conclude that, in the Crown Court, the judge should be under a duty to discharge the jury where a conviction would be unsafe because of the doubt cast on the quality of the evidence by contamination and/or collusion.

WHAT ARE CONTAMINATION AND COLLUSION?

15.3 In the leading case, Lord Mustill explored the meaning which "collusion" had been given in earlier authorities, and differentiated the true meaning of collusion from contamination:

> …, it is important to note the ambiguity of the word "collusion". In its more limited sense this may denote a wicked conspiracy in which the complainants put their heads together to tell lies about the defendant, making up things which never happened. It is however clear that the argument for the appellant, and the authorities on which it is based, give the word a much wider meaning; wide enough to embrace any communications between witnesses, even without malign intent, which may lead to the transfer of recollections between them, and hence to an unconscious elision of the differences between the stories which each would independently have told. …
>
> For convenience, the two situations may be labelled "conspiracy" and "innocent infection".[1]

15.4 The two situations thus described are the extremes of the spectrum: deliberate fabrication of allegations resulting from an agreement between two or more witnesses, and *unconscious* alteration of evidence, resulting from having become aware of what the evidence of another will be or has been. There are variations in between. We attempt below to illustrate the range within the spectrum:

(1) A and B have together decided to make false allegations against D.

---

[1] *H* [1995] 2 AC 596, 616.

(2) C, having become aware that E has made allegations against D, goes to the police (or responds to a trawl by investigators) to make false allegations on her own initiative.

(3) F and G make an agreement both to say that D was wearing a dark blue top. They may be pooling their recollection and honestly agreeing what their recollection must have been. Neither of them may be sure what colour he was wearing but they agree to say the same thing so as to give the impression that they are sure. The agreement may be the result of negotiation in which F is persuaded by G, or agrees without really being persuaded, to adopt G's recollection.

(4) H learns that J has said D's top was blue, and decides to change or add to her evidence to the same effect, without colluding with J at all. She may be telling a deliberate lie, or have been unconfident about what colour D's top was and so, on hearing that J thinks it was dark blue, resolves that she will also say it was dark blue, and believes she was mistaken in thinking it might have been green. In this scenario, the alteration is conscious, but there is no collusion in the sense of conspiracy.

(5) K is unconsciously influenced by L and changes her recollection and account so that she too says D was wearing a dark blue top, without being aware that she has changed it. That is Lord Mustill's "innocent infection".

15.5 Situations (1) and (3) involve collusion (in the first, complete concoction, and in the third, collusion as to an element of the evidence) and (1) and (2) involve concoction. Situations (2), (4) and (5) may all be described as "contamination", but only (5) is "innocent infection".

15.6 It is mistaken to correlate collusion as in (3) with false allegations, and contamination (as in (4) or (5)) with an essentially truthful story. F and G may be essentially right that D did what they allege, even though they have agreed to gild the lily to make it sound better. Conversely, K's central allegation, which chimes with L's through innocent infection, may be a complete (though unwitting) fabrication.

15.7 A jury or bench of magistrates could allow that there *had* been collusion (in the sense of (3) or contamination (as in (4) or (5)) and yet properly convict. They could not, though, accept the falsity of concoction (1) and properly convict. In (2) they could only properly convict of E's allegations, not C's.

THE QUALITY OF EVIDENCE AND ADMISSIBILITY

15.8 Contamination and collusion have the potential to affect decisions at two stages in the trial: at the time the evidence is ruled admissible or inadmissible, and after the evidence has been given. We now consider what view the court should take of the quality of bad character evidence at the time of ruling on admissibility.

The current law

15.9 The question how a court should approach such evidence was considered in *H*.[2] The defendant appealed against his convictions for sexual offences against his adopted daughter and step daughter. There were similarities in the two complainants' accounts but each denied that they had collaborated or concocted a story. The House of Lords held that, in relation to "similar fact evidence" the assessment of credibility should be left to the jury: for the purpose of deciding whether the evidence is admissible, the trial judge should not make any enquiry into the quality of the evidence. Thus the issues of collusion and contamination are not relevant considerations for the judge on the question of admissibility.

The options in the consultation paper and the response on consultation

15.10 In the consultation paper we looked at three possibilities:[3] replicating the law in *H* (option A); requiring the judge to assess the cogency of the evidence on the basis of the documents (option B); and requiring the judge to hold a voir dire to make an assessment of the quality of the evidence before ruling on admissibility (option C). We provisionally rejected option B, but expressed no view as between options A and C. We asked respondents' whether "juries can now be entrusted with the task of evaluating for themselves evidence which exhibits appreciable risks of contamination and collusion".[4]

15.11 Forty respondents addressed this issue. Twenty agreed in unequivocal terms with option A. Three agreed with it but stated that in exceptional cases option C ought to be available to the judge. (This is in fact the position under *H*, because their Lordships left open the possibility of a voir dire, although they did not give examples of when it might be appropriate.) Two expressed a preference for option B. Two suggested the use of option B as a precursor to option C. Nine preferred option C, and the remainder did not favour any of the three options.

15.12 The main argument in support of option A was that allegations of collusion and contamination essentially raise issues of credibility and ought to be left to the arbiters of fact. As one respondent wrote, "If we cannot expect juries to deal with cases in which two witnesses may have fabricated their stories together, or in which one may be feeding off or contaminating the other, we should abandon hope and do away with trial by jury."

15.13 The Law Reform Committee, General Council of the Bar thought option B merited further thought and that where there was cogent evidence of collusion and/or contamination, the judge ought to be able to express a view at the outset. We have no doubt a judge would do so where the contamination was glaring from the papers alone. Such a case would be rare, as Lord Mustill said in *H*, "I find it hard to envisage that where the committal papers are so frank or artless that they

---

[2] [1995] 2 AC 596.
[3] Paras 10.94 – 10.97.
[4] Para 10.97.

disclose on their face a real risk of fabrication the matter will ever be brought to trial."[5]

15.14 Those who supported option C appreciated that it had its failings, but nevertheless thought it preferable. As Professor Tapper wrote,

> ... even granting the valid objections to it, the least bad option is for a voire dire; to adopt any other solution must run a very severe risk of prejudice. The whole rationale of these proposals is that some evidence is too dangerous to admit; it must follow that these very dangers demand that jurors not be exposed to such evidence upon the simple decision of the prosecution, without some attempt to filter out the worst examples. It is not feasible to instruct them to eschew prejudice once the evidence has been led.

Those who criticised option C tended to do so out of hostility to voir dires, and a fear that it would be close to impossible to demonstrate no risk of collusion.

The policy considerations

15.15 The heart of the problem is the fact that the question of admissibility turns on the weight to be given to the evidence. In this context credibility is a crucial factor in deciding the probative force (and hence one limb of admissibility) of the evidence. In many cases where this problem arises, for example cases of alleged sexual misconduct, the evidence in question is likely to be very prejudicial.[6] In these cases, if the judge does not pre-test the quality of the evidence, highly prejudicial evidence of dubious quality is likely to be admitted.[7]

15.16 It appeared at the time of the consultation paper that the choice was between following *Hoch*, (option C, the Australian approach)[8] and *H* (option A). The essence of the former is encapsulated by Lord Mustill:

> The logic of the exception which permits similar fact evidence depends on the unlikelihood of coincidences between truly independent events. In some cases, the happening of the other events is undisputed, and the prosecution invites the inference that it was the defendant who was responsible for them all. In other instances the happening of all the events, including the one charged, is admitted, but the defendant maintains that they were accidental, to which the prosecution replies that whilst one accident is a possibility, it is unlikely that the same kind of event was brought [about] by the same kind of accident on so many separate occasions. In yet other cases ... all the alleged events are in dispute, and the prosecution relies on the improbability that different complainants will have spontaneously

---

[5] [1995] 2 AC 596, 616.

[6] The Jury Study concluded that hearing that a defendant had a previous conviction for indecent assault on a child was likely to colour the mock jurors' whole perception of the defendant. See paras D42 – D44 of Appendix D to the consultation paper.

[7] See C Tapper, "The Erosion of *Boardman v DPP*" (1995) 145 NLJ 1223.

[8] (1988) 81 ALR 225.

invented broadly similar accusations against the same person. In these and other situations the justification given for admitting evidence of the other occasions is that the jury should be presented with the whole picture, so that a choice can be made between an inference of guilt and an acceptance of an implausible coincidence.

Founding on this rationalisation the appellant maintains that in the third type of case the stark choice between a coincidental independent fabrication by different complainants and a finding that the complaints are true disappears once there is a possibility that the complaints may not be spontaneous and independent but fabricated in concert; and the disappearance of this choice carries away with it the logic of making an exception to the general rule.

It follows, so the argument concludes, that the prosecution, having the burden of showing that evidence which would generally be excluded is in the particular case admissible, must establish that there is no reasonably possible explanation of the similarity of the events other than guilt or coincidence. This means that the exclusion of conspiracy as a cause is a condition precedent to the admission of the evidence, and since it is the function of the judge to rule on whether the condition is satisfied he must investigate the facts, if necessary by hearing evidence on a voire dire in the absence of the jury, and reach a conclusion upon it, just as he does in other instances where the satisfaction of a factual condition precedent is in dispute.[9]

15.17 Lord Mustill decided that this conclusion cannot be accepted. The judge would, in that case, have to decide the very question that the jury has to determine:

> There are many reasons why witnesses may not be believed, and conspiracy, or the suspicion of it, is only one of them; and it may of course be alleged in cases which have nothing to do with evidence of similar facts. Credibility is always for the jury, and I can see no reason why the special feature that the testimony is adduced to support a charge concerning acts said to have been done to the person with whom the witness is suspected of conspiring, rather than to the witness herself or himself, should affect this fundamental principle in any way.[10]

15.18 The argument in favour of the judge testing the reliability of the evidence before admitting it may also be put in this way: if probative value must transcend prejudicial effect, the court must not assume the truth of the evidence tendered, because to do so means that the probative value is assumed not assessed. It appeared that the Australian courts were interpreting *Pfennig*[11] and *Hoch* to this effect, requiring the judge to pre-weigh the evidence, by a voir dire if necessary.

---

[9] [1995] 2 AC 596, 619.

[10] [1995] 2 AC 596, 620.

[11] (1995) 127 ALR 99.

15.19 There are two possible answers to this way of putting it. First, assuming the truth of evidence tendered is not the same as assuming its level of probative value. Probative value is a combination of reliability and degree of relevance. The latter has to be assessed, as well as some view being taken as to its reliability.[12] Secondly, the Australian courts have stopped short of interpreting *Hoch* as meaning that in every such case the judge has to exclude the possibility of collusion before proceeding to admit such evidence. Whereas it was once thought that the prosecution had to prove the non-collusive quality of the similar fact evidence, it then became clear that it was sufficient for the prosecution to disprove a *real* danger of concoction. It now appears that showing a real opportunity for communication between witnesses will not, without more, suffice to conjure up a possibility of concoction sufficiently real to amount to a reasonable explanation for the concert of allegations.[13] It is also noteworthy that the issue for the Australian courts is the risk of "concoction",[14] and does not extend to the risk of innocent contamination.

15.20 Lord Mustill's objections, however, remain valid even under this less rigorous interpretation of *Hoch*. Even if the court enquires only so far as to discount concoction as a reasonable explanation, it is still engaged in the very task the jury is there to perform. In any case where the complainants knew each other, or mixed together, the court would often have to assess the truthfulness of the complainants.

15.21 The practical consequences of the different policy options cannot be overlooked. First, if a voir dire were held, advocates and witnesses would learn from the voir dire, and ask questions or give answers differently or more fully, so it is not certain that the evidence on the voir dire would be the same as that given at trial.

15.22 Secondly, it is undesirable to require witnesses to testify more than once where that can be avoided, especially where their evidence may be of distressing personal matters. As Lord Mustill held in *H*, if the policy is that the prosecution is required to disprove collusion or contamination in any case in which more than one instance of sexual misconduct is relied on but there is the possibility of collusion or contamination the prosecution is required to disprove collusion or

---

[12] *Musquera* [1999] Crim LR 857 illustrates this point. The appellate court was of the view that the evidence in question was inadmissible on the other count(s), not because of the risk of collusion but because of the lack of relevance. Sexual offences were alleged against D by three complainants. Two of the complainants' allegations were of comparatively minor misconduct, while the third complainant alleged she had been raped (later amended to attempted rape). Beyond the fact that they were all allegations of sexual misconduct and that the families knew each other because they lived in the same building, the Court of Appeal could find no features which made one set of allegations relevant to another, and they held that those features were not enough to make the evidence cross-admissible.

[13] See *Colby* [1999] NSWCCA 261, para 111 which draws on *Robertson* (1997) 91 A Crim R 388, and see *OGD (No 2)* [2000] NSWCCA 404.

[14] Meaning conspiracy to make false allegations, and extending to concoction by one complainant of his or her account "after becoming aware of some like event or some like allegation concerning the accused": *BRS v The Queen* (1997) 191 CLR 275, 230, *per* Gaudron J.

contamination, then that will necessitate a voir dire in a large number of cases, with all the delays and the possible collapse of such cases which may follow:

> ... the judge will be required in almost every case to hold a preliminary trial ... solely in order to see whether the prosecution have proved a negative which will often be unprovable. This is more than I am willing to accept. The possibility of innocent infection is one amongst many factors which the jury will have to take into account; but to treat it as a unique "threshold issue" loads the scales unfairly against the prosecution, and hence against the interests of those who cannot protect themselves.[15]

We agree with this view.

15.23 We are, therefore, persuaded to favour option A. Issues of contamination and collusion ought to be decided by the jury. Of course, it *might* be the case that the evidence in the depositions would not, even if taken at their highest, prove the facts it is adduced to prove, in which case the court would not admit the evidence. Thus, if a judge *can* determine on the papers that there has been concoction, then the evidence should not be admitted. We would hope that this would be a rare occurrence. Where the court cannot make a determination on the papers it has an inherent power to hold a voir dire if it finds it necessary.[16]

15.24 We are conscious that protection against evidence which is revealed as obviously tainted must be afforded to the defendant. The purpose of the exclusionary rule is to protect the defendant. Thus, if the defendant is not going to receive the benefit of a pre-testing of the veracity of the witnesses by the court in this situation, we need to be confident that the other procedures in place to ensure a fair trial are adequate. We believe that the judge should have a duty to keep the issue of the quality of the evidence under review. If, in the course of the trial, the evidence turns out to have low probative value, because of collusion or contamination, then the judge will have the power to withdraw the case from the jury.[17]

What approach is a court to adopt to bad character evidence generally?

15.25 The quality of evidence tendered which goes to credibility or to correct a false impression[18] *is* significant, not as a pre-admission test for veracity, but on the question how far evidence on a side issue is going to distract from the central issues. The quality of the evidence might fall to be assessed by the court having regard to that factor, but not as a pre-condition of admission.

The recommendation

15.26 **We recommend that, where the court is required to assess the probative value of evidence of a person's bad character, it should be required to do**

---

[15] *H* [1995] 2 AC 596, 617.

[16] As confirmed in *H* [1995] 2 AC 596, 612C, *per* Lord Mackay.

[17] See para 15.37 below.

[18] See clauses 9 and 10 and Parts XII and XIII respectively.

so on the assumption that the evidence is true, except where it appears, on the basis of any material before the court, that no court or jury could reasonably find it to be true.

15.27 This recommendation is given effect by clause 14 in the Bill.

A DUTY TO WITHDRAW THE CASE FROM THE JURY

15.28 The House of Lords in *H* stated that if the question of collusion has been raised during the proceedings, the judge is obliged to draw the jury's attention to its importance, with a warning that, if they were not satisfied that the evidence could be relied on as free of collusion, they could not properly rely upon it for any purpose adverse to the defendant.[19] Their Lordships went on to consider the case where similar fact evidence is admitted but is later shown to be such that no reasonable jury could accept the evidence as free from collusion. In that case, they believed that the jury should be given a direction that the evidence could no longer be relied on for any purpose adverse to the defence.

15.29 This raises a stark issue: whether jurors are likely to be able to put out of their minds discredited evidence which has already been admitted and which may be extremely prejudicial. We are concerned that when such evidence has been correctly admitted, but it later transpires that the evidence has been discredited by contamination or collusion, the warnings referred to in *H* may not be effectively followed. The jury will have been seriously prejudiced.

15.30 In the consultation paper[20] we suggested that a better course might be to require the judge, if so requested, to withdraw the matter from the jury if he or she was satisfied, after hearing all the evidence, that due to the contaminated nature of the evidence given, the prejudicial effect of the bad character evidence outweighs its probative value.

15.31 In making this suggestion, we noted the existence of a similar safeguard against unreliable identification evidence.[21] A judge is obliged to withhold a case from the jury if the prosecution is based largely or entirely on identification evidence and the judge concludes that there is insufficient evidence on which a jury could properly convict.[22] The same principle could be said to apply to certain types of similar fact evidence.

Responses on consultation

15.32 Thirty-two respondents addressed this issue. Of these, eleven respondents unequivocally agreed with the proposal, and a further nine agreed with reservations. Eight disagreed, two because they thought the current law already

---

[19] [1995] 2 AC 596, 612.
[20] At para 10.105.
[21] *Turnbull* [1977] QB 224.
[22] *Daley v R* [1994] 1 AC 117.

covers the point. Two respondents were confident that a judicial direction would be sufficient to prevent injustice.

15.33 Trial judges have the *discretion* to direct an acquittal where discredited confession evidence has been admitted, so as to ensure that the defendant has a fair trial.[23] Recent cases have gone further, expressly stating that the judge *may* direct an acquittal at any time from the close of the prosecution case to the end of the trial, on the basis that there is no case to answer. This discretion should be used rarely, but it can be used for any reason, so presumably it could be exercised if the judge was concerned that some form of prejudicial evidence should not, after all, have been admitted.[24] However, this recent development runs counter to the traditional view as to the limits of a judge's power.[25] Our proposal would *oblige* the judge to direct an acquittal where discredited prejudicial evidence has been admitted, thereby making explicit what may previously have been unclear and discretionary.

15.34 Professor Tapper agreed with the proposal but felt that there may be "a danger that the judge would not sufficiently address his mind to the issue, and might be reluctant to reverse his previous considered view". We believe that the contrary is the case: a clear statutory duty will make it more, rather than less, likely that a judge would be asked to address the issue. Moreover, the judge would not be asked "to reverse his previous considered view": the evidence would have been admitted without enquiry into its quality. Once the evidence has been heard and tested, the judge need not deal in assumptions about it, but can evaluate it afresh.

15.35 A different respondent thought the issue is one for the jury, not the trial judge. We disagree. The fact that the judge must in our scheme take the reliability of the evidence at face value necessitates the introduction of this safeguard for the defendant. There already exist examples of the judge having to assess the quality of evidence placed before the jury, for example, the second limb of *Galbraith*,[26] in the case of identification evidence and, in the case of hearsay evidence, recommended by this Commission[27] (and accepted by the Government). As Lord Mustill has said, the risk that the jury may act upon evidence which is not worthy to be relied upon "may well be seen as serious enough to outweigh the general principle that the functions of the judge and jury must be kept apart".[28]

---

[23] In the case of *Watson* [1980] 1 WLR 991, the Court of Appeal accepted that the judge retains control over the evidence that should be submitted to the jury throughout the trial. If a confession is admitted, but the judge later decides that it should not have been, the judge is empowered to direct the jury to disregard it, direct an acquittal or direct a new trial (at p 995). This case was followed in *Sat-Bhambra* (1989) 88 Cr App R 55.

[24] *Boakye* (Court of Appeal, 12 March 1992, unreported); *Brown (Jamie)* [1998] Crim LR 196; *Anderson, The Independent*, 13 July 1998; *Brown (Davina)* [2001] Crim LR 675.

[25] See *Archbold* para 4–292.

[26] [1981] 1 WLR 1039: where the judge is required to consider the prosecution case, taken at its highest, the judge must make some kind of assessment of the quality of the evidence.

[27] Evidence in Criminal Proceedings: Hearsay and Related Topics (1997) Law Com No 245, para 11.31, Recommendation 47.

[28] *Daley v R* [1994] 1 AC 117, 129D.

15.36 A further respondent thought it should be left to the Court of Appeal to quash an unsafe conviction, and not for the trial judge to prevent the conviction in the first place. We do not agree. A judge has a duty to achieve a fair trial for the defendant. It is now recognised that there is a high level of coincidence, (if not total identity) between a trial which is not fair and a verdict of guilty which is "unsafe".[29] If evidence has been admitted which is highly prejudicial, and a direction from the judge may not adequately guard against prejudice, then protection for the accused from an unsafe conviction requires intervention to withdraw the case from that jury.

The recommendation

15.37 **We recommend that, in a trial on indictment, where evidence of the defendant's bad character has been admitted with leave, and the judge is satisfied that the evidence is contaminated such that, considering the importance of the evidence to the case against the defendant, a conviction would be unsafe, the judge should be required to discharge the jury or direct the jury to acquit.**[30]

15.38 We make no equivalent recommendation for the magistrates' court: if the magistrates think either that a conviction would be unsafe, or merely that the incriminating evidence has been so weakened by evidence of collusion or contamination that they cannot be sure the accused committed the offence, they will acquit.

---

[29] *Davis, Johnson and Rowe* [2000] Crim LR 1012 was the first case to consider whether the defendants' convictions were unsafe following the Strasbourg Court's finding that their trial had been unfair. The Court of Appeal agreed that the trial had been unfair, and went on to conclude that the convictions were unsafe. However, the court took the view that this was not an inevitable conclusion. The nature and the degree of the breach of Article 6 would determine whether the conviction was unsafe. *Davis, Johnson and Rowe* was considered in the case of *Togher* [2001] Crim LR 124, but slightly glossed: "We would suggest that, even if there was previously a difference of approach, that since the [HRA 1998] came into force, the circumstances in which there will be room for a different result before this Court and before the ECHR because of unfairness based on the respective tests we employ will be rare indeed ... we consider that if a defendant has been denied a fair trial it will almost be inevitable that the conviction will be regarded as unsafe." This approach was firmly endorsed by the House of Lords in *Forbes* [2001] 2 WLR 1, 13. Unfortunately the subsequent case of *Williams, The Times* 30 March 2001 was decided on the basis of *Davis, Johnson and Rowe* without reference to the more recent cases. Nonetheless, the outcome in *Williams* is consistent with the *Togher-Forbes* test, so it is now settled law that "safety" will almost inevitably follow "unfairness".

[30] Clause 13 lays a duty on the court to direct an acquittal in a trial on indictment, in specified circumstances. Under ss 6(3) and 7(1) of the Criminal Law Act 1967 and surviving common law provisions (see *Saunders* [1988] AC 148), a defendant may be convicted of a lesser offence when acquitted of the greater offence. Where the defendant has been found unfit to plead by reason of mental disability, the jury must determine whether the defendant did the act or made the omission under section 4A Criminal Procedure (Insanity) Act 1964. If evidence of the defendant's bad character is so affected by collusion or contamination that a verdict of a lesser offence or finding that the defendant did the act would be unsafe, then a duty should be laid upon the judge to direct the jury in this circumstance to acquit the defendant. This is provided for by cl 14(3).

PART XVI
SEVERANCE OF COUNTS OR INFORMATIONS

16.1 The present law governing the severance of counts or informations properly joined is set out at paragraphs 2.91 – 2.95 above. Counts may be joined if they "are founded on the same facts", or if they "form or are a part of a series of offences of the same or a similar character".[1] In *Barrell and Wilson*,[2] the Court of Appeal said that

> the phrase "founded on the same facts" does not mean that for charges to be properly joined in the same indictment, the facts in relation to the respective charges must be identical in substance or virtually contemporaneous. The test is whether the charges have a common factual origin.[3]

16.2 A judge has a discretion to order that properly-joined counts be tried separately.[4]

THE RESPONSE ON CONSULTATION

16.3 In the consultation paper we considered the argument that a defendant is prejudiced by counts being heard together where the evidence is not cross-admissible and concluded:

> The logic of this approach is very powerful but, as we have seen, it is inconsistent with general practice. We do not feel that we can make any provisional recommendations on this point, though the present practice does appear to be open to criticism on grounds of logic. We ask whether the present rules in respect of joinder of charges are adequate, or whether the courts should sever charges where prejudicial evidence is not inter-admissible between different charges, especially in sex cases.[5]

16.4 Thirty-seven respondents gave their views on this issue, of which roughly half thought there was no need for any change. One third did want to see change. The main underlying reason given by these respondents was that the prejudice caused to the defendant may be overwhelming and is unjustifiable in principle if such evidence would not be admissible under the rules governing similar fact evidence. A further four respondents thought some modification necessary, and two of those suggested a presumption in favour of severance. This is the route we have pursued.

---

[1] Indictment Rules SI 1971 No 1253, r 9.

[2] (1979) 69 Cr App R 250, 252-253.

[3] But see *Lockley and Sainsbury* [1997] Crim LR 455.

[4] Indictments Act 1915, s 5(3). The position is the same in the magistrates' courts. See paras 2.93 – 2.95 above.

[5] Para 10.111.

16.5 We have considered the following options:

(1) Leave the law as it is, governed by *Christou*.[6]

(2) Provide that where the evidence on one count *is* admissible on another count because it falls within clause 2, 7 or 8 of the draft Bill there is a presumption in favour of joinder and a discretion to sever (as now); but if evidence on one count is *not* admissible on another count, then the counts *must* be severed.

(3) Provide that if the evidence on one count *is* admissible on another count then there is a presumption in favour of joinder and a discretion to sever (as now); but if evidence on one count is not admissible on another count, and the defence so request, there is a presumption that the counts be severed *unless* the court is satisfied that the defendant can receive a fair trial without severance and it is otherwise desirable that the counts are heard together.

Joinder and fairness

16.6 There are perceived to be a number of advantages in joining counts or informations. Joinder is said to be in the interests of justice because: it makes for speedier justice with the result that it is more likely that memories will be accurate; successive trials enable the defendant and the witnesses to "rehearse" their evidence; and the fact-finders will be able to see the "complete picture" of the alleged offending.[7] It is also said that delay should be avoided because it might cause distress to witnesses and defendants, particularly those who are vulnerable. For example, one respondent complained that automatic severance of charges might lead to "appalling delays" in cases where children are complainants in cases of alleged sexual assault and "defeat the 'fast-track' system which all are agreed is necessary in such cases".

16.7 Against these arguments it may be said that, as we noted in the consultation paper, joint trials are not necessarily the most efficient option:[8] if charges are severed, the Crown will usually seek to have the most serious charges tried first. Depending on the outcome of this, guilty pleas may be offered for the remaining charges or the charges may be withdrawn. With regard to conservation of judicial resources Dawson argues in his article that joint trials may well place more of a strain upon such resources, because such trials are less likely to begin on time, will take longer to complete and are at greater risk of defence objections, leading to an appeal.

16.8 The most weighty argument must, though, be that of fairness. Neither witnesses' convenience, nor trauma and distress, nor efficient use of resources, must be put above the defendant's right to a fair trial. As for the argument that the fact-finders

---

[6] [1997] AC 117.

[7] A discussion and criticism of a number of these perceived advantages can be found in the article by R Dawson, "Joint Trials of Defendants in Criminal Cases: An Analysis of Efficiencies and Prejudices" (1979) 77 Mich LR 13.

[8] Para 10.108.

must be presented with the "complete picture", admission of evidence which is unrelated to the count in question may lead to prejudice. Clearly, the danger of a single trial for a variety of counts, where evidence on different counts is not cross-admissible, is that the fact-finders may use each count to bolster the other and support an assumption that the defendant must be guilty of at least something.

Option 1

16.9 The difficulty with leaving the law as it stands is put thus, in Professor Birch's commentary on *Wrench*:[9]

> ... the connection which justifies joinder is more slender than that which permits admissibility. For the purpose of joinder, it was held to be enough that the offences were generally similar in the sense that they both showed a "sexual interest in young female children". Thus, if the answer to the question concerning admissibility is yes, the jury will be told that they may draw inferences from the apparent connection. If the answer is no, then because the offences are heard together the evidence will be before the jury anyway and, though they will be told not to draw the inference, they cannot be prevented from doing so. There is something profoundly perverse about the latter outcome.

16.10 Since *DPP v P* evidence of bad character is permissible in a wider range of cases than it was: "striking similarity" is no longer needed. It is therefore quite likely that if the facts of some of the authorities on severance recurred now, the severance question would not be argued, because evidence on one count would be ruled sufficiently probative on another to be admissible on it.[10] The difficulty described by Professor Birch may not, therefore, be quite as acute as it has been, but it still exists. The difficulty arises in two types of case. The first is where the similarity of the facts in one count is enough to have raised the question whether that evidence on that count is admissible on other counts in the same indictment but where that application has been rejected. The second is where one count on the indictment is of a sexual nature, whether or not the other counts on the indictment are of such a nature. Certain cases, indeed most of the really difficult ones, combine both elements.

16.11 In the case of *Christou*,[11] C was charged with sexual offences against two younger female cousins. All three had been living in the same household at the time of the offences. There was sufficient connection between the offences for them to be properly joined (they formed "part of a series of offences of the same or a similar character" as required by rule 9 of the Indictment Rules 1971) but were not cross-admissible. Their Lordships held that the counts need not be severed. The law

---

[9] [1996] Crim LR 265, 267.

[10] Eg, *Flack* [1969] 1 WLR 937 where D was charged with sexual offences against his three sisters. It was obviously a close-run thing as to whether the evidence of one sister was admissible on counts relating to the others, as the judge changed his mind during the course of the trial.

[11] [1997] AC 117.

was stated by Lord Taylor of Gosforth in the leading speech in the following terms:

> Lord Lane CJ in the quoted passage, [in *Cannan*][12] refrained from specifying the factors a judge should consider when "taking into account all things he should". They will vary from case to case, but the essential criterion is the achievement of a fair resolution of the issues. That requires fairness to the accused but also to the prosecution and those involved in it. Some, but by no means an exhaustive list, of the factors which may need to be considered are: – how discrete or inter-related are the facts giving rise to the counts; the impact of ordering two or more trials on the defendant and his family, on the victims and their families and on press publicity; and importantly, whether directions the judge can give to the jury will suffice to secure a fair trial if the counts are tried together. In regard to that last factor, jury trials are conducted on the basis that the judge's directions of law are to be applied faithfully. Experience shows … that juries, where counts are jointly tried, do follow the judge's directions and consider the counts separately.
>
> Approaching the question of severance as indicated above, judges will often consider it right to order separate trials. But I reject the argument that either generally or in respect of any class of case, the judge must so order …[13]

16.12 We have no quarrel with this as a statement of what the law should provide on this issue, save for the proviso that, in our view, it must be clear that the overriding priority is that the defendant can receive a fair trial. Although we do not read this passage in any other way, it might be thought that this statement of principle may permit joinder on the grounds of the achievement of a fair resolution of the issues, in circumstances where some unfairness to the defendant in ordering joinder is overridden by the perceived need to preserve joinder in order to avoid some unfairness to other parties. We think that such an outcome would be flawed in the light of the absolute entitlement of the defendant to a fair trial pursuant to Article 6 of the ECHR. In order to avoid the possibility of such an outcome, it is our view that the statute should expressly reflect this principle. Accordingly the draft Bill does not simply reflect *Christou*.

Option 2

16.13 The logic which leads to option 2 is strong: if the evidence is either too prejudicial, and/or insufficiently probative for the court to consider that it is nevertheless fair to allow the jury or magistrates to take account of it, it is hard to see what would justify running the risk of prejudice by allowing the evidence to be heard, although not admissible. As Roskill LJ put it,[14]

---

[12] (1991) 92 Cr App R 16.

[13] [1997] AC 117, 129.

[14] *Blackstock* (1980) 70 Cr App R 34, 37.

> It is the duty of the trial Judge to see that *so far as is humanly possible* an accused person charged with more than one offence is not put in danger of conviction upon any one offence by reason of evidence being given which is not admissible in relation to that one offence.

16.14 There is, however, a difficulty with option 2. A rule which allows the judge no discretion could conceivably produce absurdities in particular cases. For example, there are many cases where offences are properly joined, where the evidence on the counts is not cross-admissible, and yet where no application to sever is even contemplated because there is no possible basis upon which there could be prejudice caused to the defendant. Juries daily up and down the land bring in verdicts on such cases which manifestly reflect their adherence to the judge's directions to consider each count separately. To recommend a blanket rule would be a recipe for administrative chaos. Furthermore it would simply discount totally the legitimate interests of those other than the defendant, which are referred to in *Christou* and would make the exercise potentially arbitrary and removed from the exercise of principle.

16.15 One kind of case which option 2 would affect is illustrated by the facts of *Christou* itself. Another example of counts properly joined but which would have to be severed under this option is *Cannan*.[15] Once the trial judge had decided the evidence relating to six counts regarding three women was not cross-admissible, the counts would have had to be severed into three separate trials. Consider also the facts of *D*.[16] D was charged with various sexual offences against two boys, ND and KC. Counts 1 – 6 concerned ND, over the period 1978 – 1984. Counts 7 and 8 concerned KC and allegedly took place in 1985. The two boys did not know each other, but it seems they and the appellant were members of the same judo club. The defence alleged collusion, but the allegation did not seem to have much weight in it. The connecting factors between the two sets of offences were the similarity of the conduct alleged, and the judo club nexus. It was expressly noted in the report that, not only was evidence relating to one boy not admissible on the counts concerning the other boy, but "the prosecution did not suggest or conduct the case on the basis that the evidence of ND was in any way supportive of KC's evidence or probative of the case of KC against the defendant" and vice versa. Yet the eight counts were heard together. The question of severance is not referred to in the report at all. In such a case, option 2 would result in two separate trials.[17] No argument for cross-admissibility was raised. Thus the assumption must be that the evidence of offences alleged regarding KC was not said to be admissible on the charges concerning ND. If option 2 were adopted then the court would have

---

[15] (1991) 92 Cr App R 16. This concerned allegations relating to three victims. The only factors which connected the victims was evidence tending to show in each case that the defendant was the attacker, and the attacks were of a similar kind, involving abduction or attempted abduction. In one case that evidence consisted of DNA, in another it was identification evidence, and in the third it was circumstantial evidence.

[16] Unreported. No 98/6262/W2. Convictions on three of the counts were quashed on the ground of delay and a misdirection on a specific finding as to one complainant's age.

[17] *Tickner* [1992] Crim LR 44 is a similar case: the defendant was deputy headmaster and the complainants were four pupils at his school. The counts were not severed.

no option but to sever the two sets of allegations notwithstanding that it may be that under the rules for joinder of counts the evidence of one set of counts is an integral part of the allegations of the other set of counts, and so the two sets should, by those lights, be heard together.

Option 3

16.16 Option 3 is that if the evidence on one count *is* admissible on another count then there is a presumption in favour of joinder and a discretion to sever (as now), but if evidence on one count is not admissible on another count, *and the defence seeks severance*, then there is a presumption in favour of severance but that the presumption may be rebutted if the defendant can have a fair trial if the counts are joined.

16.17 The differences between option 2 and 3 are: first, where no application is made to sever then no question arises of severance merely because the evidence is not cross-admissible on the various counts. This will save a great deal of court time being wasted in considering, or having to remember to consider, the question of severance when it is not seriously in issue. Second: where there is *no* basis for ruling evidence of one count admissible on another, the counts may remain joined if the defendant can still receive a fair trial under option 3, whereas under option 2 severance would have to be ordered in those circumstances. Option 3, therefore, enables the court to exercise its judgment taking into account all relevant matters, including those identified in *Christou*, but nonetheless elevates to a position of prime importance the question whether the defendant can have a fair trial. Thus option 3 still allows for the possibility of counts to be joined even though evidence is not cross-admissible, but only if the view of the court is that the defendant can still have a fair trial. In making this judgment, it would still be legitimate for the court to bear in mind the approach in *Christou* that juries do faithfully apply the judge's directions.

16.18 Thus we are putting the onus on the prosecution, who seek to have the cases heard together, to persuade the court, which must provide a fair trial for the defendant, that the defendant can have a fair trial, as that is the paramount consideration for the court in exercising its discretion. There are two reasons for adopting this discretionary route rather than an inflexible rule. First, there is some merit in the argument that, where evidence is admissible on one count and not on another, it is comparatively straightforward for the magistrates to put the evidence out of their minds when considering some charges, and, in the Crown Court, for the judge to emphasise that the jury must put the evidence entirely out of their minds when considering the latter count. This is so even though the reason the evidence is not cross-admissible is that were the magistrates or jury permitted to make use of that evidence on another count, it might be hard for them not to make irrational or unfair use of it. Second, circumstances vary infinitely as do the requirements of justice. To do justice in each individual case, the law must leave some discretion to the court.

16.19 An example of where severance would most probably follow would be where D is charged with rape of V where the issue is identity and of Y where the issue is consent. On the charge concerning V, the prosecution obtain a ruling from the judge that evidence of other alleged victims may be admitted to prove the identity of the assailant, although the other assaults are not themselves counts on the indictment. In the case of Y, neither the direct evidence of the alleged rape of V, nor the supporting evidence of other alleged victims would be admissible. The judge might well sever.

16.20 An example of where evidence is not admissible on another count, but where severance *need* not follow, would be where the defence planned to cross-examine a prosecution witness to the effect that his or her evidence has been tainted by contamination by, or is wholly the product of collusion, with the complainant on the other count. In other words, if the defence will themselves introduce evidence of other allegations of a similar nature, in order to show that the complainant on this count has been put up to it by another complainant, then the prejudicial evidence will be before the fact-finders anyway and, as long as the counts are properly joined and a fair trial is possible, severance does not serve any purpose.

THE RECOMMENDATION

16.21 **We recommend that where**

    (1) a defendant is charged with more than one offence,

    (2) evidence of the defendant's bad character is admissible on one of the offences charged but inadmissible on another, and

    (3) the defendant applies for the offences to be tried separately,

that application should be granted unless the court is satisfied that the defendant can receive a fair trial.[18]

16.22 The same rules are to apply in the magistrates' courts and in the Crown Court.

16.23 These rules are not intended to prejudice any other power to sever which a court may have.

Special rules for cases involving sexual offences?

16.24 The risk of prejudice is particularly great when the courts concern offences which are particularly likely to revolt the fact-finders, such as certain sexual offences. We noted[19] the comments made by Lord Cross and Lord Wilberforce in *Boardman*[20] that it was simply asking too much of a jury to perform the "mental gymnastics" necessary to enable them to put out of their minds, when considering each count, that other people were making similar allegations against the defendant.

16.25 There is some support in the authorities for a special rule favouring severance in cases of multiple sexual offences, the rationale being that special prejudice attaches to sexual allegations, but it was confirmed in *Christou* that no special rule

---

[18] This recommendation is given effect by cl 12 of the draft Bill.

[19] Para 10.109 of the consultation paper.

[20] [1975] AC 421, 459.

exists.[21] Most respondents did not favour special rules. Professor McEwan, on the other hand, favoured change to make it *more* likely that sexual allegations would be heard together. In one of the cases she cites, *Maloney*,[22] the trial judge was looking for "striking similarity", which of course a judge has not been obliged to find since *DPP v P* and so such a case would not now be repeated.[23] Professor McEwan's concerns are very real ones, but their target is really the rules on admissibility. Where evidence is not relevant or sufficiently relevant, but is prejudicial, our view is that the fairness of the defendant's trial must be the paramount consideration, and our recommendation makes it so.

---

[21] See, eg, Lord Goddard CJ in *Sims* [1946] KB 531, 536; Lord Cross in *Boardman* [1975] AC 459; *De Jesus* (1986) 61 ALJR 1 and *B* [1989] 2 Qd R 343, cited with approval in *Kemp* [1997] 1 Qd R 383, 396. See Roderick Munday, "Vaguely similar facts and severance of counts" (1996) 160 JP 663 – 668.

[22] *Dispatches*, "Getting away with Rape" Channel 4, February 16, 1994; cited in Professor McEwan's article "Law Commission Dodges the Nettles in Consultation Paper No. 141" [1997] Crim LR 93, 96.

[23] Looking at the facts of *Z* [2000] 3 WLR 117, in which the prosecution would have succeeded at first instance in adducing evidence of other alleged rapes admitted had it not been for the *Sambasivam* difficulty (described at para 11.62 above), it is evident that the argument is based on coincidence reasoning: it defies belief that it is just an unlucky coincidence that this number of women claim that this man dispensed with their consent to intercourse. The prosecution surely should have succeeded in *Maloney* on the same basis.

PART XVII
PROCEDURAL AND ANCILLARY MATTERS

A NOTICE REQUIREMENT

17.1 As we wrote in the consultation paper,[1] the accused may be unfairly disadvantaged in the trial if he or she has not anticipated that acts other than those alleged in the charge will be raised. This was historically one of the reasons for the rule against evidence of bad character,[2] and also justifies the view that bad character evidence which is admissible in chief should not be saved until the cross-examination of the accused.[3] Presently, there are obligations on the prosecution to disclose evidence,[4] so the defendant should not be ambushed by evidence of bad character. There is some risk that a defendant at summary trial may be ambushed by an attack by a co-defendant, as there is no obligation for the defence to disclose its case in advance (except for expert evidence)[5] but it may be that in practice this will rarely occur.[6] There is less risk of an ambush by a co-accused in the Crown Court as the defence is required to submit a defence statement in advance.[7] If one party is

---

[1] Para 7.28.

[2] Section 8 of the Treason Act 1695 provided that "no evidence shall be admitted or given of any overt act that is not expressly laid in the indictment against any person or persons whatsoever." Foster explains this as arising "lest the prisoner should be surprised or confounded by a multiplicity and variety of facts which he is to answer upon the spot": *Crown Law* (1st ed 1762) p 244. See also *Phillips' Case* (1829) 1 Lew CC 105, 168 ER 977; *Knapp and another v Haskall* (1831) 4 CAR & P 590, 172 ER 838; *Whiley and Haines* (1804) 2 Leach 983, 168 ER 589; *Gray* (1866) 4 F & F 1102, 176 ER 924.

[3] See, eg, *Jones v DPP* [1962] AC 635, 646, *per* Ashworth J (CA); at p 668, *per* Lord Denning; and at p 685, *per* Lord Morris.

[4] At least in the case of indictable offences: Magistrates' Courts (Advance Information) Rules 1985 (SI 1985 No 601) (offences triable either way); Magistrates' Courts Act 1980, s 5, as substituted by Criminal Justice and Public Order Act 1994, Sched 4 (cases transferred to the Crown Court); and *R v DPP, ex p Lee* [1999] 1 WLR 1950 (offences triable only on indictment). In practice, the prosecution frequently, but not invariably, gives disclosure of evidence in summary only cases. Whilst there is no requirement to give advance disclosure, it ought to be given in contested cases and the court must take into account the impact of non-disclosure on the fairness of the trial as a whole, see *R v Stratford Magistrates ex p Imbert* [1999] 2 Cr App R 276. A magistrates' court may order advance disclosure.

Disclosure is governed by Part I of the Criminal Procedure and Investigations Act 1996: the prosecution is required to give at least primary disclosure (s 3) irrespective of the mode of trial.

[5] Magistrates' Court (Advance Notice of Expert Evidence) Rules, SI 1997 No 705 (L11), made pursuant to the Magistrates' Courts Act 1980, s 144, and the CPIA 1996, s 20(3) and (4). If advance notice is not given, the leave of the court must be obtained before the evidence is adduced.

[6] Under s 6 CPIA 1996, defence disclosure is voluntary before summary trials, but there is an incentive to give a defence statement where evidence of bad character may be an issue as the prosecution would therefore be required to give secondary disclosure under s 7.

[7] Under the CPIA 1996 s 5 the defence is required, once primary disclosure requirements have been met by the prosecution, to disclose sufficient particulars of its case to identify the

taken by surprise, it may always apply for an adjournment. For all these reasons, this danger does not seem to be as significant as it has been historically.

17.2 In the consultation paper we stated that "Any system permitting the admission of previous misconduct evidence should contain safeguards against such evidence taking the defendant by surprise."[8] Unsurprisingly, no respondents opposed this.

17.3 **We recommend that where a party wishes to adduce evidence of the defendant's bad character which does not have to do with the offence charged, and is not evidence of misconduct in connection with the investigation or prosecution of that offence, that party should be required to give notice of the intention to do so, but that requirement may be dispensed with by the court or the defendant.**

17.4 The party against whom the evidence is to be given should be able to waive the notice requirement. We consider that the court too should be able to waive the notice requirement if it is in the interests of justice for the evidence to be admitted without the prescribed notice having been given. This might well be the case where the defendant is not in fact prejudiced by the lack of notice. Rules of court are the most appropriate way for this recommendation to be effected.[9]

17.5 This requirement applies for whatever purpose the evidence is sought to be admitted. For example, in the case of evidence being potentially admissible to correct a false impression under clause 10[10] a defendant might make a false claim about her own character in the police interview. She might be alleged to be the perpetrator of a continuing business fraud but claim in interview to be an honest but naïve business woman. The prosecution might want to adduce the interview as part of its case but suggest editing it to exclude the false claim. The defendant might not agree to such editing as she does not plan to give evidence and wants this material before the jury. In such a case, the prosecution would want to have the opportunity to contradict the false claim by seeking leave to adduce evidence of her previous convictions for offences of dishonesty or concerning the management of companies. It would be reasonable that they should have to give advance warning of wishing to do so as the decisions of the defendant may be affected by the outcome of such an application for leave.

PRE-TRIAL RULINGS

17.6 We believe that questions of admissibility should, where possible, be resolved before the trial and, where this is not possible, at the start of the trial.[11] In the case of a trial on indictment, the appropriate place and time would be at the Plea and

---

issues in dispute. A co-accused would therefore be obliged to give details of its case which could then be relayed to the defendant via secondary disclosure from the prosecution. Failure to give a defence statement may result in adverse comment being made: s 11.

[8] Provisional conclusion 6(5).

[9] See cl 16 of the draft Bill.

[10] Clause 10 is described in Part XIII.

[11] See, eg, the Hearsay Report, paras 11.8 – 11.11 and Recommendation 42.

Directions Hearing.[12] In fraud cases,[13] and in other long and complex cases on indictment,[14] the appropriate time would be at a preparatory hearing. In the case of a summary trial, it would be at a pre-trial review,[15] if one is held, but only if it was conducted by a bench.[16] In many cases rulings on the admission or exclusion of such evidence might affect the plea, or the question of whether the proceedings are to continue, so that an early ruling might well lead to an earlier conclusion of the case.

17.7 Section 40 of the Criminal Procedure and Investigations Act 1996, provides that a judge may make a ruling on the admissibility of evidence at a pre-trial hearing which is binding from the time it is made until the case is disposed of.[17] A judge may subsequently discharge or vary any ruling if it appears to be in the interests of justice to do so, and this power may be exercised on the application of any party to the case or by the court of its own motion.[18] We see no reason to exempt evidence of bad character from this general provision. We also consider that where magistrates make pre-trial rulings on evidence, their rulings should also be binding.[19]

A DUTY TO GIVE REASONS

The common law

17.8 In the civil arena, the failure to give reasons for a conclusion essential to the decision at first instance is in itself good grounds for appeal. This was held in *Flannery v Halifax Estate Agencies Ltd*[20] where the essential decision was the

---

[12] At such hearings, the prosecution and the defence are expected to inform the court of (among other things) the issues in the case, any questions as to the admissibility of the evidence which appears on the face of the papers, and any application for evidence to be given by closed circuit television or to put in a pre-recorded interview with a child witness. Any rulings made at a Plea and Directions Hearing are capable of being binding under Part IV of the CPIA 1996.

[13] A preparatory hearing may be ordered by a judge in a Crown Court trial when an indictment reveals a case of fraud of such seriousness and complexity that substantial benefits are likely to accrue from such a hearing: Criminal Justice Act 1987, s 7(1).

[14] In such cases it is possible for a judge to order a preparatory hearing under the CPIA 1996, s 29.

[15] Early Administrative Hearings, introduced under s 50 Crime and Disorder Act 1998, take place within two days of charge and are not an appropriate venue to deal with admissibility issues.

[16] The general practice is that pre-trial reviews are conducted by a single justice or justices' clerk, whose powers are limited to those contained in s 49 Crime and Disorder Act 1998 and who are therefore not able to decide admissibility issues.

[17] A case is regarded as disposed of if the defendant is acquitted or convicted, or if the prosecutor decides not to proceed with the case: CPIA 1996, s 40(3).

[18] CPIA 1996, s 40(4); but no application may be made by a party to the case unless there has been a material change of circumstances since the ruling was made: s 40(5).

[19] There are no established guidelines for pre-trial reviews and at present such rulings are rare due to the tendency for pre-trial reviews to be conducted by single justices or justices' clerks.

[20] [2000] 1 WLR 377.

preference of the evidence of one expert witness over that of another. The Court of Appeal considered the duty to give reasons to be a function of due process. A party should be in no doubt as to why they had won or lost the case and whether the court had misdirected itself so as to enable the losing party to consider whether he might appeal. The extent of the duty to give reasons varies depending on the decision and the circumstances.[21]

17.9 In the criminal sphere, the absence of a detailed ruling on the admissibility of evidence will not necessarily attract criticism,[22] but recent authority indicates this may not always be the case:

> In our judgment, on this aspect of the matter, the judge plainly did not give reasons for admitting the statements. It is clear that he should have done so. It is clear that the reasons for exercising the discretion under section 26 [of the Criminal Justice Act 1988], like the reasons for exercising any other discretion, ought to be given by the trial judge, however briefly. That has been the position in English law for many years and it is a matter to which Article 6 of the European Convention gives added emphasis.[23]

17.10 In the Crown Court, reasons should be given for the Crown Court's decision on appeal from a magistrates' court, allowing the parties to know the nature of the criminality the appeal court had found and to consider whether to apply to state a case.[24] The duty to give reasons applies equally where the court has found for the defendant as on the upholding of a conviction.[25] This duty is not absolute.[26]

17.11 Magistrates have no general duty to give judgments or reasons for their decisions and will not necessarily be criticised for their failure to give reasons.[27] However, there is support for the approach that reasons should be given, in order to assist the defence in considering possible grounds of appeal.[28]

---

[21] In *R v Secretary of State for the Home Department, ex p Doody* [1993] QB 157 Lord Mustill held that the applicants, who had been convicted of murder, were entitled to know the reasons behind the Secretary of State's decision as to the length of the penal element which they had to serve. This was because the applicant had "an obvious human desire to be told the reason for a decision so gravely affecting his future ...", and because it was necessary to have this information in order to be able to mount an effective attack on the decision.

[22] See *Moss* (1990) 91 Cr App R 371 at 375.

[23] *Denton, The Times*, 22 November 2000; judgment 19 October 2000, para 35, *per* Rose LJ.

[24] *R v Snaresbrook Crown Court ex p Input Management Ltd* (1999) 163 JP 533.

[25] *R v Inner London Crown Court, ex p London Borough of Lambeth* [2000] Crim LR 303.

[26] It was held in *R v Kingston Crown Court, ex p B (A Juvenile)* (2000) 164 JP 633 that there was no such requirement where the reasons for the decision were obvious or the subject of the appeal was unimportant.

[27] *R v The Southend Stipendiary Magistrate, ex p Rochford District Council* [1995] Env LR 1. See also *A v DPP* [2000] Crim LR 572.

[28] *Archbold* 15–440.

The ECHR jurisprudence

17.12 Article 6, the right to a fair trial, requires a court to give reasons for its judgment, enabling the defendant to challenge the court's decision on appeal,[29] but this duty does not extend to all decisions. It is dependent on the nature of the decision and the circumstances of the case. Where a submission to the judge would be decisive of the outcome of the case if accepted, specific and express reasons are required.[30]

17.13 The relevant consideration is whether the inclusion or exclusion of evidence of previous misconduct is decisive to the outcome of the trial. Reasons must be given for the ultimate judgment,[31] a major component of the complaint,[32] or a point allowing the case to be heard such as the application of time-bars:[33] these are all decisive matters. The reasoning in *Hadjianastassiou* is also relevant: reasons may be required to allow the defendant to adequately assert his right to appeal.[34]

Conclusion

17.14 In the Crown Court a judge will usually find it necessary to give reasons for a ruling on admissibility of evidence. In summary hearings, it will not necessarily be known at the time a decision is made on the admissibility of bad character evidence whether it will play a decisive role in the verdict, and even at the end of the summary trial, only the magistrates will *know* on what basis the defendant was convicted or acquitted. Thus the Strasbourg jurisprudence does not translate easily to the English context. The indications in the English case law have been that magistrates are not always *required* to give reasons, even in situations where one might expect them to have to do so. If the HRA 1998 has truly changed the position in summary trials, it will require an authoritative decision to say so. There is a trend in this direction, but so far no authority which requires magistrates to give reasons for their rulings, although where a case is appealed they may well do so.[35]

17.15 **We recommend that where a court**

  (1) **rules on whether leave is required for evidence of bad character to be admitted, or**

---

[29] *Hadjianastassiou v Greece* (1993) 16 EHRR 219.

[30] *Hiro Balani v Spain* (1995) 19 EHRR 566.

[31] *Hadjianastassiou v Greece* (1993) 16 EHRR 219.

[32] *Hiro Balani v Spain* (1995) 19 EHRR 566: whether trade mark rights could be asserted over a similar name in an action to remove a trade mark from the register.

[33] *Ruiz Torija v Spain* (1995) 19 EHRR 553.

[34] Under Article 6(3).

[35] Eg, Jackson J held in *R v Kingston Crown Court, ex p B (a juvenile)* that the Crown Court judge sitting in an appellate capacity was under a duty to give reasons, particularly as he was reversing a well-reasoned decision of the magistrates: (2000) 164 JP 633.

In *R v Crown Court at Canterbury ex p Howson-Ball* the Divisional Court quashed the Crown Court decision (rejecting the appeal from the magistrates) because "in the absence of an analysis of the evidence that the Crown Court had heard, its reasons were inadequate": (2000) JP 164 910.

(2) gives or withholds such leave, or

(3) rules on whether the case should be stopped because of such evidence being contaminated,

it must give the reasons for the ruling in open court and those reasons must be recorded.

17.16 This recommendation is given effect by clause 15. In the Crown Court, reasons announced in open court must be entered in the record, by virtue of rule 18 of the Criminal Appeal Rules 1968, so the Bill does not need to make any provision in that respect, but there is no equivalent rule in respect of the magistrates' courts, hence subsection (1)(b).

WARNINGS TO THE JURY

A warning against speculation

17.17 There will no doubt be cases where jurors become aware that evidence about the defendant's criminal record might be being withheld from them. (This is one of the reasons that some put forward for disclosing the record in all cases.)[36] Our view is that, where the defence agree, the best way to tackle this issue might be for the judge to address the jury directly on the point. As a judge may warn the jury not to speculate about any matter on which they have not heard evidence, so it may be appropriate for the warning to include the absence of evidence about the defendant's character.[37] This is a course which is currently open to the court if the defence so request.

A warning against placing too much weight on evidence of past misconduct

17.18 One of the reasons that evidence of bad character should be treated with caution is, as we have said, because of the risk that fact-finders will place too much weight on it.[38] For this reason, where the prosecution seeks to adduce such evidence against the defendant, we have recommended that there is an interests of justice test. Thus the risk of undue weight will be taken into account. The interests of justice may require the evidence to be admissible in spite of the risk of prejudice.

17.19 The current law is restrictive in that it requires the judge to direct the jury that evidence admitted under the 1898 Act goes only to credibility and is not relevant to the issue of guilt. Cases arise where such a rule sits ill with the evidence actually presented. Our view is that judges should be free to advise the jury as the individual case requires. The judge will no doubt start by pointing out the way in which the evidence is said to be relevant. The judge may well think it necessary to warn the jury of the risks of reasoning from past behaviour to a conclusion that the defendant is guilty. This will be especially so where the bad character evidence discloses misconduct of a similar nature to that alleged in the charge, and

---

[36] See para 6.18 above.

[37] As we suggest at para 6.24 above.

[38] See para 5.18 above.

especially pertinent where the purpose of adducing the bad character evidence is for its relevance to the defendant's credibility (under the corrective or credibility exceptions at the behest of the prosecution, or under the co-defendant exception).[39]

17.20 **We conclude that the jury may need to be given warnings by the judge in two situations: first, where no evidence has been adduced about the defendant's character and there is a danger of speculation about it; second, where there is a danger that the jury will give undue weight to bad character evidence which is admitted.**

SERVICE COURTS AND PROFESSIONAL TRIBUNALS

17.21 In the consultation paper we expressed the provisional view that any reforms that we recommended should apply in places where the criminal rules of evidence currently apply, namely courts-martial and professional tribunals established by statute.[40]

17.22 Eighteen respondents expressly addressed this issue. The office of the Judge Advocate General drew our attention to statutory provisions which automatically apply the rules of evidence in civilian courts to service courts. The question was whether there would be any reason to disapply those provisions in the light of our recommendations. No respondents argued that there was any reason for the rules applicable in civilian criminal proceedings not to apply in service courts and professional tribunals in the usual way.

17.23 **We recommend that the above rules should apply where the criminal rules of evidence currently apply, namely in courts-martial, summary appeal courts, the Court-Martial Appeal Court and Standing Civilian Courts, and in naval disciplinary courts and professional tribunals established by statute, but should not affect coroners' courts.**

---

[39] See paras 12.21, 13.47 - 13.48, and 14.35 above.

[40] Provisional proposal 50. See Part XV of the consultation paper.

PART XVIII
THE COLLECTED RECOMMENDATIONS AND CONCLUSIONS

In this Part we set out our recommendations and conclusions, with reference to the paragraphs of the report where they appear.

REPLACEMENT OF EXISTING RULES

1. We recommend that all the rules on the admissibility of bad character evidence in criminal proceedings be contained in a single statute, and that the common law rules (including the hearsay exception for evidence of reputation) be abolished.[1]

EVIDENCE OF BAD CHARACTER

2. We recommend that evidence of a person's bad character should be defined as evidence which shows or tends to show that that person

    (1) has committed an offence, or

    (2) has behaved, or is disposed to behave, in a way of which a reasonable person might disapprove.[2]

EVIDENCE OF BAD CHARACTER WHICH IS AUTOMATICALLY ADMISSIBLE

3. We recommend that evidence of a person's bad character should be automatically admissible if

    (1) it has to do with the offence charged, or is evidence of misconduct in connection with the investigation or prosecution of that offence; or

    (2) all parties agree to its admission; or

    (3) it is evidence of the defendant's bad character which the defendant seeks to adduce.[3]

EVIDENCE OF BAD CHARACTER WHICH IS PRIMA FACIE INADMISSIBLE

4. We recommend that

    (1) all other evidence of bad character should be admissible only with the leave of the court, and

    (2) leave should be granted only if the evidence falls within one of the exceptions we recommend below.[4]

---

[1] Para 4.85; cl 20(1) and (2) of the draft Bill.

[2] Para 8.19; cl 1 of the draft Bill.

[3] Para 8.31; cl 2 of the draft Bill.

[4] Para 8.32; cl 3 and 6 of the draft Bill.

Exceptions: non-defendants

Substantial explanatory value

5. We recommend that leave may be given to adduce evidence of the bad character of a person other than a defendant if it has substantial explanatory value.[5]

Substantial probative value

6. We recommend that leave may be given to adduce evidence of the bad character of a person other than a defendant if it has substantial probative value in relation to a matter in issue in the proceedings which is of substantial importance in the context of the case as a whole.[6]

Exceptions: defendants

Evidence of substantial explanatory value

7. We recommend that leave may be given to adduce evidence of the bad character of a defendant if it has substantial explanatory value and the interests of justice require it to be admissible, even taking account of its potentially prejudicial effect.[7]

Evidence of substantial probative value

8. We recommend that leave may be given to the prosecution to adduce evidence of the bad character of a defendant if

    (1) the evidence has substantial probative value in relation to a matter in issue (other than whether the defendant has a propensity to be untruthful) which is itself of substantial importance in the context of the case as a whole, and

    (2) the interests of justice require it to be admissible, even taking account of its potentially prejudicial effect.[8]

Evidence of the defendant's propensity to be untruthful

9. We recommend that leave may be given to the prosecution to adduce evidence of the bad character of a defendant which is relevant only to whether the defendant has a propensity to be untruthful if

    (1) the evidence has substantial probative value in showing that the defendant has such a propensity,

    (2) the defendant has suggested that another person has such a propensity,

    (3) the evidence adduced in support of that suggestion does not have to do with the offence charged, and is not evidence of misconduct in connection with the investigation or prosecution of that offence,

---

[5] Para 9.42; cl 4 of the draft Bill.

[6] Para 9.41; cl 5 of the draft Bill.

[7] Para 10.12; cl 7 of the draft Bill.

[8] Para 11.46; cl 8 of the draft Bill.

(4) without the evidence of the defendant's bad character the fact-finders would get a misleading impression of the defendant's propensity to be untruthful in comparison with that of the other person, and

(5) the interests of justice require the evidence to be admissible, even taking account of its potentially prejudicial effect.[9]

Evidence to correct a false or misleading impression about the defendant's character

10. We recommend that leave may be given to the prosecution to adduce evidence of the bad character of a defendant if

    (1) the defendant is responsible for an assertion (express or implied) which creates a false or misleading impression about the defendant,

    (2) the evidence has substantial probative value in correcting that impression, and

    (3) the interests of justice require it to be admissible, even taking account of its potentially prejudicial effect.[10]

11. We recommend that, where the prosecution seeks to rely on this exception in summary proceedings, it should first indicate to the court that the impression created is false or misleading and that the prosecution has evidence to controvert it; the bench should then rule on whether the impression is important enough to need controverting; only if the bench so rules may the prosecution detail the nature of its corrective evidence, and proceed with the full application to introduce it.[11]

Evidence of the bad character of a co-defendant

12. We recommend that leave may be given to a co-defendant to adduce evidence of the bad character of a defendant where it has substantial probative value in relation to a matter in issue between the co-defendant and the defendant where that issue is itself of substantial importance in the context of the case as a whole –

    except that, if it has probative value only in showing that the defendant has a propensity to be untruthful, leave may not be given unless, in addition, the defendant's case is such as to undermine that of the co-defendant.[12]

Statutory guidance

13. We recommend that the legislation should set out the factors to which a court is to have regard when assessing the probative value of bad character evidence or where the interests of justice lie.[13]

---

[9] Para 12.13; cl 9 of the draft Bill.

[10] Para 13.48; cl 10 of the draft Bill.

[11] Para 13.50; cl 10(9) of the draft Bill.

[12] Para 14.53; cl 11 of the draft Bill.

Assumption of truth in assessment of probative value

14. We recommend that, where the court is required to assess the probative value of evidence of a person's bad character, it should be required to do so on the assumption that the evidence is true, except where it appears, on the basis of any material before the court, that no court or jury could reasonably find it to be true.[14]

Special cases

15. We recommend that section 27(3) of the Theft Act 1968 should be repealed.[15]

16. We recommend that the admissibility of evidence of the defendant's bad character pursuant to section 1(2) of the Official Secrets Act 1911 should be determined by the above rules.[16]

PROCEDURAL AND ANCILLARY MATTERS

A notice requirement

17. We recommend that where a party wishes to adduce evidence of the defendant's bad character which does not have to do with the offence charged, and is not evidence of misconduct in connection with the investigation or prosecution of that offence, that party should be required to give notice of the intention to do so, but that requirement may be dispensed with by the court or the defendant.[17]

An additional safeguard in the case of contaminated evidence

18. We recommend that, in a trial on indictment, where evidence of the defendant's bad character has been admitted with leave, and the judge is satisfied that the evidence is contaminated such that, considering the importance of the evidence to the case against the defendant, a conviction would be unsafe, the judge should be required to discharge the jury or direct the jury to acquit.[18]

A duty to give reasons

19. We recommend that where a court

    (1) rules on whether leave is required for evidence of bad character to be admitted, or

    (2) gives or withholds such leave, or

    (3) rules on whether the case should be stopped because of such evidence being contaminated,

---

[13] Para 7.19; cl 5(2), 9(7) and 10(8) of the draft Bill.

[14] Para 15.26; cl 14 of the draft Bill.

[15] Para 11.55; cl 20(3)(b) of the draft Bill.

[16] Para 11.61.

[17] Para 17.3; cl 16 of the draft Bill.

[18] Para 15.37; cl 13 of the draft Bill.

it must give the reasons for the ruling in open court and those reasons must be recorded.[19]

Warnings to the jury

20. We conclude that the jury may need to be given warnings by the judge in two situations: first, where no evidence has been adduced about the defendant's character and there is a danger of speculation about it; second, where there is a danger that the jury will give undue weight to bad character evidence which is admitted.[20]

Severance of counts/informations

21. We recommend that where

    (1) a defendant is charged with more than one offence,

    (2) evidence of the defendant's bad character is admissible on one of the offences charged but inadmissible on another, and

    (3) the defendant applies for the offences to be tried separately,

    that application should be granted unless the court is satisfied that the defendant can receive a fair trial.[21]

GENERAL

22. We recommend that the above rules should apply where the criminal rules of evidence currently apply, namely in courts-martial, summary appeal courts, the Court-Martial Appeal Court and Standing Civilian Courts, and in naval disciplinary courts and professional tribunals established by statute, but should not affect coroners' courts.[22]

(*Signed*) ROBERT CARNWATH, *Chairman*
HUGH BEALE
STUART BRIDGE
MARTIN PARTINGTON
ALAN WILKIE

MICHAEL SAYERS, *Secretary*
8 August 2001

---

[19] Para 17.15; cl 15 of the draft Bill.

[20] Para 17.20.

[21] Para 16.20; cl 12 of the draft Bill.

[22] Para 17.23; cl 18 and Sched 1 to the draft Bill.

Criminal Evidence Bill

CONTENTS

Bad character evidence generally

1. "Bad character"
2. Requirement of leave

Persons other than defendants

3. Non-defendant's bad character
4. Evidence with explanatory value
5. Evidence going to a matter in issue

Defendants

6. Defendant's bad character
7. Evidence with explanatory value
8. Evidence going to a matter in issue
9. Evidence going to credibility
10. Evidence to correct false impression
11. Evidence going to an issue between co-defendants
12. Trying more than one offence together
13. Stopping the case where evidence contaminated

General

14. Assumption of truth in assessment of probative value
15. Court's duty to give reasons for rulings
16. Rules of court
17. Interpretation
18. Armed forces
19. Minor and consequential amendments
20. Repeals etc
21. Citation, commencement and extent

Schedule 1 — Armed forces
Schedule 2 — Repeals

Criminal Evidence Bill 1

DRAFT

OF A

BILL

TO

Make provision about evidence of bad character in criminal proceedings.

B E IT ENACTED by the Queen's most Excellent Majesty, by and with the advice and consent of the Lords Spiritual and Temporal, and Commons, in this present Parliament assembled, and by the authority of the same, as follows:—

Bad character evidence generally

1 **"Bad character"**

References in this Act to evidence of a person's bad character are references to evidence which shows or tends to show that—
- (a) he has committed an offence, or
- (b) he has behaved, or is disposed to behave, in a way that, in the opinion of the court, might be viewed with disapproval by a reasonable person.

2 **Requirement of leave**

(1) In criminal proceedings evidence of a person's bad character is admissible only with leave of the court, unless the evidence—
- (a) has to do with the alleged facts of the offence with which the defendant is charged, or
- (b) is evidence of misconduct in connection with the investigation or prosecution of that offence.

(2) This section does not apply in relation to an item of evidence if—
- (a) all parties to the proceedings agree to the evidence being admissible, or
- (b) in the case of evidence of the defendant's bad character, the evidence is adduced by the defendant himself or is given in answer to a question asked by him in cross-examination and intended to elicit it.

EXPLANATORY NOTES

Bad character evidence generally

Clause 1

This clause defines evidence of bad character.

Clause 2

This clause provides that, with certain exceptions, bad character evidence is admissible in criminal proceedings *only* with leave of the court. Clauses 3–11 then describe the circumstances in which leave may be given, where it is required.

Subsection (1) ensures that leave is *not* required for evidence of the central facts of the case. Evidence is admissible under this exception if, though it falls within the definition of evidence of bad character, it has to do with the alleged facts of the offence charged, or the investigation or prosecution of that offence. Leave is required *only* for evidence of bad character which falls *outside* that central set of facts. For example, D is charged with burglary. Evidence that he committed that burglary is evidence of bad character as defined by clause 1, because it is evidence which tends to show that he has committed an offence; but it does not require leave, because it is evidence of the offence *with which he is charged*. Evidence that he committed an assault in the course of the burglary is also evidence of bad character, for the same reason; but it too does not require leave because, though not actually evidence of the offence charged, it *has to do with* the alleged facts of that offence. Evidence that D had tried to intimidate a prosecution witness would also not require leave, because it is evidence of misconduct in connection with the *investigation or prosecution* of the offence charged. Evidence that D had committed burglary *on another occasion*, however, would satisfy none of these conditions, and would therefore require leave.

The clause applies equally where the evidence is of the bad character of a person who is not a defendant. For example, evidence that a police officer planted evidence on the defendant, or fabricated a confession, would be admissible without leave because it has to do with the alleged facts of the offence charged or is connected with the investigation or prosecution of that offence. Evidence that the officer had planted evidence or fabricated confessions *on other occasions*, however, would satisfy none of these conditions, and would therefore require leave.

Subsection (2) provides that leave is not required if all parties consent to the evidence being admitted, or if it is the defendant who wishes to adduce evidence of his or her own bad character.

Persons other than defendants

3 Non-defendant's bad character

In the case of evidence of the bad character of a person other than the defendant, the court is not to give leave under section 2 unless the evidence falls within section 4 or 5.

4 Evidence with explanatory value

Evidence falls within this section if—
- (a) without it, the court or jury would find it impossible or difficult properly to understand other evidence in the case, and
- (b) its value for understanding the case as a whole is substantial.

5 Evidence going to a matter in issue

(1) Evidence falls within this section if it has substantial probative value in relation to a matter which—
- (a) is a matter in issue in the proceedings, and
- (b) is of substantial importance in the context of the case as a whole.

(2) In assessing the probative value of evidence for the purposes of this section the court must have regard to the following factors (and to any others it considers relevant)—
- (a) the nature and number of the events, or other things, to which the evidence relates;
- (b) when those events or things are alleged to have happened or existed;
- (c) where—
    - (i) the evidence is evidence of a person's misconduct, and
    - (ii) it is suggested that the evidence has probative value by reason of similarity between that misconduct and other alleged misconduct,

  the nature and extent of the similarities and the dissimilarities between each of the alleged instances of misconduct;
- (d) where—
    - (i) the evidence is evidence of a person's misconduct,
    - (ii) it is suggested that that person is also responsible for the misconduct charged, and
    - (iii) the identity of the person responsible for the misconduct charged is disputed,

  the extent to which the evidence shows or tends to show that the same person was responsible each time.

(3) In subsection (2)(d) "misconduct charged" means the misconduct constituting the offence with which the defendant is charged.

EXPLANATORY NOTES

Persons other than defendants

Clause 3

Where leave is required to adduce evidence of the bad character of someone who is *not a defendant*, this clause provides that leave may only be given if the evidence falls within clause 4 or 5.

Clause 4

This clause concerns evidence of the bad character of someone who is not a defendant which any party wishes to adduce for the sake of its *explanatory* value.

Leave may be given under this clause if

- without the evidence it would be impossible or difficult for the magistrates or jury properly to understand other evidence in the case; *and*
- the evidence has substantial value for the understanding of the case as a whole.

Clause 5

This clause concerns evidence of the bad character of someone who is not a defendant which any party wishes to adduce for the sake of its *probative* value.

Leave may be given under this clause if the evidence has substantial probative value in relation to a matter in issue which is itself of substantial importance in the context of the case as a whole.

Subsection (2) lists a number of factors to which the court must have regard in assessing the probative value of the evidence. For this purpose the court must assume that the evidence is true unless it appears that no court or jury could reasonably find it to be true (see clause 14).

Defendants

6 Defendant's bad character

In the case of evidence of the defendant's bad character, the court is not to give leave under section 2 unless the evidence falls within section 7, 8, 9, 10 or 11.

7 Evidence with explanatory value

(1) Evidence falls within this section if the following three conditions are met.

(2) The first condition is that, without the evidence, the court or jury would find it impossible or difficult properly to understand other evidence in the case.

(3) The second condition is that the value of the evidence for understanding the case as a whole is substantial.

(4) The third condition is that the court is satisfied—
 (a) that, in all the circumstances of the case, the evidence carries no risk of prejudice to the defendant, or
 (b) that the value of the evidence for understanding the case as a whole is such that, taking account of the risk of prejudice, the interests of justice nevertheless require the evidence to be admissible.

8 Evidence going to a matter in issue

(1) Evidence falls within this section if the following two conditions are met.

(2) The first condition is that the evidence has substantial probative value in relation to a matter which—
 (a) is a matter in issue in the proceedings, and
 (b) is of substantial importance in the context of the case as a whole.

(3) The second condition is that the court is satisfied—
 (a) that, in all the circumstances of the case, the evidence carries no risk of prejudice to the defendant, or
 (b) that, taking account of the risk of prejudice, the interests of justice nevertheless require the evidence to be admissible in view of—
  (i) how much probative value it has in relation to the matter in issue,
  (ii) what other evidence has been, or can be, given on that matter, and
  (iii) how important that matter is in the context of the case as a whole.

(4) In determining whether the two conditions are met the court must have regard to the factors listed in section 5(2) (and to any others it considers relevant).

(5) For the purposes of this section, whether the defendant has a propensity to be untruthful is not to be regarded as a matter in issue in the proceedings.

(6) Only prosecution evidence can fall within this section.

9 Evidence going to credibility

(1) This section applies only where—

EXPLANATORY NOTES

Defendants

Clause 6

Where leave is required to adduce evidence of a *defendant's* bad character, it may only be given if the evidence falls within (at least) one of clauses 7, 8, 9, 10 or 11.

Clause 7

This clause concerns evidence of a defendant's bad character which the prosecution or a co-defendant wishes to adduce for the sake of its *explanatory* value.

To obtain leave under this clause, the party seeking to adduce the evidence must satisfy the court that

- without the evidence, it would be impossible or difficult for the magistrates or jury properly to understand other evidence in the case; *and*
- the evidence has substantial value for the understanding of the case as a whole; *and*
- *either* the evidence is unprejudicial, *or* its explanatory value is such that, even taking account of the risks of prejudice which do attach to it, the interests of justice *require* it to be admitted. "Prejudice" is defined at clause 17(2).

Clause 8

This clause concerns evidence of the bad character of a defendant which the prosecution wishes to adduce for the sake of its *probative* value.

To obtain leave under this clause, the prosecution must satisfy the court that

- the evidence has substantial probative value in relation to a matter in issue which is itself of substantial importance in the context of the case as a whole; *and*
- *either* the evidence is unprejudicial, *or* it is so probative that, even taking account of the risks of prejudice which do attach to it, the interests of justice *require* it to be admissible. Subsection (3)(b) sets out the factors that the court must take into account in determining whether the evidence has enough probative value to outweigh any risk of prejudice. ("Prejudice" is defined at clause 17(2).)

In assessing whether the evidence has enough probative value to satisfy these conditions, the court must have regard to the factors listed at clause 5(2). For this purpose the court must assume that the evidence is true unless it appears that no court or jury could reasonably find it to be true (see clause 14).

The purpose of subsection (5) is to ensure that the prosecution may *not* advance its case under this exception by seeking only to prove that the defendant has a propensity to be untruthful. If, for example, the defendant has a conviction for perjury, the prosecution may not seek leave to adduce evidence of that conviction under clause 8 on the basis that the defendant's propensity to lie on oath is a matter in issue. To adduce this evidence it would have to satisfy the more stringent requirements of clause 9.

This rule does not, however, prevent the prosecution from seeking to adduce evidence which shows that the defendant has advanced a *similar defence* before.

Clause 9

This clause concerns evidence of a defendant's bad character which the prosecution wishes to adduce to show that the defendant has a *propensity to be untruthful*. The essence of this exception is to ensure that the magistrates or the jury are not given a false impression of the defendant's propensity to be untruthful *as compared with that of another person*.

(a) the defendant makes an attack on a person's character, and
(b) the effect of the attack is to suggest, or to support a suggestion, that the person has a propensity to be untruthful.

(2) For the purposes of this section a defendant makes an attack on a person's character where—
   (a) he adduces evidence of the person's bad character, other than—
      (i) evidence that has to do with the alleged facts of the offence with which the defendant is charged, or
      (ii) evidence of misconduct in connection with the investigation or prosecution of that offence,
   (b) he asks questions in cross-examination that are intended to elicit evidence of the kind referred to in paragraph (a), or
   (c) evidence is given of an assertion made about the person by the defendant—
      (i) on being questioned under caution, before charge, about the offence with which he is charged, or
      (ii) on being charged with the offence or officially informed that he might be prosecuted for it,
   and the assertion is such that, if it were made in evidence, the evidence containing the assertion would be evidence of the kind referred to in paragraph (a).

(3) Evidence falls within this section if the following three conditions are met.

(4) The first condition is that the evidence has substantial probative value in showing that the defendant has a propensity to be untruthful.

(5) The second condition is that, without the evidence, the court or jury would get an inaccurate impression of the defendant's propensity to be untruthful in comparison with that of the other person.

(6) The third condition is that the court is satisfied—
   (a) that, in all the circumstances of the case, the evidence carries no risk of prejudice to the defendant, or
   (b) that, taking account of the risk of prejudice, the interests of justice nevertheless require the evidence to be admissible in view of—
      (i) how much probative value it has in showing that the defendant has a propensity to be untruthful,
      (ii) what other evidence has been, or can be, given on that matter, and
      (iii) how important it is, in the context of the case of a whole, to prevent the impression mentioned in subsection (5).

(7) In determining whether the three conditions are met the court must have regard to the following factors (and to any others it considers relevant)—
   (a) the nature and number of the events, or other things, to which the defendant's attack relates and of those to which the evidence in question ("the responding evidence") relates;
   (b) when those events or things are alleged to have happened or existed;
   (c) how important is the defendant's propensity to be untruthful, and that of the other person, in the context of the prosecution case and of the defence case;

EXPLANATORY NOTES

Clause 9 (cont'd)

This clause applies only where the defendant has suggested that another person has a propensity to be untruthful. The defendant may do this by adducing evidence of that person's propensity, by cross-examining to that effect, or by making an assertion to that effect after being cautioned (whether when being questioned or on being charged) of which evidence is then given.

The clause does *not* apply where the allegation of untruthfulness has to do with the facts of the offence charged or the investigation or prosecution of that offence. For example, the defendant would not open the door to evidence of his own past untruthfulness merely by suggesting that prosecution witnesses are lying about the offence charged, or that the prosecution's evidence has been fabricated by the police.

To obtain leave under this clause, the prosecution must satisfy the court that

- the evidence it wishes to adduce has substantial probative value in showing that the defendant has a propensity to be untruthful; *and*

- without that evidence, the magistrates or jury would get an inaccurate impression of the defendant's propensity to be untruthful in comparison with that of the other person; *and*

- *either* the evidence is unprejudicial, *or* it is so probative that, even taking account of the risks of prejudice which do attach to it, the interests of justice *require* it to be admissible. Subsection (6)(b) sets out the factors that the court must take into account in determining whether the evidence has enough probative value to outweigh any risk of prejudice. ("Prejudice" is defined at clause 17(2).)

Subsection (7) sets out a number of further factors to which the court must have regard in determining whether these conditions are met.

In assessing the probative value of the evidence, the court must assume that it is true unless it appears that no court or jury could reasonably find it to be true (see clause 14).

(d) in a case where this section applies by virtue of subsection (2)(b), whether or not the evidence intended to be elicited is actually given;

(e) how inaccurate the impression mentioned in subsection (5) would be;

(f) where the responding evidence is of a spent conviction, the fact that the conviction is spent;

(g) any risk that admitting the responding evidence would be confusing or misleading, or would unduly prolong the proceedings.

(8) Only prosecution evidence can fall within this section.

10 Evidence to correct false impression

(1) This section applies only where the defendant is responsible for the making of an express or implied assertion which is apt to give the court or jury a false or misleading impression about the defendant.

(2) Evidence falls within this section if the following two conditions are met.

(3) The first condition is that the evidence has substantial probative value in correcting the false or misleading impression.

(4) The second condition is that the court is satisfied —
   (a) that, in all the circumstances of the case, the evidence carries no risk of prejudice to the defendant, or
   (b) that, taking account of the risk of prejudice, the interests of justice nevertheless require the evidence to be admissible in view of —
      (i) how much probative value it has in correcting the false or misleading impression,
      (ii) what other evidence has been, or can be, given to correct that impression, and
      (iii) how important it is, in the context of the case as a whole, for that impression to be corrected.

(5) For the purposes of this section a defendant is responsible for the making of an assertion if —
   (a) the assertion is made by the defendant in the proceedings (whether or not in evidence given by him),
   (b) the assertion was made by the defendant —
      (i) on being questioned under caution, before charge, about the offence with which he is charged, or
      (ii) on being charged with the offence or officially informed that he might be prosecuted for it,
      and evidence of the assertion is given in the proceedings,
   (c) the assertion is made by a witness called by the defendant,
   (d) the assertion is made by any witness in cross-examination in response to a question asked by the defendant and intended, in the opinion of the court, to elicit it, or
   (e) the assertion was made by any person out of court, and the defendant adduces evidence of it in the proceedings.

(6) Where it appears to the court that a defendant, by means of his conduct (other than the giving of evidence) in the proceedings, is seeking to give the court or jury an impression about himself that is false or misleading, the court may if it

EXPLANATORY NOTES

Clause 10

This clause concerns evidence of a defendant's bad character which the prosecution wishes to adduce to correct a *false or misleading impression about the defendant* for which the defendant is responsible. A defendant is responsible for such an impression if it results from an assertion which is made

- by the defendant in the proceedings (either in the course of giving evidence, or through his or her representative);
- in an assertion made out of court by the defendant after caution, and evidence of the assertion is before the court;
- by a defence witness;
- by any witness in cross-examination by the defendant, unless the question was not intended to produce the answer given; or
- by anyone out of court, and the defendant adduces evidence of it.

Under subsection (6) the court may also treat the defendant as responsible for creating a false or misleading impression about himself or herself where it appears to the court that the defendant is seeking to give the magistrates or jury such an impression by means of his or her conduct.

To obtain leave under this clause, the prosecution must satisfy the court that

- the evidence has substantial probative value in correcting the false or misleading impression; *and*
- *either* the evidence is unprejudicial, *or* it has such corrective value that, even taking account of the risks of prejudice which do attach to it, the interests of justice *require* it to be admissible. Subsection (4)(b) sets out the factors that the court must take into account in determining whether the evidence has enough corrective value to outweigh any risk of prejudice. ("Prejudice" is defined at clause 17(2).)

appears just to do so treat the defendant as being responsible for the making of an assertion which is apt to give that impression.

(7) In subsection (6) "conduct" includes appearance or dress.

(8) In determining whether the two conditions are met the court must have regard to the following factors (and to any others it considers relevant)—
   (a) the nature of the impression given by the assertion referred to in subsection (1), and how false or misleading that impression is;
   (b) by whom and in what circumstances the assertion is or was made;
   (c) the nature and number of the events, or other things, to which the evidence in question ("the correcting evidence") relates;
   (d) when those events or things are alleged to have happened or existed;
   (e) where the correcting evidence is of a spent conviction, the fact that the conviction is spent;
   (f) any risk that admitting the correcting evidence would be confusing or misleading, or would unduly prolong the proceedings.

(9) Where in proceedings before a magistrates' court—
   (a) the defendant is responsible for the making of an assertion which is apt to give the court a certain impression about the defendant,
   (b) the prosecution allege that the impression is false or misleading, and
   (c) in reliance on this section the prosecution propose to apply for leave under section 2 to adduce or elicit evidence to correct the impression,
the court must first rule (without being given any details about the evidence) whether, however false or misleading the impression may be, it is unimportant in the context of the case as a whole for it to be corrected; and if the court makes a ruling to that effect, no evidence can fall within this section in relation to the assertion in question.

(10) Only prosecution evidence can fall within this section.

11 Evidence going to an issue between co-defendants

(1) Evidence falls within this section if it has substantial probative value in relation to a matter which—
   (a) is a matter in issue between the defendant and a co-defendant, and
   (b) is of substantial importance in the context of the case as a whole.

(2) For the purposes of this section, evidence is not to be treated as having the probative value mentioned in subsection (1) by virtue of its relevance to the question whether the defendant has a propensity to be untruthful unless the nature or conduct of his defence is such as to undermine the co-defendant's defence.

(3) In assessing the probative value of evidence for the purposes of this section the court must have regard to the factors listed in section 5(2) (and to any others it considers relevant).

(4) Only evidence—
   (a) which is to be (or has been) adduced by the co-defendant, or
   (b) which a witness is to be invited to give (or has given) in cross-examination by the co-defendant,
can fall within this section.

EXPLANATORY NOTES

Clause 10 (cont'd)

Subsection (8) sets out a number of further factors that the court must take into account in determining whether these two conditions are met.

In assessing the corrective value of the evidence, the court must assume that it is true unless it appears that no court or jury could reasonably find it to be true (see clause 14).

Subsection (9) provides that, where the prosecution proposes to apply for leave under this clause in the *magistrates'* court, the court must first rule whether, in the context of the case as a whole, the impression in question is sufficiently important to need correcting. If the court rules that it is not, the prosecution may not pursue that application. The court must make its ruling without hearing about the evidence which it is said would correct the impression given.

Clause 11

This clause concerns evidence of a defendant's bad character which a *co-defendant* wishes to adduce (or to elicit in cross-examination) for the sake of its *probative* value. (If the co-defendant wishes to adduce it for the sake of its *explanatory* value, leave may be sought under clause 7.) The prosecution may not apply under this clause.

Leave will be given under this clause if the evidence has substantial probative value in relation to a matter in issue between the defendants concerned, which is of substantial importance in the context of the case as a whole. For this purpose the court must have regard to the factors listed at clause 5(2), and must assume that the evidence is true unless it appears that no court or jury could reasonably find it to be true (see clause 14). There is no need for the court to consider whether the evidence is prejudicial or, if so, whether the interests of justice require it to be admitted despite that risk.

Subsection (2), however, provides that evidence of a defendant's *propensity to be untruthful* cannot be admitted under this clause unless that defendant has undermined the co-defendant's defence. The defendant may do this either by running a particular defence (for example, that the co-defendant was solely responsible) or by running the defence in a particular way (for example, by attacking the credibility of the co-defendant's witnesses).

12 Trying more than one offence together

(1) In section 5 of the Indictments Act 1915 (c. 90) (orders for separate trial etc) insert after subsection (2)—

"(2A) Where—
(a) a person is charged with more than one offence in the same indictment,
(b) the prosecution propose to adduce evidence which is admissible in relation to one of the offences but which, in relation to another, is evidence of the person's bad character and is inadmissible, and
(c) the person applies before trial for an order that the offences mentioned in paragraph (b) above be tried separately,

the court shall grant the application unless satisfied that trying the offences together would not prevent the defendant having a fair trial.

(2B) The reference in subsection (2A) above to evidence of the person's bad character shall be read in accordance with section 1 of the Criminal Evidence Act 2001."

(2) In subsection (3) of that section, after "before trial" insert "(in a case not falling within subsection (2A) above)".

(3) Where in proceedings before a magistrates' court—
(a) it is proposed that the defendant be tried for two or more offences together,
(b) the prosecution propose to adduce evidence which is admissible in relation to one of the offences but which, in relation to another, is evidence of the person's bad character and is inadmissible, and
(c) the defendant objects before trial to the offences mentioned in paragraph (b) being tried together,

the court may order those offences to be tried together only if satisfied that doing so would not prevent the defendant having a fair trial.

13 Stopping the case where evidence contaminated

(1) If on a defendant's trial on indictment for an offence—
(a) evidence of his bad character has been admitted with leave under section 2, and
(b) the court is satisfied at any time after the close of the case for the prosecution that—
(i) the evidence is contaminated, and
(ii) the contamination is such that, considering the importance of the evidence to the case against the defendant, his conviction of the offence would be unsafe,

the court must either direct the jury to acquit the defendant of the offence or, if it considers that there ought to be a retrial, discharge the jury.

(2) Where—
(a) a jury is directed under subsection (1) to acquit a defendant of an offence, and

EXPLANATORY NOTES

Clause 12

Subsection (1) amends section (5) of the Indictments Act 1915 so as to provide for the situation where counts are properly joined in an indictment and where evidence of the defendant's bad character is admissible on one count but inadmissible on another. If the defendant applies for the counts to be tried separately, the paramount consideration for the court is whether the defendant can receive a fair trial. If the court is not so satisfied, there must be separate trials.

Subsection (3) makes similar provision for summary trials.

Clause 13

This clause comes into play where, in a trial on indictment, evidence of a defendant's bad character has been admitted with leave, but, after the close of the prosecution's case, the court is satisfied that that evidence is "contaminated". By virtue of subsection (5), evidence might be "contaminated" as a result of: deliberate fabrication of allegations resulting from an agreement between witnesses; concoction of an allegation by one person (no conspiracy); collusion between witnesses to make their evidence sound more credible falling short of concoction of allegations; deliberate alteration of evidence or unconscious alteration of evidence, resulting from having become aware of what the evidence of another will be or has been.

Where the court is satisfied that the contamination is such that a conviction would be unsafe, it must stop the trial on that charge (and on any lesser offence: subsection (2)).

(b) the circumstances are such that, apart from this subsection, the defendant could if acquitted of that offence be found guilty of another offence,

the defendant may not be found guilty of that other offence if the court is satisfied as mentioned in subsection (1)(b) in respect of it.

(3) If—
  (a) a jury is required to determine under section 4A(2) of the Criminal Procedure (Insanity) Act 1964 (c. 84) whether a person charged on an indictment with an offence did the act or made the omission charged,
  (b) evidence of the person's bad character has been admitted with leave under section 2, and
  (c) the court is satisfied at any time after the close of the case for the prosecution that—
    (i) the evidence is contaminated, and
    (ii) the contamination is such that, considering the importance of the evidence to the case against the person, a finding that he did the act or made the omission would be unsafe,

the court must either direct the jury to acquit the defendant of the offence or, if it considers that there ought to be a rehearing, discharge the jury.

(4) This section does not prejudice any other power a court may have to direct a jury to acquit a person of an offence or to discharge a jury.

(5) For the purposes of this section, a person's evidence is contaminated where—
  (a) as a result of an agreement or understanding between the person and one or more others, or
  (b) as a result of the person being aware of anything alleged by one or more others who are, or could be, witnesses in the proceedings,

the evidence is false or misleading in any respect, or is different from what it would otherwise have been.

General

14 Assumption of truth in assessment of probative value

(1) Subject to subsection (2), a reference in this Act to the probative value of evidence is a reference to its probative value on the assumption that it is true.

(2) In assessing the probative value of an item of evidence for any purpose of this Act, a court need not assume that the evidence is true if it appears, on the basis of any material before the court (including any evidence it decides to hear on the matter), that no court or jury could reasonably find it to be true.

15 Court's duty to give reasons for rulings

(1) Where the court makes a relevant ruling—
  (a) it must state in open court (but in the absence of the jury, if there is one) its reasons for the ruling;
  (b) if it is a magistrates' court, it must cause the ruling and the reasons for it to be entered in the register of the court's proceedings.

(2) In this section "relevant ruling" means—

EXPLANATORY NOTES

Clause 13 (cont'd)

Subsection (3) achieves the same result where the defendant has been found unfit to plead by reason of mental disability, and (under section 4A(2) of the Criminal Procedure (Insanity) Act 1964) the jury therefore has to determine not whether the defendant is guilty, but only whether he or she did the act or made the omission charged.

This clause does not apply to summary trials.

General

Clause 14

Subsection (1) provides that the probative value of bad character evidence is to be assessed on the assumption that it is true.

Subsection (2), however, provides for an exception to this rule where it appears that no court or jury could reasonably find the tendered evidence to be true. In that case the court need not assume that it is true, but may assess the reliability of the evidence for itself, and has an inherent power to arrive at that decision in whatever way is thought most appropriate. It might be possible to make the assessment on the basis of the papers alone, taking submissions by the advocates into account; or the court might think it necessary to hear evidence, in which case it would do so on a voir dire.

Clause 15

This clause provides that, where a court

- rules on whether bad character evidence is admissible only with leave,
- gives or refuses leave, or
- rules on an application to stop the trial under clause 13 (on the ground that contaminated evidence of the defendant's bad character has been admitted),

it must give its reasons, and those reasons must be recorded.

Criminal Evidence Bill

(a) a ruling on whether an item of evidence is admissible only with leave under section 2;
(b) a decision whether to give leave under that section;
(c) a ruling under section 13.

16 Rules of court

(1) Rules of court may make such provision as appears to the appropriate authority to be necessary or expedient for the purposes of this Act; and the appropriate authority is the authority entitled to make the rules.

(2) The rules may require a party who—
   (a) proposes to adduce evidence of a defendant's bad character that is admissible only with leave under section 2, or
   (b) proposes to cross-examine a witness with a view to eliciting such evidence,
to serve on the defendant such notice, and such particulars of or relating to the evidence, as may be prescribed.

(3) The rules may provide that the court or the defendant may, in such circumstances as may be prescribed, dispense with a requirement imposed by virtue of subsection (2).

(4) If a party fails to comply with a requirement that has been imposed in relation to an item of evidence by virtue of subsection (2) (and not dispensed with by virtue of subsection (3)) the court may take the failure into account—
   (a) in deciding whether to grant leave under section 2;
   (b) where leave is given, in considering the exercise of its powers with respect to costs.

(5) The rules may—
   (a) limit the application of any provision of the rules to prescribed circumstances;
   (b) subject any provision of the rules to prescribed exceptions;
   (c) make different provision for different cases or circumstances.

(6) Nothing in this section prejudices the generality of any enactment conferring power to make rules of court; and no particular provision of this section prejudices any general provision of it.

(7) In this section—
   "prescribed" means prescribed by rules of court;
   "rules of court" means—
      (a) Crown Court Rules;
      (b) Criminal Appeal Rules;
      (c) rules under section 144 of the Magistrates' Courts Act 1980 (c. 43).

17 Interpretation

(1) In this Act—
   "bad character" is to be read in accordance with section 1;
   "criminal proceedings" means criminal proceedings in relation to which the strict rules of evidence apply;

EXPLANATORY NOTES

Clause 16

This clause provides for rules of court to be drawn up concerning notice that a party will have to give to a defendant that it intends to adduce evidence of that defendant's bad character, and gives the court or defendant the power to dispense with such a requirement.

Clause 17

This clause defines various expressions used in the Bill.

"defendant", in relation to criminal proceedings, means a person charged with an offence in those proceedings; and "co-defendant", in relation to a defendant, means a person charged with an offence in the same proceedings;

"misconduct" means—
  (a) the commission of an offence, or
  (b) behaviour of a kind that, in the opinion of the court, might be viewed with disapproval by a reasonable person;

"prejudice", in relation to an item of evidence and a defendant, is to be read in accordance with subsection (2);

"probative value" is to be read in accordance with section 14;

"prosecution evidence" means evidence which is to be (or has been) adduced by the prosecution, or which a witness is to be invited to give (or has given) in cross-examination by the prosecution.

(2) For the purposes of this Act evidence carries a risk of prejudice to a defendant where—
  (a) there is a risk that the court or jury would attach undue weight to the evidence, or
  (b) the nature of the matters with which the evidence deals is such as to give rise to a risk that the court or jury would find the defendant guilty without being satisfied that he was.

(3) Where a defendant is charged with two or more offences in the same criminal proceedings, this Act has effect as if each offence were charged in separate proceedings; and references to the offence with which the defendant is charged are to be read accordingly.

18 Armed forces

Schedule 1 (armed forces) has effect.

19 Minor and consequential amendments

(1) In section 6 of the Criminal Procedure Act 1865 (c. 18) (witness's conviction for offence may be proved if not admitted)—
  (a) for "A witness may be" substitute "If, upon a witness being lawfully";
  (b) omit "and upon being so questioned, if".

(2) In section 1(2) of the Criminal Evidence Act 1898 (c. 36) (restriction of privilege against self-incrimination where defendant gives evidence) at the beginning insert "Subject to section 6 of the Criminal Evidence Act 2001 (inadmissibility of evidence of defendant's bad character),".

(3) In section 16(2) of the Children and Young Persons Act 1963 (c. 37) (offences committed by person under 14 disregarded for purposes of evidence relating to previous convictions) for the words from "notwithstanding" to the end substitute "even though the Criminal Evidence Act 2001 would not prevent the question from being asked."

20 Repeals etc

(1) The common law rules governing the admissibility of evidence of bad character in criminal proceedings are abolished.

EXPLANATORY NOTES

Clause 17 (cont'd)

Subsection (3) has the effect that, in applying clause 8 where the defendant faces more than one charge, the court approaches the question of admissibility for each offence in isolation. Thus evidence might be admissible in relation to offence A but inadmissible in relation to offence B.

Clause 18

This clause gives effect to Schedule 1, which makes provision for the use of bad character evidence in courts-martial and other service courts.

Clause 19

This clause makes various minor and consequential amendments to existing statutes.

Clause 20

Subsection (1) abolishes the existing common law rules on bad character evidence, and subsection (3)(a) repeals section 1(3) (formerly section 1(f)) of the Criminal Evidence Act 1898. (The Bill has been drafted on the basis that paragraph 4 of Schedule 1 to the Youth Justice and Criminal Evidence Act 1999 is already in force although it is not in force at the time of writing.) Thus the Bill sets out *all* the rules applicable to bad character evidence in criminal proceedings.

Criminal Evidence Bill 11

(2) The rules referred to in subsection (1) include any rule under which, as an exception to the inadmissibility of hearsay evidence, evidence of a person's reputation is admissible for the purpose of proving his character, but only so far as the rule relates to evidence of bad character.

(3) The following cease to have effect—
  (a) section 1(3) of the Criminal Evidence Act 1898 (c. 36) (which makes provision as to the questions that a defendant may be asked about his bad character in cross-examination);
  (b) section 27(3) of the Theft Act 1968 (c. 60) (admission of evidence of previous convictions for theft etc to prove that defendant knew goods to be stolen).

(4) The enactments specified in Schedule 2 are repealed to the extent specified.

21 Citation, commencement and extent

(1) This Act may be cited as the Criminal Evidence Act 2001.

(2) This Act comes into force on such day as the Secretary of State may appoint by order made by statutory instrument; and different days may be appointed for different purposes.

(3) No provision of this Act applies in relation to a hearing begun before the day appointed for the purposes of that provision under subsection (2).

(4) An order under subsection (2) may include such supplementary, incidental or consequential provisions as appear to the Secretary of State to be necessary or expedient.

(5) This Act, except section 18 and Schedule 1, extends to England and Wales only.

(6) Section 18 and Schedule 1, so far as relating to proceedings before a particular service court, have the same extent as the Act under which the court is constituted.

EXPLANATORY NOTES

Clause 20 (cont'd)

Subsection (2) abolishes the common law hearsay exception which permits evidence of character to be proved by evidence of a person's reputation, but only in respect of evidence of *bad* character.

Subsection (3)(b) repeals section 27(3) of the Theft Act 1968, which provides for the admissibility of certain previous convictions of a defendant charged with handling stolen goods. Such cases will no longer be governed by special rules.

Subsection (4) gives effect to Schedule 2, which repeals various existing provisions.

Clause 21

This clause provides for the Bill's short title, the date of its coming into force, and its territorial extent.

SCHEDULES

SCHEDULE 1

Section 18

ARMED FORCES

1 (1) The relevant sections of this Act, in so far as they are not applied in relation to proceedings before service courts by provision contained in or made under any other Act, have effect in relation to such proceedings (whether in the United Kingdom or elsewhere) as they have effect in relation to criminal proceedings.

   (2) The relevant sections are sections 1 to 11 (except section 10(9)) and sections 14, 15 and 17.

2 Section 10(9) has effect in relation to proceedings before Standing Civilian Courts (whether in the United Kingdom or elsewhere) with the substitution of "Standing Civilian Court" for "magistrates' court".

3 (1) Section 13 has effect in relation to proceedings before courts-martial (whether in the United Kingdom or elsewhere) with the following modifications.

   (2) In subsection (1) —
      (a) for "on indictment" substitute "before a court-martial";
      (b) for "the court is satisfied" substitute "the judge advocate is satisfied";
      (c) for the words after paragraph (b) substitute "the judge advocate must either direct the court to acquit the defendant of the offence or, if he considers that there ought to be a retrial, dissolve the court."

   (3) In subsection (2) —
      (a) for "a jury" substitute "a court";
      (b) for "the court is satisfied" substitute "the judge advocate is satisfied".

   (4) In subsection (3) —
      (a) for paragraph (a) substitute —
         "(a) a court is required to determine under section 115B(2) of the Army Act 1955, section 115B(2) of the Air Force Act 1955 or section 62B(2) of the Naval Discipline Act 1957 whether a person charged with an offence did the act or made the omission charged,";
      (b) for "the court is satisfied" substitute "the judge advocate is satisfied";
      (c) for the words after paragraph (c) substitute "the judge advocate must either direct the court to acquit the defendant of the offence or, if he considers that there ought to be a rehearing, dissolve the court."

   (5) For subsection (4) substitute —

4 "(4) This section does not prejudice any other power a judge advocate may have to direct a court to acquit a person of an offence or to dissolve a court."

4 Section 15, as it applies in relation to proceedings before service courts, has effect with the substitution of the following for subsection (1)—

"(1) Where the court makes a relevant ruling—
 (a) it must state in open court (but, in the case of a ruling by a judge advocate, in the absence of the other members of the court) its reasons for the ruling;
 (b) if it is a Standing Civilian Court, it must cause the ruling and the reasons for it to be entered in the note of the court's proceedings."

5 Section 16 has effect as if, in subsection (7), the definition of "rules of court" included rules regulating the practice and procedure of service courts.

6 (1) In this Schedule, and in section 13 as applied by this Schedule, "court-martial" means a court-martial constituted under the Army Act 1955 (3 & 4 Eliz. 2 c. 18), the Air Force Act 1955 (3 & 4 Eliz. 2 c. 19) or the Naval Discipline Act 1957 (c. 53).

(2) In this Schedule "service court" means—
 (a) a court-martial;
 (b) a summary appeal court constituted under section 83ZA of the Army Act 1955, section 83ZA of the Air Force Act 1955 or section 52FF of the Naval Discipline Act 1957;
 (c) the Courts-Martial Appeal Court;
 (d) a Standing Civilian Court.

(3) In relation to any time before the coming into force of section 18 of the Armed Forces Act 2001 (c. 19) (abolition of naval disciplinary courts), this Schedule has effect as if the definition of "service court" in sub-paragraph (2) included a disciplinary court constituted under section 52G of the Naval Discipline Act 1957.

SCHEDULE 2

Section 20(4).

Repeals

Short title and chapter	Extent of repeal
Criminal Procedure Act 1865 (c. 18)	In section 6, the words "and upon being so questioned, if".
Criminal Evidence Act 1898 (c. 36)	Section 1(3).
Theft Act 1968 (c. 60)	In section 27— (a) subsection (3); (b) in subsection (5), the words from "and in subsection (3)(b)" to the end.
Criminal Evidence Act 1979 (c. 16)	In section 1, the words from "each of the following" to "1898, and".

Short title and chapter	Extent of repeal
Criminal Justice and Public Order Act 1994 (c. 33)	Section 31.
Youth Justice and Criminal Evidence Act 1999 (c. 23)	In Schedule 4, paragraph 1(5).

APPENDIX A
RESEARCH: THE EFFECT ON MAGISTRATES OF KNOWING OF A DEFENDANT'S CRIMINAL RECORD

A.1 In the consultation paper we referred to research into the effect on juries of knowing of a defendant's previous convictions conducted by Dr Sally Lloyd-Bostock, Research Fellow of the Centre for Socio-Legal Studies and of Wolfson College, University of Oxford. Dr Lloyd-Bostock has since completed a second project addressing how the same evidence affects magistrates. This research has been published in the Criminal Law Review.[1] We summarise it here.

OUTLINE OF THE STUDY

A.2 This project was modelled closely on its forerunner.[2] The study focused on how the knowledge that the defendant had a previous conviction affected magistrates and whether that effect differed depending on the nature of the conviction, including its similarity to the offence charged and the age of the conviction. The study also considered what assumptions magistrates made, on the basis of knowledge of a previous conviction, about the defendant's likelihood to reoffend. Magistrates were also questioned about whether they thought it was useful or appropriate to disclose previous convictions to fact-finders and what problems might arise for them from such disclosure. In total, 222 magistrates participated in the research.[3]

Methodology

A.3 The research was conducted by way of simulation experiment. Groups of magistrates viewed a video of a condensed reconstruction of one of two trials: one relating to a charge of handling stolen goods, the other to one of indecent assault on a woman. There were eight versions of the trial of each offence. In each there was a neutral voice-over, when the defendant came to the witness box. In each the judge in his summing up gave either no, or differing information about the defendant's criminal history as follows:

(1) no mention of previous conviction or good character (the base condition);

(2) good character;

(3) recent[4] similar conviction (to offence charged);

(4) old[5] similar conviction (to offence charged);

---

[1] [2000] Crim LR 734.

[2] Detailed in the consultation paper at Appendix D.

[3] All of whom were volunteers. Most were female (60%), over 45 (90%) and white (97%).

[4] Fifteen months old.

[5] Five years old.

(5) recent dissimilar conviction;[6]

(6) old dissimilar conviction;

(7) recent conviction for indecent assault on a child; or

(8) old conviction for indecent assault on a child.

A.4 The judge gave the appropriate standard direction depending on whether a previous conviction was disclosed or not. Where it had been stated that the defendant was of good character, the judge gave the following direction:

> You have heard that the defendant has no previous convictions. In deciding whether the prosecution has made you sure of his guilt, you should have regard to the fact that he is a man of good character. You should take it into account in his favour in the following two ways.[7]

A.5 Where nothing was disclosed about the defendant's character, the judge did not say anything about the defendant's character. Where a previous conviction had been mentioned, the judge said,

> You have heard about the defendant's previous conviction for [...]. You must not assume that the defendant is guilty or that he is not telling the truth because he has been convicted on a previous occasion. It is for you to decide the extent to which his previous conviction assists you.

A.6 The magistrates watched a single version of the video in groups of between 12 and 18. Immediately after watching it they completed Questionnaire 1 in which they expressed their initial verdict, a rating of confidence in that verdict, and two ratings (one on a five-point scale and one on a 0–100% scale) of the likelihood that the defendant committed the offence.

A.7 They were then divided into groups of three to arrive at a bench verdict. After group deliberation they then completed Questionnaires 2 and 3. Questionnaire 2 asked for the bench's decision, the individual magistrate's personal verdict and again, ratings of the likelihood that the defendant committed the offence. Questionnaire 3 asked the magistrates for (i) their impressions of the defendant (giving ratings for credibility, trustworthiness and propensity to commit particular crimes); (ii) their views on whether fact-finders should be told of previous convictions; (iii) their beliefs about people's propensity to re-offend or to lie in court depending on previous convictions and (iv) their experiences of discovering or realising that the defendant has previous convictions and the extent to which this is a source of difficulty for them.

A.8 The results were tested for statistical significance: that is the probability that such data would be produced by chance. In this study, as in that conducted with juries,

---

[6] Intentionally causing grievous bodily harm (contrary to s 18 of the Offences Against the Person Act 1861) in the handling stolen goods trial and handling stolen goods in the indecent assault trial.

[7] The direction then goes on to explain that good character supports credibility and the lack of propensity to commit the offence charged.

a significance level of less than 0.05 (one in twenty) is used, meaning that a result which has a less than one in twenty likelihood of occurring randomly is treated as significant. Naturally, the significance level of particular results and confidence in the reliability of the findings is increased where analyses of different variables show a similar result or pattern of results. Where a large number of statistical tests are carried out, however, the probability of one reaching a significance level by chance increases.

SUMMARY OF RESULTS AND ANALYSIS

A.9 The first part of this analysis, concerning likelihood and belief in guilt, examines only the results of the groups that viewed the videos concerning previous conviction scenarios one to six. The results generated by the videos involving indecent assault on a child are discussed at paragraph A.24 below.

Likelihood scores

A.10 Below is a table of the average score (from one to a hundred) given by magistrates on their immediate individual analysis and after deliberation in a bench, of the likelihood that the defendant committed the offence.

Table 1

Previous conviction information	Average likelihood rating Individual (pre-deliberation)	Average likelihood rating Bench (post-deliberation)
Old similar	65.5	65.3
Recent similar	60.9	59.1
Old dissimilar	56	58.5
Base	41.6	37.8
Good character	39.1	41.5
Recent dissimilar	37.4	34.9

A.11 The significance level between the sets of the differing conviction information only reached 0.05 in the three highest-scoring groups. The relationship between category of previous conviction and likelihood score is more significant after deliberation, following the same general pattern.

A.12 As occurred in the Jury Study, a *similar* previous conviction is associated with the higher perceived probability that the defendant committed the offence currently charged. In the present study both old and recent similar convictions have a significant effect. However, in the Jury Study, whilst *recent* similar convictions had the greatest effect on the likelihood score, old convictions made little or no difference to the likelihood estimates.

A.13 A recent *dis*similar previous conviction appeared, as in the Jury Study, to be of positive help to the defendant. The dissimilarity neutralises the effect of a conviction, possibly invoking a stereotype of a person who commits *that* type of offence, not the type of offence charged. Unlike in the Jury Study, however, the small advantage of a recent dissimilar conviction over no information or good character is not significant.

Effect of previous conviction information on verdict

Individual magistrates

A.14 The table below shows the percentage of magistrates recording guilty verdicts and not-guilty verdicts (in brackets) before deliberation, after deliberation, and as a bench.

Table 2

Conviction information	Pre-deliberation [%]	Post-deliberation [%]	Bench verdict [%]
Old dissimilar	24.2 (75.8)	24.2 (75.8)	20 (80)
Old similar	23.1 (76.9)	23.1 (76.9)	12.5 (87.5)
Recent similar	21.4 (78.6)	21.4 (78.6)	25 (75)
Good character	19.2 (80.8)	11.5 (88.5)	0 (100)
Base	17.2 (82.8)	13.8 (86.2)	0 (100)
Recent dissimilar	11.1 (88.9)	7.4 (92.6)	0 (100)

A.15 Unexpectedly, old dissimilar convictions were associated with the highest rate of guilty verdicts before and after deliberation. This was not the case in the Jury Study. This finding was consistent amongst the three groups that watched the video in question, but did not appear at a statistically significant level of variance. The "dissimilar conviction" was for a section 18 assault. It appears that a conviction for violent assault was associated with a consistently negative view of the defendant by magistrates.[8] Only where the conviction is recent does the dissimilarity outweigh this negative impression.

Bench verdict in relation to magistrates' belief in guilt.

A.16 The table on the following page demonstrates the relationship between the likelihood scores and the bench verdict. The likelihood scores were recorded on a five-point scale relating to belief in the defendant's guilt.

---

[8] See para A.21 below.

Table 3

Belief (pre-deliberation) (likelihood score)	Convictions (%) Pre-deliberation	Convictions (%) Post-deliberation
Definitely committed offence	88.26	71.4
Almost certainly committed offence	55.4	35.3
Probably committed offence	6.3	6.9
Probably did not commit offence	2.5	2.6
Definitely did not commit offence	0	11.1

Effect of nature of previous conviction on the perception of the defendant

A.17 The magistrates were asked to score (between one and five) their initial impressions relating to the defendant's honesty and propensity to commit different offences. These results may not entirely reflect the effect previous convictions have on magistrates' opinions of the defendant because some magistrates were reluctant to answer the questions, seeing this as an invitation to express prejudices, or did not answer at all. It is possible that others may even have underestimated their own unconscious prejudices. The results follow a similar trend to the previous analysis concerning likelihood of guilt. However, the magistrates consistently viewed good character favourably and any conviction, recent or old and of any nature, unfavourably.

A.18 The following tables show the average rating (between one and five) given to defendants with each type of conviction information.

Table 4

Previous conviction information	Belief in evidence as witness	Propensity to commit type of offence charged	Trustworthiness
Section 18 assault	2.33 (1)	2.72 (5) [1]	1.87 (1)
Indecent assault on a child	2.87 (2)	2.57 (4) [1]	2.23 (2)
Handing stolen goods	2.87 (3)	2.33 (2) [1]	2.46 (4) [1]
Indecent assault on a woman	3 (4) [1]	3.29 (6) [1,2,3,4]	2.29 (3)
Good character	3.46 (5) [1]	1.52 (1)	3.18 (5) [1,2,3,4]
Base	3.48 (6) [1,2,3]	2.34 (3) [1]	2.69 (6) [1,2]

A.19 The scores are numbered in order by the numbers in round brackets. Significant variation between sets is denoted by the latter set's corresponding number in square brackets; this tended to occur in the highest rated categories. In interpreting the table it should be remembered that a previous conviction for handling stolen goods was used both as a similar conviction to the same charge and as a dissimilar offence where indecent assault was charged, whereas indecent assault was only used as a similar offence.

No information

A.20 Where no information was given about the defendant's previous convictions, the magistrates were asked how many convictions they assumed the defendant had. Just over half the respondents (55.2%) thought that the defendant would have one or two convictions and a further 14% thought that the defendant had more convictions. Around a third (31%) assumed the defendant had no previous convictions.

Other aspects of magistrates' impressions of the defendant

A.21 Magistrates viewed defendants with a conviction for section 18 assault as more deserving of punishment and more likely to have got away with criminal offences in the past than all other categories. This was seen as the most relevant conviction in terms of employment of the defendant, more so than a dishonesty offence, except where the job involved caring for children where the indecent assault convictions produced worse scores.

FUTURE OFFENCES

A.22 Magistrates were asked to assess the likelihood that the defendant would commit various offences in the future. These offences included those used as previous convictions and currently charged, plus some offences with common attributes (burglary, robbery with violence, indecent exposure to children and rape).

A.23 Those with a previous conviction for section 18 assault were seen as more likely than others to commit offences of burglary, robbery with violence, section 18 assault and, second only to the defendant with a previous conviction for handling, handling stolen goods. However, this defendant was regarded as least likely to commit a sexual offence.

A.24 A previous conviction for indecently assaulting a child made the defendant perceived as more likely to commit sexual offences or intentionally cause grievous bodily harm, but not commit burglary, handling stolen goods or robbery. The Jury Study found that such a conviction produced a consistent statistically significant increase in the likelihood of the defendant committing all other offences, but this was not the view of magistrates.

A.25 These results suggest that dishonesty, violence and sexual offending are seen as significant components of offences likely to be repeated. It is perceived that a previous conviction for one offence with such a component makes it more likely that other offences with the same component will be committed by that defendant.

Experiences and beliefs about previous conviction information

A.26 All the magistrates were asked whether they or juries should be told of previous convictions. A large majority of magistrates thought that previous convictions should never be disclosed to either magistrates or juries.[9] The primary reason for this was the risk of bias,[10] but some magistrates cited lack of relevance or importance of the information.[11] Around 10% of magistrates considered the fact that juries did not benefit from the training that magistrates had received to disregard certain evidence. This training and awareness of current debates might also explain some of their reservations about the disclosure of previous conviction information.

A.27 Fifteen magistrates thought that they ought to be told about the defendant's previous convictions and a further 55 thought that they should sometimes be told. Ten magistrates said that it depended on the type or gravity of offence and four that the information should only be revealed if relevant to the current case. Rather more magistrates, 35 in relation to telling magistrates and 34 in relation to juries, thought that in the case of crimes involving patterns[12] previous conviction information should be revealed. However, some limited this to cases where the information was of strict relevance.[13]

A.28 The magistrates were asked how many convictions a person would need before being described as a persistent offender. The magistrates' responses ranged from two convictions to ten, with the majority responding between three and six.[14]

A.29 The magistrates were also asked to consider how recent a conviction needed to be to be helpful to fact-finders. The responses were diverse: 64 said within three years, 56 said within five years, 19 thought within ten years, three thought within 15 years and three thought within 20 years.

---

[9] 152 magistrates (68%) in respect of magistrates and 172 magistrates (77%) for juries.

[10] 36.9% of magistrates in relation to magistrates and 38.2% in relation to juries.

[11] 29.3% in relation to magistrates and 20.3% in relation to juries.

[12] For example, sex offences, murder and burglary.

[13] Ten in relation to magistrates and 15 in respect of juries.

[14] The number of magistrates opting for each number (3-6) was almost evenly spread.

ASSISTING IN REACHING VERDICT

A.30 Magistrates were asked whether the fact that they had been told about the defendant's previous conviction helped them arrive at their verdict.

Table 5

Comment	Frequency (Percentage)
Very much	1 (0.6%)
Quite a lot	10 (6%)
A little	25 (14.9%)
Not at all	132 (78.6%)
TOTAL	168[15]

A.31 It is possible – indeed likely – that previous conviction information would affect the judgment of magistrates in ways of which they are not aware. These results are significantly different from those in the Jury Study where the simulated jurors found the information significantly more helpful.

OWN EXPERIENCES

A.32 Whilst the study showed that it was common for magistrates to learn of the defendant's previous convictions, only 22% said that difficulties arose as a result. The magistrates were asked whether knowledge of the defendant's previous convictions means that magistrates should withdraw. Forty-six magistrates thought that this was always cause for withdrawal. Twenty-six regarded this as necessary only where it would cause bias, eleven thought it necessary if the clerk advised it and ten where the defendant was known or the crime affected the magistrate personally.

A.33 Only 10% of magistrates had never realised that a defendant had previous conviction from recognising the defendant or family from previous court appearances. Experiences of such recognition were wide-ranging: three magistrates had this experience in over 200 cases, six in 100–200 cases, 22 in over 51–100 cases, 41 between 21–50, 27 in 11–20, 40 in 6–10 cases, 39 in 2–5 and only two had recognised a defendant just once.

A.34 There is no direct parallel between the figures relating to magistrates knowing that a defendant has previous convictions and those relating to withdrawal due to such knowledge. Asked approximately how often they had withdrawn because of knowing or learning of the defendant's previous conviction, 161 magistrates (72.5%) said they had never withdrawn for that reason. Those that had had occasion to do so had withdrawn once (6.3%) or twice (9%).

---

[15] Four groups did not watch a video featuring a previous conviction.

CONCLUSION

A.35 Any previous conviction unfavourably affected the magistrates' impressions and verdicts, except where the defendant had a recent conviction dissimilar to that charged. The effects are not large but they are significant and follow a consistent pattern which broadly mirrors that found in the Jury Study.

A.36 The main difference between the results of the two studies relates to assumptions made by the mock jurors about a defendant with a previous conviction for indecent assault on a child and those made by magistrates in relation to a previous conviction for section 18 assault. The mock jurors consistently associated a previous conviction for indecent assault on a child with a negative evaluation of the defendant, including a greater perceived likelihood that the defendant would commit further offences, whether sexual in nature or not. The magistrates, however, had a less favourable impression of the defendant with a previous conviction for section 18 assault, also assuming that that defendant had a greater likelihood of commiting further offences. This virtually supplanted the effect of indecent assault on a child found in the Jury Study, although it was not as strong or consistent. This effect may be explained by the magistrates' greater awareness of the kind of offence a section 18 assault represents.

A.37 Other differences between the studies include the effect of good character, which impressed magistrates far more than the mock jurors. Magistrates were more influenced by old convictions than the mock jurors. Furthermore, magistrates tended to be more confident in their verdicts: the likelihood of guilt ratings altered less before and after deliberation.

A.38 In general the results indicate that information about previous conviction is likely to affect magistrates' decisions despite their awareness of the dangers and their efforts to avoid bias. These findings do not offer confidence that the rules on admitting previous convictions can be safely relaxed for magistrates any more than for juries.

APPENDIX B
PERSONS AND ORGANISATIONS WHO COMMENTED ON THE CONSULTATION PAPER

INDIVIDUALS AND GROUP RESPONSES

Duncan Alexander, Jackie Pearcey, and Richard Faulkner

R E Arnold-Shrubb JP

Their Honours Judge Francis Allen, Judge Richard Bray and Judge Julian Hall

Mr Justice Alliott

His Honour Judge Michael Baker

His Honour Judge Bathurst-Norman

Paul Batterbury

Judge Peter Beaumont

Mr Justice Bell

Mr Justice Blofeld

Sir Wilfrid Bourne KCB QC

P D Brown JP

The Right Honourable Sir Stephen Brown

Mr Justice Buckley

The Right Honourable Lord Justice Buxton

The Right Honourable Lord Justice Carswell

Peter Carter QC, Wadham College, University of Oxford

Dr Andrew L-T Choo, University of Leicester

His Honour Judge Colston QC

D S Cottrell

His Honour Judge Cowell

Stephen Cretney

Mr Justice Curtis

Dr Penny Darbyshire, Kingston Law School

His Honour Judge Rhys Davies QC, Honorary Recorder of Manchester

His Honour Judge Neil Denison QC, The Common Serjeant of London

His Honour Judge John Devaux

Sean Doran, Queen's University Belfast

John Duckett JP

His Honour Judge Mark Dyer

Mr Justice Dyson

Andrew Edis, Northern Circuit

His Honour Judge G O Edwards QC

B E Evans JP

David Faulkner, University of Oxford, Centre for Criminological Research

Mr Justice French

Mr Justice Garland

His Honour Judge Gerald Gordon QC

His Honour Judge Richard Havery QC

Michael Hirst, Reader in Law, University of Wales in Aberystwyth

John Hodgson, Association of Law Teachers

His Honour Judge Michael Hucker

Professor John Jackson, Queen's University Belfast

David Jeffreys QC

Mr Justice Ian Kennedy

His Honour Judge Kenny

His Honour Judge Esyr Lewis QC

Mr Justice Longmore

His Honour Judge David Lynch

His Honour Judge R G May

Norman Marsh

Professor Jenny McEwan, Keele University

His Honour Michael McMullan

His Honour Judge Mettyear

Peter Mirfield, Jesus College, University of Oxford

Mr Justice Morland

Professor Peter W Murphy, South Texas College of Law

Michael Neligan

Mr Justice Newman

Sir John Nutting QC

S J Odgers and Justice Tim Smith, Supreme Court of Victoria

David Pannick QC

The Right Honourable Lord Justice Phillips

His Honour J W Rant CB QC, Judge Advocate General

Dr M Redmayne, University of Manchester

His Honour Judge Rivlin QC

Paul Roberts, Reader in Criminal Justice, University of Nottingham

Peter Roe

Peter Rook QC

Mr Justice Rougier

Ian G Sampson

Alec Samuels JP

Mr Justice Sedley

The Right Honourable Lord Justice Schiemann

His Honour Judge Peter Smith

Professor Sir John Smith CBE QC FBA, University of Nottingham

South Eastern Circuit

Alan Suckling QC

The Right Honourable Lord Justice Swinton Thomas

Professor Colin Tapper, Magdalen College, University of Oxford

His Honour Judge Tetlow

His Honour Judge Anthony Thorpe

Mr Justice Toulson

Treasury Counsel at the Central Criminal Court, (David Calvert-Smith QC, Nicholas Loraine-Smith, Jonathan Laidlaw)

The Justices of Uxbridge Magistrates' Court

Wales and Chester Circuit (Wales and Chester branches submitted separate responses)

His Honour Judge Brian Walsh, Recorder of Leeds

Professor Martin Wasik, University of Manchester

His Honour Judge Wickham

Stephen Williamson QC

Michael Worsley QC

Mr Justice Wright

ORGANISATIONS

Association of Chief Police Officers

Criminal Bar Association

Crown Prosecution Service

Department of Trade and Industry

Foreign and Commonwealth Office

General Council of the Bar, Law Reform Committee

H M Customs and Excise

Inland Revenue

Joint Council of Metropolitan and Provincial Stipendiary Magistrates, Legal Committee

JUSTICE

Justices' Clerks' Society

Liberty

London Criminal Courts Solicitors' Association and City of Westminster Law Society (joint response)

Magistrates' Association

National Association for the Care and Resettlement of Offenders

Office of the Solicitor, Departments of Health and Social Security

Royal Ulster Constabulary (R White BEM OBE LLB, Assistant Chief Constable)

Serious Fraud Office